**Praise for *Alabama v. King*
by Dan Abrams and Fred D. Gray with David Fisher**

"A fascinating story of grit, determination and courtroom acumen... The stirring tale of how an inexperienced 25-year-old lawyer, only two years out of law school, played a pivotal role in King's emergence as the 'American Gandhi' is a story for the ages."

—*New York Times*

"Poignant, sometimes harrowing."

—*Wall Street Journal*

Praise for Dan Abrams and David Fisher

"Dan Abrams and David Fisher write the heart-pounding pulse of history."

—Diane Sawyer on *Lincoln's Last Trial*

"Abrams and Fisher do a superb job of clearly presenting the issues in this remarkable and intensely dramatic trial."

—Scott Turow on *Theodore Roosevelt for the Defense*

"Abrams and Fisher are gifted writers, and their prose is neither overly spare nor showy; they're clearly fascinated by the trial, and their enthusiasm for their subject matter shows."

—NPR on *Theodore Roosevelt for the Defense*

"The authors do a remarkable job of spinning the court transcripts into a fascinating tale of intrigue and underscoring the men and the issues at play."

—*Fredericksburg Book Review* on *John Adams Under Fire*

"An engrossing, lively and expertly crafted courtroom drama filled with colorful characters and having significant resonance for the present."

—*Washington Post* on *Kennedy's Avenger*

"Clear, straightforward writing and superb research that pays attention to tension as well as humor make this riveting courtroom drama that feels as alive as it did it 1963."

—NPR on *Kennedy's Avenger*

ALABAMA v. KING

ALABAMA v. KING

MARTIN LUTHER KING JR. AND THE CRIMINAL TRIAL THAT LAUNCHED THE CIVIL RIGHTS MOVEMENT

DAN ABRAMS AND FRED D. GRAY
WITH DAVID FISHER

HANOVER
SQUARE
PRESS

HANOVER
SQUARE
PRESS™

Recycling programs
for this product may
not exist in your area.

ISBN-13: 978-1-335-44959-7

Alabama v. King

First published in 2022. This edition published in 2023.
Copyright © 2022 by Dan Abrams and Fred D. Gray with David Fisher

Hanover Square Press
22 Adelaide St. West, 41st Floor
Toronto, Ontario M5H 4E3, Canada
HanoverSqPress.com
BookClubbish.com

Printed in U.S.A.

Lawyers often talk about "fighting for justice," but what they typically mean is that inside a courtroom, they vigorously represent a client's position. Sometimes they even take unpopular or controversial positions of public significance and pay a price for fighting on behalf of a noble cause. But Fred Gray literally lived these fights. When he was battling for equality throughout his career, he was both attorney and in many cases, indirectly, client as well. He, like so many others, was being forced to sit in the backs of buses and to stay outside "whites only" public facilities. He was being discriminated against, threatened, mistreated and underestimated. Yet through it all, he always kept his eye on how to best affect change, strategically determining which cases to file, which arguments to make and which plaintiffs to include in an effort to walk that fine line between principle and chance of success. That made Fred not just a great lawyer, but a great leader. Even as we were writing this book, various honors and awards were bestowed on Fred that felt overdue. Thank you, Fred Gray, for allowing us entry into your world.

Dan Abrams and David Fisher

CONTENTS

FOREWORD

Looking back, sixty-seven years after my admission to the bar, after representing Claudette Colvin, Rosa Parks, Martin Luther King Jr., Ralph Abernathy, the NAACP, the plaintiffs in *Gomillion v. Lightfoot*, the men in the infamous Tuskegee Syphilis Study, the Freedom Riders, the Selma to Montgomery marchers, and the plaintiffs in the cases that desegregated the schools in Alabama from kindergarten to the universities, I never imagined that I would be invited to join Dan Abrams and David Fisher to tell this story. However, it happened. That has been the history of my life, helping to make the impossible possible.

When I was approached by them to coauthor this book, I was surprised, shocked, astonished, and didn't really believe it was happening, but it did.

I did not set out to play a role in history. I was just determined to change conditions in Alabama. Growing up in segregated Montgomery in the 1940s and early 1950s, I came to understand the promises of America were being denied to African Americans solely because of the color of our skin. I knew what the US

Constitution said and I knew what the Alabama laws said, and I knew for sure that they weren't the same thing. As I was sitting in the back of a bus, going back and forth across the city to Alabama State College for Negroes, I decided I was going to be a lawyer in Alabama, I was going to fight segregation anywhere, anytime, I was going to destroy segregation wherever I found it and I was going to do that for the rest of my life.

So far, so good.

Segregation was insidious. It poisoned every aspect of African American life. It was designed and applied not simply to control actions but, perhaps more importantly, to create a mindset of inferiority that would limit dreams. My mother fought that every day for her five children's lives. I don't know exactly why I believed I could rely on the law to change the law in order to fight segregation when the law had been used for so long to make segregation legal. But I did. I always did. Perhaps my religious background and my ministerial training gave me the faith and courage that I needed.

I had no specific plans for how I was going to fight for civil rights. When I opened my first office, there was no national unified civil rights movement. There were no national African American leaders. My primary concern was figuring out how to obtain clients and pay the fifty-dollar-a-month rent. At that time there was only one African American lawyer in Montgomery and he had been practicing for only a year. However, I was fortunate to be guided by some very smart, very determined people within the Black community. Many of them are represented by statues and plaques today, but at that time they were of flesh and blood, and they were willing to risk their lives and livelihoods in order to obtain equal justice. Many of them are well-known, E. D. Nixon, Rufus Lewis, Jo Ann Robinson, Rosa Parks, Dr. Martin Luther King, Ralph Abernathy, Claudette Colvin and John Lewis, for example, but there were others, and so many of the mostly forgotten people mentioned in the following pages stood up when that wasn't a safe or easy thing to do.

As we write about in this book, I was there at the birth of the civil rights movement.

This book is the story of *Alabama v. King*, the first civil rights trial of Dr. King's career. When it began, no one, absolutely no one, understood how important it would be in history. That's why so few photographs exist. I was a young Montgomerian and I knew from experience not to have any great expectations about obtaining justice on a local level. Even that early in what was to evolve into a national movement, it was my belief that our victories in the war against legal segregation would come on the federal level and that's where I intended to make my fight. This trial began as just another step on a long climb to the "promised land of equal justice for all."

The county solicitor believed it would not take long to convict Dr. King. That result would serve as a warning to the rest of the community about what was going to happen if they didn't end this protest.

When Judge Eugene Carter gaveled the trial to order in March 1956 before an all-white jury, Dr. Martin Luther King was the little-known minister of a small, upscale church located one block from the state capitol. The trial introduced him to America, putting him on the front pages of the country's leading newspapers for the first time. The *New York Times* profiled him as its Man in the News. By the time the trial ended four days later, he was the leader of the burgeoning movement.

But the trial accomplished far more than that. As you will read in these pages, in defense of Dr. King, actually in defense of the bus protest, we produced a series of witnesses who painted a broad and disgusting portrait of segregation that white America could not ignore. Many of them were not educated people. They were people who had grown up "knowing their place." Second-class citizens for life. But finally given the opportunity to be heard, they stood up—at times defiantly—to the white prosecutors and told their stories their way. Although it took place a long time ago, on occasion I can still hear the distant echoes of the packed courtroom cheering for people finally standing up for their rights.

The extraordinary bus protest highlighted by this trial served as a message to this country that African Americans would no longer accept second-class citizenship. For me, like Dr. King, it was just a beginning. My career took me from that fifty-dollar-a-month office above a Sears to arguing in front of the Supreme Court. And almost exactly a decade after the *Times* had profiled Dr. King, on May 6, 1966, I was the Man in the News, "A Voice for Negroes," as they referred to me, quoting me as explaining that I "wanted to be a lawyer because I felt that if there were more Negro lawyers, they could do something about our situation."

It is impossible to know how many civil rights cases I have fought in my career. Impossible. It was a case that I initiated, *Browder v. Gayle*, that eventually overturned *Plessy v. Ferguson*, outlawing segregation on public transportation, and another federal case of mine, *Gomillion v. Lightfoot*, outlawed gerrymandering on a racial basis. I discuss many of those cases in my earlier book *Bus Ride to Justice*. I did what I set out to do, fight segregation anywhere, anytime. I'm ninety-one years old and still doing so, but certainly the situation has changed. For example, I am now working out of my office in the firm I started, Gray, Langford, Sapp, McGowan, Gray, Gray & Nathanson, PC, located on the appropriately named Fred Gray Street in Tuskegee. That street connects on the south to Martin Luther King Hwy and on the north to Rosa Parks Plaza. Across the street on the west, the Square is where a Confederate monument still stands. My most recently filed civil rights case involves that property. It was filed September 1, 2021, *Macon County, a political subdivision of the State of Alabama, et al. v. United Daughters of the Confederacy, et al.*, for the purpose of having the court to declare Macon County is the owner of the old courthouse site that the then governing body of Macon County in 1906 gave without any consideration and ordered conveyed to the Tuskegee Chapter of the United Daughters of the Confederacy "for the purpose of converting the same to a park for white people and for the purpose of erecting a monument to the memory of the confederate soldiers from Macon County who were in the war between the states and for no other purpose." As I write this, the case is pending.

When Dan and David first approached me to work with them on this book, I mistakenly believed they intended to write about Dr. King's highly publicized 1960 case in which I also defended him. In that case he became the first person in Alabama history to be prosecuted for felony state tax evasion. By that time Dr. King had become respected around the world and we knew this simply was another effort to stop his influence from spreading. But I was pleasantly surprised when Dan and David corrected me. I have always believed the civil rights movement started with the bus protest and this trial, *Alabama v. King*, and I am so pleased to be able to bring long-overdue attention to it—not just for Dr. King but for all those other people who found the courage to stand up for their rights. During that trial, I took great pride in the courage of ordinary people standing up to injustice, and as you read their words, I suspect you will feel the emotion present in that courtroom.

Several symbolic events that took place while we were working on this book reminded me how far we have come since this trial. In December 2021, a Montgomery Juvenile Court expunged Claudette Colvin's 1955 conviction. A month later, the governor of Louisiana officially pardoned Homer Plessy, whose 1892 arrest for refusing to leave a whites-only railroad car led directly to the 1896 Supreme Court decision legalizing segregated facilities. And last fall, the City of Montgomery officially changed the name of the street on which I grew up from Jeff Davis Avenue to Fred D. Gray Avenue. Since the Montgomery bus protest, at least two generations of people have grown up knowing far too little about the problems that African Americans suffered as a result of segregation. It is therefore necessary that we have history museums across the country in various communities telling the story. I am delighted that over twenty years ago, I was cofounder of the Tuskegee Human & Civil Rights Multicultural Center, also known as the Tuskegee History Center, located in Tuskegee, Alabama, which not only shows the contributions made to this country by Native Americans, Americans of European descent and Americans of African descent, but also serves as a permanent memorial for the men in the infamous Tuskegee Syphilis Study. Finally, it gives a brief history of the struggle that African Americans have had from slavery times to the present. If you are unable to visit, we welcome your support.

Admittedly, we have made substantial and significant progress toward eliminating racism and inequality in this country. But still not enough. Not nearly enough. The struggle for equal justice and the elimination of racism and inequality continues. People of good will and good intentions are trying, but still we have a ways to go. I first met John Lewis when he was a teenager trying to figure out how he was going to afford college. I spoke with him for the last time in July 2020, only a few days before he died. We talked about many things, and as our conversation ended, I asked him for his thoughts on what we needed to do. "Brother," he told me, "keep going, keep pushing, set the record straight."

This book is part of that effort. So as you read it, remember this is where we started, and keep going, keep pushing, set the record straight, and do it in a nonviolent manner until justice rolls down like water and righteous as a mighty stream.

Fred D. Gray

PREFACE

Saturday, August 12, 1950, was a dreary overcast day in downtown Montgomery, Alabama. "A chance of thunderstorms" warned the *Montgomery Advertiser*. It had been a dry summer; the city needed the rain. At three o'clock in the afternoon the temperature was still edging up to a humid ninety degrees. At 3:45 the Cloverdale bus that would carry passengers into the Black neighborhoods stopped on the north side of Dexter Avenue. Twenty-two-year-old army veteran Hilliard Brooks, a married father of two, dressed neatly in his pressed khakis, put his dime in the slot, then started walking toward the back of the bus, to the rear seats set aside by law and Jim Crow tradition for Black passengers.

The bus driver yelled for him to stop. The regulations were specific: when ordered to by the driver, usually when white passengers were standing in the aisle, Black passengers were not permitted to walk down that center aisle to the rear. Instead, they were required to pay their fare, get off the bus, then walk to the back door and reboard.

Hilliard Brooks was slight; he couldn't have weighed more than 145 pounds and had just been honorably discharged from the army. He may have been celebrating. He had been drinking heavily, no one disputed that. He stopped in the aisle and turned. He'd had enough; he'd served his country. He wasn't going to be humiliated. Maybe the liquor pushed him. He refused, responding that he was only a few steps from the back, no need to get off. The driver ordered him off the bus. Okay, Brooks agreed, he'd get off—but he wanted his dime back. The driver would not return the fare; the situation escalated quickly.

Brooks started cursing at him. The driver banged down on his horn, attracting a white police traffic officer named Marvin Mills, who was standing on the other side of Dexter Avenue. A witness reported that the driver told Officer Mills, "I got a n——r on here who won't act right. I need your help."

The police officer boarded the bus and ordered Brooks, "Get down here, n——r."

Brooks glared at him.

Mills took a couple more steps. "Get your black ass off the bus. Now!"

The young soldier stood his ground. Witnesses offered differing accounts about exactly what happened next, but it seems Brooks was beaten to the floor. The officer and the driver took hold of Brooks and pushed and dragged him toward the front door. Somehow Brooks got free, pushed the white men aside, then yanked the officer's whistle and chain off his neck. Officer Mills pulled his gun. As Brooks reached the sidewalk, Mills fired one shot, according to some reports, hitting him in the back. The bullet ripped through the soldier's body and struck two innocent bystanders, a white man and a Black woman.

Mills told reporters that the soldier was coming toward him, ignoring orders to stop. "Then I shot him."

Witness G. W. Ruppert disputed that. "It was a shame. The Negro never had a chance."

Mrs. A. W. Robertson agreed. "I did not see the boy attempt to strike the policeman. I do not think the policeman shot in self-defense."

Hilliard Brooks was grievously wounded, but even after being placed in an ambulance he fought to get off the stretcher. He was taken to a local hospital; hours later he was dead.

In response, civil rights activist Thomas Gray secretly organized a veterans' protest march. Organized Black demonstrations were extremely rare in Montgomery. To prevent city officials from stopping it, no printed announcements were made. No public instructions were issued. Details were spread by voice, person-to-person. To avoid being arrested for loitering, demonstrators had to march to a specific destination. Gray decided they would walk to the courthouse, where many of them would register to vote.

On a hot Alabama August morning, an estimated four hundred protesters marched two by two on the sidewalk, moving purposefully and carefully to avoid arrest for blocking the walk. When warned by police to put down their signs, they did so. This protest continued for almost a week; fewer people showed up each day until it finally ended.

The protest accomplished nothing substantive and created barely a ripple among Montgomery's forty thousand Black residents. It was generally accepted that "raisin' up" had few benefits—and getting involved meant risking confrontations with white authorities who held all the power. The thousands of Black people working for white folks were not ready to put their jobs at stake.

Demonstrations didn't work. Mostly they caused problems for people who already had a bundle of them. Things weren't going to change. Everybody knew that. It was as simple as Black and white.

CHAPTER ONE

At about 9:15 p.m. on January 30, 1956, twenty-seven-year-old Martin Luther King Jr. was advocating nonviolent protest to approximately two thousand people at the cavernous First Baptist Church. Dr. King told the enthralled audience, "If all I have to pay is going to jail a few times and getting about twenty threatening calls a day... I think that is a very small price to pay for what we are fighting for." Little did he know that literally as he spoke, that price was becoming significantly higher.

A white supremacist had driven to his home that night, walked up half the steps of his white clapboard house in a quiet neighborhood and tossed a live stick of dynamite onto the front porch. His wife, Coretta Scott King, and a friend had been in the living room, and their newborn daughter, Yolanda, asleep in a back room. When the dynamite exploded a few moments later, windows were blown out and portions of the house destroyed or in shambles.

Upon hearing of the incident, King immediately rushed home and was relieved to find his wife, her friend and his daughter all uninjured. A furious and fearful crowd of about three hundred quickly gathered to support the King family, and with the remnant smell of explosives still wafting through the night air, Dr. King stepped out onto his only partially standing porch and declared: "We believe in law and order. Don't get your weapons… We are not advocating violence. We want to love our enemies." With those words, a potentially volatile situation had been defused.

The local authorities never arrested the perpetrator of the crime, but less than two months later they did arrest Dr. King for organizing the peaceful protests he was championing the night his house was bombed. The trial that followed would introduce the young minister to America.

It had required an extraordinary, unexpected and fortuitous chain of events to place the young Dr. King in the spotlight of history. It was not a role he had pursued. "When Martin Luther King came to Montgomery in September 1954," remembers Fred Gray, his friend and first civil rights attorney, who coincidentally had been admitted to the Alabama bar that same week, "he didn't have civil rights on his mind. In fact, the preacher before him had gotten run out of town because he was too liberal."

But after civil rights activist Rosa Parks was arrested on December 1, 1955, for violating a city ordinance by refusing to give up her seat on a crowded bus to a white person, a small group of Montgomery's leading Black citizens and ministers had urged a one-day bus boycott to protest the way Black Montgomerians were being treated on public transit. The protest was scheduled for December 5, the day of Parks's trial. "This was a long time coming," remembers Fred Gray. "This wasn't just an isolated incident. We had been complaining about the way Black people were treated on the buses for a long time. But the bus company had done nothing at all about it. Initially, we would have settled for minor changes; but they just ignored us. They treated us like we had no rights. So when Mrs. Parks was arrested, the

UNDERWOOD ARCHIVES/GETTY IMAGES

It is a great American myth that Rosa Parks had acted spontaneously when she refused to give up her seat on a bus to a white passenger. Parks and Fred Gray had spent count-less hours, mostly in his office, preparing for that eventuality, and when she was arrested and fingerprinted, Gray defended her.

community just said, 'This is it. We're going to do something about it right now. They are going to give us respect or we are not going to continue riding their buses.'"

At her thirty-minute trial on December 5, Rosa Parks pleaded not guilty to charges of disorderly conduct and violating a local statute. Fred Gray defended her. She was convicted and fined $10, plus $4 in court costs. Gray immediately appealed the conviction. But by that time the protest had begun.

Now, the concept of a citywide boycott was seriously discussed for the first time. In 1953, a two-week-long boycott of city buses in Baton Rouge, Louisiana, had led to compromise that made the middle seats in the buses first come, first served. "Unfortunately," Gray recalls, "there were some Black leaders in Montgomery, including some Black ministers, who felt that before we filed a lawsuit to desegregate the buses we ought to try to get the city to agree to something less than that. Personally, I didn't have any problems with that because I felt certain the city was not going to be willing to make any sort of deal. The city's attitude seemed to be, if you give them a seat, they'll take the whole bus."

Montgomery's Black community comprised only a small part of the electorate—less than 8 percent of the city's forty thousand Black residents were registered to vote—and yet in recent elections those Black votes had proved key to victory. Politicians needed those votes, so, at the least, they had to act like they were listening. In 1954, Professor Jo Ann Robinson, president of Montgomery's Women's Political Council, an activist organization for Black women, had sent a letter to Mayor William Gayle, noting that "Three-fourths of the riders of these public conveyances are Negroes. If Negroes did not patronize them, they could not possibly operate." She requested a variety of changes to the existing regulations. These included the right for Blacks to be seated from back forward on a first-come, first-seat basis and that "Negroes not be asked or forced to pay fare at the front and go to the rear of the bus to enter."

City officials agreed to other requests such as that buses stop at every block in the Black section of the city, as they did in white sections, rather than every other block. The officials also agreed to investigate claims that certain drivers were abusive. But seating remained the unsolvable problem. Generally, the front seats were reserved for white people, Blacks sat in the back—but the middle sixteen seats had no permanent designation. Drivers were empowered to determine who would sit where—with the understanding that white people would always be given priority. Each driver operated his bus essentially as a fiefdom; he could order seated Black passengers to give up their seats to whites, and if they refused they were subject to arrest.

That was the line that the city and bus company refused to cross—no matter where individual drivers set that line. They had no choice in the matter, they claimed. That was the law. Gray had expected that response. "I told Jo Ann Robinson that we were going to have to be prepared to stay off the buses for more than one day if we really wanted to get the attention of the city. Otherwise they just were not going to listen to us."

Robinson had put her teaching position at Alabama State College for Negroes at risk by secretly printing thousands of flyers urging people to stay off the buses on Monday, December 5. Black citizens were asked not to share this information; leaders were fearful that if the white community learned of these plans they would take steps—including threatening to fire anyone who participated in the protest—to stop it. It leaked out. Supposedly a Black domestic worker gave a copy of the leaflet to her white employer. In reality, prominent Black activist leader E. D. Nixon had given a flyer to a reporter he trusted, and the next day, December 4, it had appeared on the *Montgomery Advertiser*'s front page. Within hours the city's white leaders, the police department, the bus company and the media knew about it. Montgomery's two local TV and four radio stations reported the planned protest, ensuring that just about every Black citizen of the city became aware of it.

The *Montgomery Advertiser* quoted unnamed police sources as saying that roving "Negro goon squads" had been organized to prevent people from riding the buses, and that every police officer and reserve officer in the city was ready to intervene to stop them. While there were no such squads, ironically, that story had the effect of frightening many people who might otherwise have ignored the protest, keeping them off the buses.

The unexpectedly complete success of the "protest," as it was referred to in the Black community, or the "boycott," as white Montgomery called it, led to the formation of the Montgomery Improvement Association, which was created to plan strategy going forward—and then to coordinate and administer the details of the continuing effort. There were many Black organizations already in existence, among them the NAACP, the Women's Political Council and Citizens Coordinating Committee, Fred Gray recalls, "and we needed to have all of their support, which is why I suggested that rather than using the NAACP, for example, which had a stigma in the minds of white people, we should start a new organization to bring all of these Black groups together without affecting any of them, and their leaders would also be the leaders of this new organization."

Gray knew one thing was critical: "We needed a leader, a person who would be able to organize, motivate and keep the people together." Robinson suggested the pastor of her church, the Dexter Avenue Baptist Church, Martin Luther King. Fred Gray did not know Dr. King, who had arrived in Montgomery from Atlanta slightly more than a year earlier, and he remembers asking Robinson, why King?

"As she told me that night, 'He could move people with his words and that's what we need.' As a practical matter, she pointed out, selecting a minister to lead the MIA also prevented the white power structure from bringing economic pressure on him. There was some talk about Dr. King because of his known commitment to nonviolence. For some people that seemed like what we had been doing for a long time, without seeing any change. I remember my brother Thomas Walter Gray, who also was an activist and a member of the MIA executive board, didn't believe in that concept. I remember him telling Martin that it was a nice thought, but nonviolence never accomplished anything. In fact, one day the *Montgomery Advertiser* ran a story about Dr. King's strong belief that nonviolence was essential to the success of any protest movement. The next day Tom told Dr. King that this was a very clever ploy and the newspapers had believed it. Martin looked surprised. I'll never forget his response. 'Oh no, Brother Gray, this is no ploy at all. If we're going to succeed,

I am convinced that an absolutely nonviolent method must be ours amid the vast hostilities we face.'

"I don't recall Tom responding, but I doubt he was convinced that he could adopt that philosophy or successfully follow it. But Dr. King was insistent, and eventually we followed him."

Dr. King had accepted the pulpit of this relatively small, somewhat conservative upper-crust church on September 1, 1954. He had been recruited to replace Reverend Vernon Johns, whose outspoken support of civil rights activism (in addition to other issues) had irritated some members of his congregation. Dr. King was an ideal compromise candidate: he was especially eloquent and, perhaps more importantly, he had not been in the city long enough to become embroiled in local politics.

King was not in the meeting when he was nominated by Ralph Abernathy and unanimously elected. Later he said he might have rejected the nomination if he had been present. "I neither started the protest nor suggested it," he later wrote. "I simply responded to the call of the people... I just happened to be there."

Hours later King addressed the boisterous and supportive crowd gathered inside and outside the Holt Street church. It was arguably the most important speech of his budding career: "There comes a time when people get tired of being trampled over by the iron feet of oppression..." he said. He spoke extemporaneously, he had not had time to write a speech; but within moments, Fred Gray remembers, "We knew we had found the leader we needed."

At the urging of Robinson and Gray, E. D. Nixon, who held a prestigious job as a Pullman porter and had organized and led the local chapter of the International Brotherhood of Sleeping Car Porters, as well as having served as president of the state's NAACP, was elected treasurer. A year earlier Nixon had become Montgomery's first Black candidate for public office since

Reconstruction when he ran—unsuccessfully—for a seat on the County Democratic Executive Committee.

Rufus Lewis, a popular longtime athletic coach, was also the owner of a fashionable social club, the Citizens Club, which admitted only registered voters—and registered them. His wife, Jewel, was co-owner of the Ross-Clayton Funeral Home, the largest Black funeral chapel in the city. Rufus Lewis was placed in charge of the MIA's transportation committee and made co-chairman of the registration and voting committee. He was a great choice, Gray says, but also a practical one: "We knew we were going to have to find a way of moving people around if they stayed off the buses. In addition to the funeral home's fleet of cars, Coach Lewis knew all the other funeral home operators and they all had some cars."

The twenty-five-year-old Gray, one of only two Black attorneys in Montgomery and a close friend and adviser to Rosa Parks, was named the association's legal adviser. Under the guidance of the MIA, the boycott continued into the New Year far more effectively than anyone might have expected. More than forty thousand people stayed off the buses, driving their own cars, utilizing a jerry-rigged transport system or walking.

Initially, the MIA, Dr. King and his adviser Ralph Abernathy intentionally made moderate requests so the city, if it wanted to, could easily comply. City officials met several times with Black leaders, among them Gray, Dr. King and Jo Ann Robinson, to try to forge a compromise about bus seating. Mayor Gayle said publicly that the boycott was an attempt to end segregation, which he claimed was required by state law. There was nothing the bus line could do.

According to its attorney, Jack Crenshaw, the company was legally bound to follow existing city ordinances. At a December 16 meeting, Dr. King offered a solution devised by Gray; as state law only governed travel between cities, the Montgomery bus company was free to make its own rules—just as the city of

Mobile had done. This was a way for the city to end the boy-cott without addressing segregation.

They weren't interested. Mayor Gayle and other leaders remained confident the boycott would collapse within a few weeks. People had to get to work, so while publicly negotiating, privately they were determined to tough it out, to break the boycott.

Rather than breaking apart, the boycott grew stronger every day. In desperation, the city shut down the bus lines for several days, then resumed service on a limited basis. The rapidly growing Montgomery chapter of the White Citizens Council—a supposedly nonviolent organization that had been founded a year earlier to fight court-ordered integration—conducted a massive advertising campaign urging people to ride the buses. In early January, the same day the city proposed raising the bus fare, Mayor Gayle issued a statement essentially pleading with all residents of the city "to patronize the existing transportation systems…so that everyone may be assured of continuation of bus transportation in the city."

Days later, Governor Jim Folsom called for renewed harmony. "Naturally," he said, "there is a fundamental difference between races and tribes since the beginning of time. The great masses of Alabama Negroes do not fear their white brothers as much as they do some of their overanxious leaders… I say to the great masses of both races, let us approach our problems in the spirit of calmness, understanding, debate and deliberation."

By the seventh week, the MIA was holding weekly pep sessions that had taken on the spirit of old-time revival meetings. They had become well organized, with many people finding the volunteer car pools more convenient and economical than the buses had been. While the protesters adhered strictly to Dr. King's insistence on nonviolence, the white community had no such compunctions, and leaders of the boycott had their tires slashed and received threatening phone calls and letters.

Suddenly, in the eighth week, the city announced triumphantly it had reached an agreement with three Black ministers to end the boycott. That turned out to be a scam; as Dr. King quickly pointed out, those ministers were not associated with the MIA and had not been authorized to speak for the MIA. The city had picked out these pastors, Black men who were not actively involved in the protest, and invited them to a meeting under largely false pretenses. They then pressured the men to announce some type of deal that no one even knew about, much less had agreed to. One of those ministers explained that he had been invited to city hall to discuss selling insurance policies, but when he arrived he was told he would have to help end the boycott before insurance could be discussed. He apologized to the Black community.

Mayor Gayle was growing increasingly desperate. On January 25 he told a reporter from the *Advertiser* that boycotters were "fighting to destroy our social fabric." He was especially critical of white people who supported the movement by providing transportation for their Black employees, sometimes even personally picking them up or bringing them home. "The Negroes are laughing at white people behind their back," the mayor said. "They think it's very funny and amusing that whites who are opposed to the Negro boycott will act as chauffeurs to Negroes who are boycotting the buses."

Violence finally erupted days later when that bomb detonated outside Dr. King's house. The Black newspaper *Alabama Citizen* reported that among the people who gathered outside King's house that night "were Mayor W. A. Gayle and Police Commissioner Clyde Sellers who possibly gave courage to the reactionary forces by joining the White Citizens Council."

With the transit system collapsing from a lack of revenue, desperate city officials turned to the law, a strategy that had been used successfully against Black Americans literally throughout the nation's history. The city had an obscure state anti-boycott statute that had been passed in 1921 to prevent Birmingham, Alabama, coal miners from organizing and striking. That labor unrest, according to then governor Thomas Kilby, was caused by "foreign agitators," who were attempting to promote socialism, "which often results in anarchy." The statute prohibited "two or more persons who, without a just cause or legal excuse for so doing, enter into any combination, conspiracy, agreement, arrangement or understanding for the purpose of hindering, delaying or preventing any other persons, firms, corporations from carrying on any lawful business."

When this law was originally passed, a state representative had offered a bit of blunt advice to striking coal miners: "Hang your orators."

The statute hadn't been used in more than three decades, and while it was quite a stretch to use it to force people to put their dimes in the fare box, it was the only grounds the city could find. City officials believed, hoped really, they could break the boycott by threatening to arrest its leaders. An eighteen-member grand jury, which included one Black man, the headwaiter at the all-white Montgomery Country Club named E. T. Sinclair, was impaneled to consider bringing charges. Judge Eugene Carter instructed the grand jury that "The right to conduct one's business without wrongful interference of others is a valuable property right which will be protected, if necessary, by injunctive relief..."

A boycott, he explained, "is a confederation, generally secret, of many persons whose intent is to injure another by preventing any and all persons from doing business with him through fear of incurring the displeasure, persecution and vengeance of the conspirators."

The judge then added a bit of conciliatory advice, reminding the grand jurors "Montgomery has been a city that both races have had the pleasure of living in. I say to both black and white, let's continue to live as neighbors."

The grand jury met for eight days in February, hearing more than two hundred witnesses. Eventually they indicted ninety-three people, reporting, "There is a growing tension between the races in this community. The bus boycott is but one manifestation of this feeling. Distrust, dislike and hatred are being taught in a community which for more than a generation has enjoyed exemplary race relations... It is the feeling of this grand jury that if we continue on our present course of race relations, violence is inevitable... In this state we are committed to segregation by custom and by law; we intend to maintain it. The settlement of differences over school attendance, public transportation and other public facilities must be made within those laws that reflect our way of life."

The White Citizens Council supported the indictments, its leaders saying aloud the hidden fear of most white Alabamians: "If these people succeed in getting the Negroes of Montgomery to break the law, and get away with it, then who's to say what unlawful act they will advocate next."

The objectives of Montgomery's Black community had been simple and clear: they just wanted to be treated fairly, if not even totally equally, on the city's public buses. This was not an attempt to overthrow Jim Crow, to eliminate segregation in all forms; it was not an effort to upset the city's social structure, and it certainly was not an attempt to destroy the bus company. "And it was not," Gray remembers, "an attempt to solve the nation's racial problems." The Black community actually needed the buses far more than white people. In fact, a substantial majority of daily passengers were Black. They just wanted to be treated with respect and to be able to sit in any available seat.

But they ended up achieving far more than even they imagined.

"Negroes from almost every walk of life" had been indicted, according to the *Advertiser*. Among those people indicted were

MONTGOMERY COUNTY ARCHIVES

After being verbally abused by a white bus driver, Jo Ann Robinson, as president of the Women's Political Council, began fighting for a bus protest as early as 1949. She was an unofficial leader of the MIA, fearing that accepting a public position might force Alabama State University to fire her.

Rosa Parks and her husband Raymond, Tom Gray, Jo Ann Robinson, E. D. Nixon and Rufus Lewis, Dr. King, and eighteen other ministers.

The roundup began a day later. The first person arrested was Reverend Ralph Abernathy, who was heading negotiations with the bus company. "We are law-abiding citizens," he told reporters. "We are ready to be governed by the law." Asked by a reporter if that included Alabama's segregation laws, he smiled and responded, "Oh no. No. By the law of the land."

When word spread of the arrests, a large crowd of supporters gathered outside the police station, cheering as each person was brought in to be fingerprinted, photographed and booked. As soon as the process was completed, they were released on $300 bond put up by members of the community. Fred Gray was named the defense attorney for every one of them.

MONTGOMERY COUNTY ARCHIVES

Among the eighty-nine people arrested were E. D. Nixon and Professor Jo Ann Robin-son, mostly overlooked activists who laid the groundwork for the civil rights movement. Dr. King described Nixon as "a symbol of the hopes and aspirations of the long oppressed people of the state of Alabama."

Under Alabama privacy laws, the names of indicted people were not made public until they were physically arrested. Interested people began calling the solicitor's office to see if their name was on the list. By late morning people began showing up to be voluntarily arrested. Rather than being intimidated by the move, Montgomery's Black community was aroused, inspired and united as they had never been before. Dr. King later described these mass arrests: "Those who had previously trembled before the law were now proud to be arrested for the cause of freedom." When one person arrived to be arrested, a friend greeted him by bragging, "Man, you're late. I've been here an hour." Some people actually were upset when they were told they had not been indicted. As E. D. Nixon was being processed, he politely asked deputies to move as rapidly as possible. Asked why, he explained, "I'm on jury duty in circuit court."

Among the last of the eighty-nine people arrested for violation of a 1921 ordinance was Dr. Martin Luther King. These booking photographs, which obviously were intended to be a warning, instead solidified resistance to segregation in the city, then in the state and finally throughout the nation.

But then he wondered, "I don't know if I can serve on the jury if I'm under arrest."

People were lining up to be arrested into the early evening. A white man arrested for public intoxication watched the process and said with approval, "Looks like y'all are doing a real good job at arresting today."

Among the last people to be arrested was Martin Luther King. He had been in Tennessee conducting a religious program when the roundup began. He showed up the following morning, accompanied by his far-better-known father, Reverend M. L. King Sr., "Daddy King," the pastor of Atlanta's renowned Ebenezer Baptist Church. Eventually a total of eighty-nine people were arraigned. Those four others originally believed to have been indicted were dismissed or not processed for a variety of causes. Two of them, for example, were airmen being sent overseas. A total of $27,900 in bail bonds was posted, the money coming from local individuals, especially the successful Black businessman D. Caffey, as well as contributions from organizations around the country, which were beginning to pour in to support the boycott.

Reverend King was the first to be tried. The first and, as it turned out, the only one.

The irony of the trial was irrefutable: for more than two centuries, the law in America had been used to prevent Black people from exercising their constitutionally granted and Civil War–won rights. It had been used to keep them out of public and private buildings and businesses and deprive them of the equal use of public facilities; it had kept them out of neighborhoods and schools and been used to defend white people who had committed heinous crimes against them.

But this time the white community was using the law in a different way: to force boycotting Black Montgomery residents to resume riding the city's segregated public buses. Prosecutors were threatening to penalize people for joining together for their common interest with substantial fines as well as six months in prison at hard labor.

It was not the first time that a white city government had tried this strategy. Less than a year earlier, Fred Gray had represented the Tuskegee Civic Association, whose members were boycotting shops in downtown Tuskegee in retaliation for a statute that changed the city limits, legally excluding most Black residents of the city from voting in city elections. Alabama attorney general John Patterson filed a suit in the circuit court in Macon County to essentially force the Black citizens of Tuskegee to patronize white businesses downtown. Gray won that case when courageous white judge Will O. Walton ruled, as Gray had argued, that people had a constitutional right to trade—or not trade— with whomever they pleased.

Gray had been preparing for this type of legal challenge since the beginning of the protest. "I knew I would need assistance," he said. "I was barely out of law school and was now responsible for all this legal work connected to the protest. At the beginning I didn't know what legal problems I might have to deal with, but I didn't want to have to start running around when I needed help."

Following the mass arrests, he hastily assembled a defense team. "There weren't many Black lawyers in the state of Alabama at that time, and I knew all of them. No one turned me down." Consisting of six Black lawyers, this team was led by the well-respected Birmingham attorney Arthur Davis Shores, who had been fighting the white legal establishment for more than two decades. Arthur Shores was the first Black attorney to represent his own Black clients in an Alabama courtroom. A year after being admitted to the Alabama bar in 1937 as the state's third Black lawyer, Shores had successfully represented seven Black teachers who had been denied the right to vote, and since then had battled the legal establishment almost continuously in every area in which equal rights were being denied—on occasion risking his life to do so. For a considerable time he waged lonely battles as the only Black lawyer in the entire state. Only months before this case began, he had successfully represented Autherine Lucy in front of the United States Supreme Court. Lucy, a young Black woman, had been denied admission to the University of Alabama because of her race. After the high court ruled in her favor, Lucy had integrated the university on February 3, 1956, but hostile crowds prevented her from attending classes and the school suspended her, claiming it could not ensure her safety. Shores was still deeply embroiled in that situation when this case began.

When Fred Gray had applied for admission to the Alabama bar, it was Shores who had helped him find the five practicing lawyers he needed to attest to his character. And when Gray began putting together his legal team, Shores was one of the first people he contacted. "He had been doing this for a long time," Gray recalls, "and I wanted to learn how to do it like he did, and maybe even better if I could. I was very, very happy to have him with me on the first major case of my career."

Among the other members of this team was thirty-one-year-old Howard University law school graduate Orzell Billingsley. Billingsley was just beginning to establish himself in Democratic Party politics, and eventually would become an adviser to presidents John Kennedy and Lyndon Johnson. But at this point he was earning a reputation as a bulldog criminal attorney, just then beginning his effort to abolish all-white juries.

Suave and debonair forty-three-year-old Peter Hall, the first Black attorney to try a case in Selma, Alabama, had earned a reputation as a tireless fighter for racial justice. He had garnered considerable attention during a 1955 rape trial when he told the judge, "I don't know whether my client is guilty or not but it's damn sure the system is. I'm going to try the system while the circuit solicitor tries my client."

After earning his law degree at Catholic University, World War II veteran Charles Langford had been admitted to the Alabama bar in 1953, preceding Fred Gray by a year. Later he served in both the state's House then Senate. Initially he had shied away from participating in civil rights cases, fearful his involvement might result in his sisters losing their jobs; but when his activist sisters urged him to join the protest movement, he accepted Gray's invitation to join the defense team and later became Gray's longtime law partner.

Shores had mentored most of the Black lawyers in Alabama, including Fred Gray. But Gray had grown up in Montgomery and so knew the city and its attitudes and policies well. He also had plenty of experience riding its segregated buses, sitting dutifully in the back as he crossed the city twice or more every day on his way to work or classes at Alabama State.

At the suggestion of E. D. Nixon, soon after the protest had begun, Gray had contacted Thurgood Marshall, then head of the National Association for the Advancement of Colored

People's Legal Defense Fund. Nixon knew Marshall through his own work with the Montgomery chapter of the NAACP. Marshall invited Gray to meet with him in New York a week before Christmas. The NAACP was carefully selecting cases in which to become involved, looking for situations that might have greater national impact. Marshall introduced Gray to his associate, Robert Carter, telling him Carter was going to be his contact man. "With that, the NAACP was on board to supply us with whatever legal work we needed. I was thrilled I was able to convince them to give me the help I needed down in Alabama to get done what I needed to do." Any doubts about the importance of this trial were immediately erased with the arrival in Montgomery of the NAACP's Carter.

Robert Carter was one of the nation's most successful Black litigators and had been working alongside Thurgood Marshall since 1948. In the 1950 case *Sweatt v. Painter*, he and Marshall had successfully challenged the Supreme Court's 1896 decision in *Plessy v. Ferguson* that had legalized the "separate by equal" doctrine by demonstrating that a Black law school created by the State of Texas was in no way equal to the University of Texas School of Law. As a result, the state was compelled to integrate that university's law school.

More recently Carter had presented key oral arguments to the Supreme Court in the landmark *Brown v. Board of Education* case that ended legal segregation in public schools. While *Brown* had abolished the Plessy doctrine in public education, it remained in force in other areas of society, especially public transportation, which was strictly segregated in many parts of the country. The NAACP viewed this boycott trial in the "Cradle of the Confederacy" as an opportunity to press its attack on *Plessy v. Ferguson* into those other sectors.

The arrival of this prominent nationally respected attorney clearly shook the local white legal establishment. An important factor in the success of the Southern states to maintain segregation for the past half century had been the ability to contain and isolate challenges. Keeping it local protected the entrenched power structure, which could quietly bring all levels of threats and punishment to anyone who dared challenge the system. Shining a national spotlight on this local case significantly reduced that tactical advantage.

To mitigate that as much as possible, Judge Eugene Carter refused to allow Robert Carter to participate publicly in the trial. While Alabama judges almost always granted visiting lawyers temporary permission to practice law in the state, Judge Carter made this case a rare exception.

Carter was permitted to sit at the defense table during the trial, and confer with the other attorneys, but he would not be allowed to question witnesses or offer objections. The defense challenged this seemingly petty ruling, then warned it would be used as part of any appeal should Dr. King be convicted.

Initially the bus protest had been viewed as a local issue with the modest goals of changing the policies of the bus company rather than a much broader attack on segregation. In fact, in the early days of the boycott Dr. King told reporters, "We are not asking an end to segregation. That's a matter for the legislature and the courts." But after the city's government refused all efforts at compromise, the objectives became greater.

The American legal system is an ascending, often unwieldy maze of traditions, rules and regulations, consisting of a myriad of different courts, appeals and jurisdictions, sometimes overlapping. Years earlier a popular vaudeville sketch began with a man carrying a briefcase walking nonchalantly across the stage; when asked where he was going, he replied, "I'm taking my case to court." Much later on the bill he reappeared, this time carrying his briefcase and a ladder. Asked once again his destination, he explained, "I'm taking my case to a higher court!"

In particular, during this time of upheaval in the legal system over racial issues, losing a verdict at a lower level was just the beginning. Establishing a record for appeal to the next level was paramount. This case would be tried in the Montgomery Circuit Court, which had been established when Alabama joined the Union in 1819.

The trial began on paper, long before it would be heard in the courtroom. The defense began its case by filing a series of motions, knowing that they would be denied. But should King be found guilty, as everyone expected was likely, those denials on the record would form part of the basis for an appeal. Arthur Shores and Fred Gray filed a demurrer, a legal term essentially meaning an objection to the charges. In this instance Shores and Gray argued that the indictments were flawed for a variety of reasons and that this case, and the eighty-eight others, should be dismissed. The allegations, they claimed, "are so vague and indefinite" that the defendants didn't even know what actions they were defending. And that the statute the prosecutor was claiming had been violated "constitutes an abridgement of... rights and liberties secured to all persons by the First and Fourteenth Amendments to the United States Constitution."

That was key; by making a claim that King's constitutional rights were being denied, the defense was laying the groundwork to move the case into the federal system, which, over the previous few years, had been much more accommodating to civil rights actions.

Shores also included another essential claim. "The said statute, in so far as it is applied to enforce laws requiring the segregation of passengers in intrastate transportation, constitutes a denial of the equal protection of the laws in violation of the Fourteenth Amendment."

This was another far-reaching claim. The US Supreme Court had outlawed segregation in interstate travel a decade earlier; cocounsel Thurgood Marshall had argued successfully in *Morgan v. Virginia* that segregating passengers on trains and buses traveling between states violated the Constitution's Interstate

Commerce Clause. But until *Brown*, the courts had usually recognized the rights of states to make and enforce laws within their borders. This claim was a direct attack on a zealously protected states' right.

In response, Montgomery's no-nonsense solicitor William Thetford answered by citing the state supreme court, which years earlier had upheld the anti-boycott law, adding that the United States Supreme Court by refusing to review that decision had essentially supported it.

As anticipated, Judge Carter rejected the arguments made in the demurrer.

The stage was set by several other pretrial rulings and agreements.

The defense began by agreeing to a bench trial, meaning that rather than seating an entire jury and having twelve people agree on a verdict, Judge Carter by himself would hear the case and issue a verdict. It was an interesting decision: seating a jury including at least one Black member might have significantly improved chances of at least getting a hung jury, a jury unable to reach a verdict, while seating an all-white jury might provide additional grounds for an appeal and give Orzell Billingsley additional fodder for his attack on the existing jury system.

Putting the decision in Judge Carter's hands was not intended to be a vote of confidence in him. Like most members of the Alabama judiciary, Judge Carter was a product of the segregated system; he had received his law degree from the University of Alabama forty years earlier and been elected to the bench in 1934. He was an experienced, competent judge who also happened to be a segregationist. Once, for example, he had co-sponsored a resolution that barred Black men and women from his church—unless they were part of the janitorial crew. He had been involved in the legal cases against the boycott from its beginning, previously upholding Rosa Parks's conviction for violating state and municipal law by refusing to give up her seat

ALABAMA DEPARTMENT OF ARCHIVES AND HISTORY

When the protest began, segregation was legal throughout the United States, defended fiercely by men like circuit court judge Eugene Carter, who presided over several significant civil rights trials, including those of Dr. King and Rosa Parks. The very few African American attorneys in the South believed they could use the law to change the law.

and then—on his own volition—putting this case in front of the grand jury he supervised.

Judge Carter had spent his career defending and protecting legal segregation, so expecting him to suddenly deviate from that was a long shot. But there was no better alternative; changing judges would make no difference. In so many ways this trial was legal theater: everyone expected that it would be conducted as a real trial, the participants would play their roles, it would sound and look like a trial. But as with any theater the outcome was predetermined. There really was no reason to think that this case, a seemingly minor case about where people had to sit on a bus, would be any different. It would take a day or so to try and within a few weeks or months would be forgotten. Eventually the city would return to normal.

No one could envision what was about to happen.

The defense also had demanded and received a severance in this case, meaning that each one of the defendants would "be tried separately, alone and apart from each other." Each of the eighty-nine defendants was entitled to a separate trial, complete with a jury and witnesses, which would have clogged the city's court system for a year or more and been inordinately expensive for both sides.

The prosecution, with the assent of the defense, would make this the test case. If King were to be convicted and it survived any appeal, the prosecutors hoped it would send a clear message to the other eighty-eight—plead guilty in exchange for a minimum punishment. While the defense wanted King's case tried alone, they also did not want dozens of trials either. The burden of defending each case would be far too great for them to bear.

The *State of Alabama v. Martin Luther King Jr.* was called to order at 9:00 a.m. on March 19, 1956. The Honorable Eugene W. Carter acting "without a jury" told Solicitor Thetford, "They have asked for a severance. Which case are you going to try first?"

Thetford responded, "The King case."

Until that moment the quest for civil rights in America had been a movement without a leader, moving forward sluggishly from case to case, state to state. King's father, Reverend Martin Luther King Sr., had been fighting for civil rights long before his son was born. He had led the fight for equal pay for Black teachers and integrated the elevators in the city courthouse. Men like Thurgood Marshall and Robert Carter had been poking at the deeply entrenched system and making some critical inroads, but there had been no single, charismatic person able to speak universally for Black Americans, no one with the ability to bring together the entire community.

Now, by putting him on trial as the face of Montgomery's bus boycott, Alabama had inadvertently picked the man around

AUTHOR COLLECTION—FRED D. GRAY

Fred Gray and Martin Luther King Jr. in Gray's small office in 1956. They met there al-most daily to plan Gray's defense of Dr. King in the trial that would lead to both men pio-neering the movement that morally and legally changed America forever.

whom the movement could coalesce and provided him a na-tional platform. In their effort to legally punish the Black pop-ulation of Montgomery, the people who had shaken the power structure by refusing to ride the city buses, the city government would be giving the civil rights movement its leader.

As Fred Gray remembers, "It certainly is accurate to say that none of the people who picked him thought of him as someone who would lead Black folks all over the country. We were just dealing with the situation on the buses in Montgomery. For me, this was an important step in achieving my goal of destroying segregation wherever I could find it. It was only later that we understood that this sort of casual selection had made all the difference in the world."

CHAPTER TWO

On March 20, 1956, the *New York Times* reported on Dr. King for the first time with the headline "First Negro Tried in Bus Boycotting." "The leader of the Negro protest against the segregation policies of the Montgomery bus lines went on trial today on a charge of conducting an illegal boycott," the story began. It wasn't until the second paragraph that King was mentioned by name. "The Rev. Martin Luther King Jr. was the first of ninety-three persons, including twenty-five ministers, arrested in connection with the movement to be tried. He is the president of the Montgomery Improvement Association, which is directing the protest."

Reporting that the NAACP was considering "whether the passive resistance pattern developed here could be applied elsewhere in the fight on segregation," the paper credited King for "having applied that policy to the racial struggle in the South."

A day later, as the trial began capturing national attention, Dr. King was profiled as the *Times'* Man in the News: "Dr. King is a rather soft-spoken man with a learning and maturity far beyond his twenty-seven years. His clothes are in conservative good taste and he has a small trim mustache. He heads an upper middle-class group of Negro Baptists with dignity and restraint.

"Dr. King came here as pastor of the church in September, 1954, after finishing work on his Doctor of Philosophy degree at Boston University. He is particularly well read in Kant and Hegel, and the concepts of struggle as a law of growth."

And then, finally, the obviously enraptured reporter explained his appeal. "Dr. King is a Baptist preacher in a great southern tradition of resounding, repetitive rhetoric. And he can build to his climax with a crescendo of impassioned pulpit-pounding that overwhelms the listener with the depth of his convictions.

"Among his convictions are these: That all men are basically good; that ultimately good will triumph over the evil in their nature; that segregation in all its aspects is evil, and that ultimately it must be swept away.

"'Frankly, I am for immediate integration,' he said. 'Segregation is evil and as a minister I cannot condone evil.'"

As his trial began, Martin Luther King Jr. sat quietly next to Fred Gray at the defense table. While it was Dr. King on trial, the six Black lawyers comprising the defense team had decided they were going to put a Southern way of life on trial. They were going to show America the ugly reality of racism, about the daily slurs and insults that were part of everyday life for Black people in this country.

The attorney representing the Montgomery City Lines bus company, Jack Crenshaw, claimed to be sympathetic to the requests from the Black community, but as he told Mayor Gayle soon after the boycott had begun, "I don't see how we can do it within the law. If it were legal I would be the first to go along with it, but it just isn't legal. The only way that it can be done is to change your segregation laws."

The *Montgomery Advertiser* agreed, explaining in an editorial,

"The boycott makes an innocent sufferer of the bus company. Had the company defied city and state laws its franchise would have been canceled. The quarrel of the Negroes is with the law."

The law is often confused with justice. They are very different concepts. The law is simply a body of rules and regulations governing behavior in life and commerce created by the existing power structure to ensure its desired form of civilization might survive and prosper. It does not necessarily guarantee justice or even fairness. The law may be ambiguous or contradictory, definitive or inexact, unpredictable, obvious or confusing, contrarian, inexplicable, inconsistent, irrational, incomprehensible and even absurd; but it is always open to interpretation. The law, in fact, is what the judicial system says it is. And whatever that is, the entire law enforcement community and the vast majority of citizens will support it.

There was always an uneasy debate in the Black community about the need to respect or follow clearly discriminatory laws. "Dr. King and I used to talk about that," Fred Gray recalls. "There were times when he told me, 'Fred, I understand what you say the law is, but our conscience says that the law is unjust and we cannot obey it. However, there is a higher law.' He was a realist, though. 'So if we are arrested, we will be calling on you to defend us.'"

Beginning on June 21, 1788, the day the Constitution was ratified, the law in America effectively institutionalized systemic racism. Each state, in turn, passed its own body of laws that codified two parallel but unequal societies; one white, one "Negro." These laws ensured that the rights of Black Americans, originally both free and enslaved, would be restricted. The laws gave legitimacy to always humiliating, often cruel and sometimes brutal treatment of Black men and women.

Even the equality supposedly granted to Blacks after the Civil War by the Fourteenth and Fifteenth Amendments was narrowly defined by state courts under the doctrine of states' rights.

It was these laws that Fred Gray had vowed to fight, laws that were carefully drawn to protect and perpetuate the system. Laws that, as much as possible, denied "equal protection under the law" to African Americans. In many states, Blacks could not even bring a lawsuit, either because they were denied the right to do so or couldn't find or afford a white attorney to represent them. It wasn't until 1844 that the nation's first Black lawyer, Macon Bolling Allen, was admitted to the bar in Maine, causing a local newspaper to respond to angry protesters, "Is the practice of law so much more respectable than hoeing potatoes that a lawyer can be disgraced by contact with a black man, and not a farmer?"

After Bolling moved to Massachusetts and was admitted to practice there, that same newspaper praised him as "a better looking man than two or three members of the Boston Bar and it is hardly possible that he can be a worse lawyer than at least six of them, whom we can name…"

Even those few practicing Black lawyers had difficulty attracting clients, as every judge and jury was white. It is believed that in 1847 Boston's Robert Morris Sr. became the first Black lawyer to represent a client in a trial. While details of that trial are largely lost to history, Morris later wrote, "There was something in the courtroom that made me feel like a giant. The courtroom was filled with colored people and I could see, expressed on the faces of every one of them, a wish that I might win the first case that had ever been tried before a jury by a colored attorney in this country." When the jury found for his client, he continued, "My heart pounded up and my people in the courtroom acted as if they would shout for joy."

State bar associations were slowly integrated. Alabama admitted its first Black attorney, Howard University law school graduate Moses Wenslydale Moore, to the state bar in 1871, resulting in the *Montgomery Daily State Journal* calling it, "An age of progress; ten years ago whom would have believed that a Negro was capable of learning the law sufficiently to practice in the (state) Supreme Court."

The amount of real progress was questionable; almost twenty-five years later the first Black lawyer to establish a practice in Tuskegee was shot and chased out of town by a lynch mob.

In many states it remained illegal for a Black man to practice law. As late as 1877, for example, Maryland's highest court upheld a state law barring the admission of Black lawyers to practice.

Initially young men learned the law by apprenticing for a judge or working in an office. Few of the early law schools admitted Black people. It wasn't until the 1860s that Black students were permitted to attend any public law schools. The cost also was prohibitive, which led Mark Twain to voluntarily pay tuition for Warner McGuinn, one of Yale Law School's first Black students.

This forced the Black community to become reliant on white lawyers to represent them in both civil and criminal proceedings. Most places in nineteenth-century America were strictly segregated, so people were able to go about their daily lives almost entirely within their own community. While most segregated public venues, restaurants, sports stadiums, department stores and hotels might be avoided, the use of public transportation was an absolute necessity. It was there that the races came together. As Gray points out, "If the Black residents of Montgomery had attempted to solve any other racial problem by boycotting, it would not have worked. Stores and theaters in the white part of the city were not economically dependent on our business. The bus system needed our patronage. And we weren't trying to put them out of business—we needed the buses. We just wanted to be treated fairly when we paid their fare."

By law, common carriers, public transportation, were required to carry any person who paid the designated fare. But they were allowed to set regulations for the safety and convenience of their passengers. So on virtually all forms of transport, on railroads and stagecoaches, streetcars, trolleys and steamboats, the law was straightforward: if Blacks were permitted at all, they were forced to sit in designated "Jim Crow" sections—although in the South before the Civil War, slaves were permitted to ride with their owners.

To prevent confrontation, cities employed all types of remedies. In the 1840s, for example, New York City designated twenty horse-drawn streetcars for its Black residents. Those streetcars, which ran irregularly, hung signs in their windows reading Colored Persons Allowed. All other streetcar drivers were legally permitted to pick up or put off anyone they chose at their discretion. In July 1854, more than a century before the Rosa Parks case made national headlines, twenty-four-year-old Black schoolteacher Elizabeth Jennings refused a driver's order to get off his streetcar in lower Manhattan. Eventually the driver and a police officer forcibly dragged her off the car. As the *New York World* reported, "The conductor got her down on the platform, jammed her bonnet, soiled her dress and injured her person. Quite a crowd gathered, but she effectually resisted."

Frederick Douglass published details about the case in his newspaper, turning it into a national story. Jennings's wealthy father decided to file a lawsuit against the Third Avenue Railway Company. Miss Jennings was represented in court by twenty-four-year-old white attorney Chester A. Arthur. In awarding her $500, later reduced by half, the presiding judge said, "Colored persons if sober, well-behaved and free from disease had the same rights as others and could neither be excluded by any rules of the company, nor by force or violence." Within another decade New York City's public transportation system was completely integrated. Arthur used the publicity surrounding the case as a springboard that eventually led to him becoming the twentieth vice president of the United States, and ultimately succeeding the assassinated James Garfield as the nation's twenty-first president.

Attempts to integrate public conveyances continued throughout the country with sporadic success. As the Civil War ended in 1865, sixty-eight-year-old Sojourner Truth, an abolitionist and former slave, was thrown off a Washington, DC, streetcar while attempting to challenge the segregated system in the nation's capital. Although her effort failed, she did have the conductor arrested for assault and battery.

In 1883, investigative journalist Ida Wells, a founder of the NAACP, bought a first-class ticket in the ladies' car on a train in Tennessee running from Memphis to the town of Woodstock. When three employees literally dragged her down the aisle into the smoking car where African Americans were permitted, she sued the railroad. The court awarded her $200. Months later she tried again, and after being physically removed once again, she won a $500 judgment.

To avoid these repeated legal challenges, carriers created what became known as separate but equal facilities. In response to a legal challenge to that concept, in 1887 the federal government's Interstate Commerce Commission ruled "The right of the carrier to assign...a colored man to a car for his own race, takes nothing from the right...to have accommodations substantially equal to others paying the same fare."

The Supreme Court codified the concept in its 1896 decision *Plessy v. Ferguson*, which made racial segregation the law of the land. In reality, though, it was the illusion of equality. Facilities always were separate but rarely equal.

Few cities embraced segregation more readily than Montgomery, Alabama. Montgomery had become the state capital in 1847, and it was there in 1861 that the Confederacy was founded. The Southern anthem "Dixie" was played there for the first time during the inauguration of Jefferson Davis, the president of the Confederate States of America. The Confederate flag, the Stars and Bars, flew for the first time from Davis's home, the Confederacy's first White House. Those traditions endured even after the end of the Civil War, embodied by the state's code of arms, which included the Latin phrase meaning We Dare Defend Our Rights. At the beginning of the twentieth century, every aspect of life in Montgomery was segregated, from the public parks to the schools.

So it was astonishing that one of the rare successful actions against segregated streetcars took place there.

In 1900, among many indignities mandated by law, Black riders were forced to board public streetcars by the rear door and remain in the back. In midsummer that year, Black ministers organized a boycott, appealing to their congregations to walk rather than ride until they were treated fairly. That boycott lasted five weeks, and threatened to bankrupt the streetcar company. Having no alternative, the struggling company finally surrendered, and for a time Montgomery's public transportation system was integrated. But within a decade, as the city continued to grow, Jim Crow laws had once again taken hold and Black passengers were sent to the back of the bus.

This temporary victory was a rare exception. The scarcity of Black lawyers meant there were few challenges to that doctrine. In fact, when the NAACP was founded in 1909, incredibly, it was forced to rely mostly on white lawyers to spearhead the attack on racial discrimination. Throughout the early decades of the century, there was never more than a light sprinkling of Black lawyers in Alabama. In 1903, for example, Wilford Horace Smith, a Black graduate of Boston University's law school, challenged an Alabama state constitutional provision that made it much more difficult for Blacks to vote, in a case that eventually went to the Supreme Court. This was the first voting rights case ever heard by the high court. Smith's fee and all costs in this case, *Giles v. Harris*, were quietly paid by Booker T. Washington. Responding for the court, Justice Oliver Wendell Holmes let the controversial law stand, the court refusing to interfere with Alabama's right to set its own voting registration laws—as long as they were applied equally to all citizens. *Equally*, once again, being the operative word.

It had always been especially difficult for Black lawyers to establish a viable legal practice. They rarely attracted white clients, and many Black people needing representation often preferred hiring a white lawyer to do battle in white offices and courtrooms. Over decades that slowly began changing, as the children, then grandchildren, of former slaves became adults in a changing world, shedding their collective history as they did.

The real assault on legal segregation began when NAACP lawyers led by a young Thurgood Marshall sued the state of Maryland in 1936 to force the state university law school to admit Black Amherst graduate Donald Murray. Marshall, who eventually would become the first African American justice on the United States Supreme Court, had been born in Baltimore but had been unable to attend the University of Maryland law school because it did not accept Blacks. This was his opportunity to attack that policy. After rejecting Murray because he was Black, the university offered to fulfill its obligation under separate but equal by helping him gain admission to an out-of-state law school. Thurgood Marshall argued that such a remedy might be separate but it certainly wasn't equal; there was only one law school in the entire state of Maryland, and any out-of-state school by definition taught the law of an entirely different state, which would make it extremely difficult for applicants seeking admission to the Maryland bar.

Maryland was ordered to admit Murray to its law school. "Separate but equal" remained the law of the land, but this was the first chip in the wall that separated the races. And suddenly other lawyers began chipping away at it as well.

This decision was part of an extraordinary foundation. For the first time, young Black lawyers had decided to use those same laws that had for so long been used against them to win the rights that had been taken away from them. They did this in the belief that the white community would respond to its legal losses just as they did: they respected the law.

Almost two decades later the decision in Donald Murray's case finally led to *Brown v. Board of Education*, in which the Supreme Court recognized the inequality of separate schools. Segregated schools were outlawed. Simultaneous with this effort, other lawyers attacked voting restrictions and segregation on public transportation.

Progress in integrating public transportation was equally slow. The Supreme Court ruled in the 1946 decision in *Morgan v. Virginia* that "no state law can reach beyond its own border nor bar transportation of passengers across its boundaries, diverse seating requirements for the races in interstate journeys result," which basically outlawed segregated seating in interstate travel legally if not in actuality.

It took courage for Black lawyers to challenge the system since it could involve real personal danger. Their lives, as well as their livelihood, were threatened. There were so few Black lawyers in Alabama that in 1925 the Protective National Detective Association was founded to provide representation for Black people in both civil and criminal matters. An advertisement for their services pointed out, "Hundreds of poor colored people are hard labor prisoners today because they did not have a lawyer to represent them."

When Arthur Shores successfully sued the state of Alabama in 1938 for denying the right to vote to seven teachers, he understood he was making himself a target. In addition to the entrenched white establishment, the Ku Klux Klan was operating with impunity. In response to that lawsuit, the Klan warned Shores to get out of Birmingham—or Bombingham, as it later became known to civil rights activists. He had learned to ignore the countless threats he had received—in 1944 he was physically attacked in a courthouse corridor during a trial, and years later his home would be bombed. There was no powerful organization protecting Shores; he was literally risking his life.

Out of necessity, Gray recalls, most of the Black lawyers in Alabama obtained pistol permits and carried a weapon. He decided not to carry, he says, "Because I felt if I would have had a pistol and used it, even for self-protection, they were going to convict me. So I just thought it would be better for me not to have a weapon and figure out how to deal with situations without it."

Change came very slowly. Gray had been born and raised in Montgomery, the son of a carpenter who had died when Fred was two years old. His home in the early years of his childhood did not have running water or electricity. There was an outhouse in the backyard. With the help of the Holt Street church, his mother raised him to believe he and his four siblings "could be anything we wanted to be—then she gave us the necessary shove to fulfill that prophecy." He had also helped support his family, doing everything from shining shoes to managing the delivery of the *Alabama Journal*. Growing up, segregation was all Gray had known. "I lived in the Black community on the west side of town. I went to a Black church. All of the people I knew were Black. I never had come in contact with white people, so I don't recall any racist encounters during that time. But we knew that there was a Black world and a white world and there were problems. We knew what segregation was and how it worked. We definitely knew that."

Gray had grown up believing he would become a minister or a teacher, the two professions open to Black men and women. As he admits, "After graduating from Alabama State, I briefly considered becoming a teacher. But when I interviewed for a job in Lowndes County, the superintendent referred to me as 'boy'; that was the end of that for me. If teachers are called 'boy' I wanted no part of that.

DON CRAVENS/GETTY IMAGES

Fred Gray was raised by his widowed mother, Nancy Jones Gray, seen here outside her tiny shop on West Jeff Davis Avenue, to believe he could be anything he wanted to be—although she hoped he would become a minister. About seven decades later, to honor Gray's legal achievements, the City of Montgomery changed the name of that street to Fred D. Gray Avenue.

"I decided to become a lawyer while riding the segregated buses back and forth to Alabama State. Other than an uncle who was a lawyer practicing in Chicago, I didn't know any lawyers. It was while I was riding the buses back and forth to school and work I found out that lawyers could help people solve problems. The Black community had a lot of problems, but we didn't have many lawyers. I realized that if I got to be a lawyer I could help to change things."

Becoming an attorney can be difficult for anyone, but the hurdles were considerably higher for a Black Southerner. Knowing a Black student would not be admitted to the segregated

University of Alabama law school, he applied and was accepted to Case Western Reserve in Cleveland.

"I didn't even tell my mother I had applied to law school. After I had gotten accepted we were having dinner and I just sort of put the acceptance letter in front of her. She read it and said, 'Well, Mr. Smarty, now that you've been accepted, where you get your money from?' Then she went out and found another job to raise some of the money I needed. The only advice she ever gave me about that was 'You can be anything you want to be, but I don't ever want you to stop preaching.' I made her that promise."

Under a complicated formula created as a way to legally circumvent separate but equal restrictions, the state would pay the difference in cost between attending the state university and an out-of-state school. The catch was that the state would only reimburse students later, meaning they would have to find the money to pay tuition, fees and living expenses up front, which in many cases was prohibitive. At the last minute Gray received a $250 scholarship from his college fraternity, Omega Psi Phi.

While attending law school, Gray simultaneously prepared for both the Alabama and Ohio bar exams, passing both and being admitted to practice in both states in late 1954.

He was officially the ninth Black attorney in the entire state. Upon Gray's return to Montgomery, Reverend Solomon Seay offered to sublease space in his office above the Sears Roebuck on Monroe Street, where most of the upscale Black businesses were located. "It won't cost you but $50 a month," he'd told Gray, "and if you don't have the $50, you don't have to pay that!"

When Gray hosted a reception to officially open his office, his fiancée, Bernice Hill, filled the otherwise empty shelves with impressive-looking law books borrowed from the white lawyer whose wife she worked for.

Not unexpectedly, he struggled to build his practice. Ironically,

Gray's ministerial training also made it harder for him to build a business; when people looking for a divorce lawyer came into his office, he tried to counsel them, offering ways to solve their marital problems. While he probably saved some marriages, he certainly lost potential clients. But he never lost sight of that driving force that had sent him to law school, and Gray intended to fulfill that mission of using the law to attack segregation head-on.

To raise his visibility, and perhaps attract a few clients, he began regularly attending NAACP meetings. It was there he'd become close to the soft-spoken, fiercely determined chapter secretary and youth leader Rosa Parks, who was then working as an assistant tailor at Montgomery Fair, the city's leading department store. Parks had been one of the hostesses celebrating the arrival of a second Black lawyer in Montgomery. She, along with Gray's family, even helped him open his law office. Gray and Parks began meeting there almost daily for lunch. Day after day, she'd pick up something in the store, where she was not permitted to sit at the lunch counter, and bring it to his office. On occasion, when he had an appointment or his "secretary," his sister Pearl, was out, she would stay and answer the phone. They would discuss and debate strategies for enacting change and shared a commitment and determination to attack segregation; but much of it was hypothetical.

The hypothetical became reality on March 2, 1955, when Claudette Colvin and an elderly Black woman, Mrs. Hamilton, refused to surrender their seats just in front of the rear door to a white person who had just boarded a Montgomery, Alabama, bus. The police were called. A Black man offered his seat to Mrs. Hamilton, who moved, but Colvin—who had been studying Black history at Booker T. Washington High—refused. When the police officers grabbed her, she resisted, kicking, scratching and screaming. She was arrested for violation of the city's segregation laws, as well as assault and battery.

★ ★ ★

E. D. Nixon, who had been a close friend of Fred Gray's family for many years, stepped in and arranged for Gray to defend her. This was the first civil rights case of his career. "It may have even been my first appearance in a courtroom," says Gray. "This was just what we had spent all those days talking about, and I thought this might be a good test case to challenge segregation on public transportation."

As he would do for the following decades, Gray began searching for an opportunity to attack legal segregation. While Claudette Colvin was only the latest in a series of similar arrests, under the direction of her then twenty-four-year-old attorney, she became the first person known to plead not guilty to violating the Montgomery bus ordinance.

Appearing in Juvenile Court, the newly minted attorney argued that Colvin was not a delinquent; she was an honor student coming home from school. She was not disorderly; she did not resist arrest. "I reminded the court that because of the Fourteenth Amendment we were supposed to have the same rights as white people, and a white person would not have been treated that way," Gray recalls.

After that was rejected, he introduced a much more direct assault on the prosecution's case: in settling the 1900 trolley boycott, the Montgomery city council agreed that people could be forced to give up their seat only if there was another available seat. The bus on which Colvin had been riding was completely full. There was no other seat. So it appeared the bus driver, rather than the teenager, had violated the city ordinance.

In this first courtroom confrontation between Gray and circuit solicitor William Thetford, offering a taste of the trial to come, the prosecutor quickly amended his complaint against Colvin, instead invoking a recently passed state statute requiring buses to enforce segregated seating regulations. The legal maneuvering had begun, each side poking at the law to support their arguments.

While the legality of that ordinance was questionable, its application was not. "The judge was nice and respectful," Gray later remembered, "but he found Miss Colvin to be a delinquent and placed her on unsupervised probation." Gray's appeal was denied by Judge Eugene Carter, but he urged Parks and other community leaders to use this case to challenge the constitutionality of the segregation laws.

"There were some people who claimed later that we didn't use Claudette Colvin to attack the system because she was sixteen years old, unmarried and pregnant, and therefore not the right person to become the public face of this challenge, but that had nothing at all to do with it. It was simply that the community wasn't ready."

Bus seating was a real problem for the Black community, but for the white residents it also was symbolic. Their world was changing. The *Brown* decision was an assault on their traditional way of life. Once they started moving the line, there was no way of knowing where it would stop. Black leaders continued to insist that this protest was not an attack on segregation; they just wanted hardworking people to be able to sit down in peace, without being degraded or humiliated. The city's government saw it very differently; this was another step toward complete integration. And so it had to be resisted. The laws that had served them so well for so long had to be upheld.

Throughout 1955, Gray and Parks continued meeting almost daily at his office to prepare for the next case, and the case after that one. They discussed what Parks would do if she were in this situation. "I think I could be cool as a cucumber," she told Gray. "I would just sit there and wait for police to take me away." That preparation would become necessary late in the afternoon of December 1, 1955, when Rosa Parks boarded the Cleveland

Avenue bus at Court Square and ignored a bus driver's order to give up her seat.

She had not planned to be arrested that day and, had she not been preoccupied, probably would have waited for the next bus. But rather than the passive role depicted by history, Parks, with legal guidance from Gray, had prepared to actively challenge the system.

Admittedly, Gray was not optimistic about the protest. After being retained by Parks to represent her, Gray met with E. D. Nixon and then sat with Jo Ann Robinson in her small living room to determine if this was the opportunity they had been waiting for. "I was more interested in the legal situation, while she wanted to get the community involved," Gray explained. "We agreed that if we were going to do anything, now was the time to do it. We talked about staying off the buses. I did not believe that would be an effective way to accomplish our aim. It takes a long time for a lawsuit to go through, I told her, and wondered how we were going to keep people off the buses until they could ride on a nonsegregated basis. It wasn't going to be one day. In order to accomplish that, we needed to figure out how we were going to help people get to where they needed to go."

Gray himself risked disbarment by laying the strategic and legal groundwork for both Parks and the ensuing protests. "I knew my career was at stake. A decade earlier, the Board of Bar Commissioners had disbarred Black attorney Arthur Madison, claiming he had not been authorized to file an appeal on behalf of Black citizens who had sued after being denied the right to vote. But that was just an excuse to stop him."

Parks, Robinson, Gray and others had set the stage for what led to the mass arrests and the trial of then local minister Dr. Martin Luther King.

CHAPTER THREE

"It was a good day," reported the *Pittsburgh Courier,* a Black newspaper, on March 19, 1956, as the trial began. "The softness and the quiet of the South was everywhere. There was music. Church kind of music. It suited the day... So with the music and the beauty of the day there was nothing to suggest that this was a tense, divided city that might hold the destiny of a whole race of people."

Trials often had been treated as theater, but given the newspaper coverage from around the country as well as several nations, this was the biggest "opening night" in this city's history. The *Boston Globe* described it as "A tense drama of profound national importance," adding, "Here in the shadow of the statue of Jefferson Davis, most white leaders feel that to give in on the bus boycott would end in destroying the Southern way of life by encouraging the Negroes to demand more." They then quoted Mississippi senator James Eastland's recent racist warning: "If we don't stop these Africans we'll wake up one day and find Martin Luther King in the White House."

BETTMANN ARCHIVE/GETTY IMAGES

After years of being humiliated by being pushed to the backs of buses, the Black community finally grasped this opportunity to express its anger. Rather than breaking the protest, the trial of the Reverend Martin Luther King actually solidified the community's determination to end segregation on Montgomery's buses and later, everywhere.

Also that morning four hundred Black and white American clergymen from all denominations had released a statement expressing support for the ministers of Montgomery and urging President Dwight D. Eisenhower to "speak out against segregation in every form" as well as consider "personally going to Alabama and Mississippi."

Several hundred Black men and women had gathered outside the courthouse as the trial began. Many of them remained there throughout the first morning of the trial, quietly demonstrating support. Others crammed the hallways of the county court building or stood at the windows of the east courtroom, allowing them to watch the proceedings across the open courtyard. The 238 seats in the west courtroom in downtown Montgomery had been filled early in the morning. Most taken by Black Montgomery residents, many of them bearing cloth crosses pinned to their dresses or on the left lapel of their jackets reading "Father, forgive them." The only white people in the courtroom were the folksy Judge Eugene Carter, the three-man prosecution team led by solicitor William Thetford, a few spectators sitting in the jury box and journalists from around the country, as well as England, France and India.

Among those spectators who brought attention to the trial was Congressman Charles Diggs, a Democrat from Michigan and one of only three Black members of the 84th Congress. Diggs was accompanied by his aide, Basil Brown. The light-skinned Brown had been stopped at the entrance by Bailiff Addie Mosley and forced to prove he was "a Negro" before being permitted to sit next to Diggs in the segregated courtroom.

"It was the largest courtroom in the county," Gray recalls, "and it was entirely filled. Courtrooms always were segregated, whites on one side, Blacks on the other. We filed a motion to desegregate the courtroom because the number of Black participants and spectators was far greater than the designed space. Ironically, considering this trial was about seating, Judge Carter granted that request. Most of the white spectators were seated in the empty jury box. Members of the media were sitting in the front rows. Dozens of seats behind them were filled by other defendants.

"Coretta King was sitting by the railing, and at times Martin would exchange a glance with her. I believe my brother Tom and my sister Pearl were there too, but I know for certain my mother was not. In my memory my mother never came to see me in a courtroom. She just kind of felt, I believe, that she was going to leave the legal stuff up to me; she had done everything she could to get me there, what happened there was up to me.

But it was a typically noisy, busy courtroom. Certainly no one at that moment fully realized the historical impact of what was taking place."

The world, as the Black citizens of Montgomery had known it for their entire lives, had suddenly moved just slightly off its axis, the balance of power shifting. It was not yet a seismic change, rather just a rumbling, but it was real. In the sermon Martin Luther King had delivered to his congregation at the Dexter Avenue church a day earlier, he had discussed what he referred to as "this bus situation." He related a conversation he'd had in which a man "discussed the peace being destroyed in the community, the destroying of good race relations. I agree that it is more tension now—but peace is not merely the absence of tension, but the presence of justice.... It is true if the Negro accepts his place, accepts exploitation and injustice, there will be peace...and if peace means this, I don't want peace."

"Aw right," Judge Eugene Carter drawled, opening his court early in the morning. "You can smoke, but just keep quiet. Aw right, I'm ready." Sitting directly in front of a large American flag affixed to the wall, Judge Carter almost immediately repeatedly banged his gavel, warning boisterous spectators that if they wanted to remain in his courtroom they had to be silent. "This is no vaudeville," he told them. "If you came to be entertained you're in the wrong place."

After dealing with the business of preparation, the judge turned to "Lawyer" Shores. In transcripts Black attorneys were always identified as "Lawyer," never "Mr.," a term of respect reserved for white practitioners. "Your plea, I take it, is not guilty?"

Shores stood up ramrod straight. He was dressed in a black pin-striped three-piece suit. "That is right."

The three prosecutors and six lawyers for Dr. King sat at either end of the same long table. Dr. King sat silently between Fred Gray and Arthur Shores.

"The state is ready," said the "solicitor," William Thetford. Thetford also was a young man, still at the beginning of a career that would eventually put him on the bench. He was a tall man, six feet four inches, and bulky. "Not a difficult man to talk to," Fred Gray remembers. "What I always tried to do in any courtroom was present myself in a way that my opponent would respond to in a decent manner. I was not trying to beat him personally, I was trying to represent my client, and I understood he was doing the same thing. Thetford seemed to feel the same way. As I had not done many criminal cases, I hadn't spent much time in a courtroom with him.

"He was not one of the viciously racist prosecutors, who acted with disdain when dealing with Black lawyers, but like most of them, he believed in segregation. I never thought of him as a good man or a bad man. He was the product of the system that he had been raised in and trained to protect."

The first witness called to the stand was James H. Bagley, who identified himself in a clear, crisp voice as "transportation superintendent of the Montgomery City Lines," the bus company that had been providing public transportation under a city franchise for twenty years. Bagley had been caught in the center of the boycott between the city, the company and the Black community; while supposedly he ran the bus lines and therefore became the most visible target, in fact his power to do anything more than manage day-to-day operations was limited.

Thetford's objective was to show that the Montgomery Improvement Association, headed by the defendant King, had been created to support and sustain a boycott that was illegal under the city anti-boycott ordinance. As a legal matter, the statute was broad enough that the prosecution would only have to prove that King conspired to "hinder" or "delay" a "lawful business." Even though it was not required, the city's case would be enhanced if it could prove that the boycott was not entirely voluntary, that the MIA had physically intimidated and restrained people from riding the buses.

Conversely, the defense sought to demonstrate that the Black citizens of Montgomery had "just cause" to stay off the buses, which legally would justify their actions under the 1921 statute. "We had a fine legal excuse," Gray recalls, "for failure to ride segregated buses, particularly where we had been mistreated and humiliated." The defense intended to put James Bagley's bus company on trial.

The solicitor began by trying to show the devastating effect the boycott was having on the bus company. "Have you experienced any slackening of your business since December the 5th?"

"We object," Peter Hall said loudly, his voice echoing through the courtroom. Hall was a physically large man, and his girth and booming voice gave him an intimidating presence. Having successfully fought through all the barriers in place to prevent young Black men from becoming members of the Alabama bar, there was no back-down in him. The defense team wanted to limit testimony to the direct involvement of Dr. King. "Right at that time it (the economic impact) had absolutely nothing to do with the conspiracy and is irrelevant."

Judge Carter responded, "I expect he is leading up to that now. Really, no one has testified to any so-called boycott as yet, so for the purpose of saving time I will let him testify while he is on the stand... Unless there is some testimony of a conspiracy not to use the buses—if it isn't connected I will rule it out."

Bagley finally was permitted to answer. "We had... There is not as many people riding the buses as there were before December 5th." It would be decades later before the devastating effect of the boycott would become known. During the boycott, bus revenues declined by almost 70 percent.

When the defense again objected, Thetford told the court, "I think this witness will connect King with the boycott... The state will assure you we will connect King." Then he asked

Bagley, "Do you know the defendant in this case, King, have you seen him?"

Perhaps speaking for the entire white population of the city, Bagley responded, "I know him now." He had been invited to the meeting at city hall by Mayor Gayle to meet with Dr. King and the committee, he continued, including "Attorney Gray and, I believe, Attorney Langford... There was three women there, I think one of their names was, I believe, Jo Ann Robinson."

Asked who acted as the spokesman at this meeting, he replied, "Reverend King."

When Bagley said that Dr. King acted as the spokesman for the entire committee, the judge asked, "Was it for the colored people there, or not?"

"Yes, sir."

"And he presented certain demands upon the bus company?"

"He did..."

And then he discussed the Resolution that Fred Gray had prepared. It consisted of three basic demands that Gray, Jo Ann Robinson and E. D. Nixon had settled on. What it did not include was any suggestion that the buses be desegregated.

"...Number one was requesting more courtesy from the bus drivers when riding the buses. Number two was a request for a change in the seating arrangements on the buses for the different races. He said that they were requesting that colored people sit from the rear to the front and white people from the front to the rear. No seats reserved for anyone. That is about the extent of the request for number two. Number three, they were requesting Montgomery City Lines hire some colored drivers on routes which were predominantly colored people... We didn't go into any exact number as to what he was requesting."

The prosecution then attempted to introduce a copy of Gray's three-page Resolution, which supposedly had been passed by the Montgomery Improvement Association at the December 5 mass meeting and mailed to Bagley the following day. After outlining the outrageous manner in which Black citizens were treated on city buses—"There are thousands of Negroes in the city and county who ride buses owned and operated by the Montgomery City Lines…on many occasions have been insulted, embarrassed and have been made to suffer great fear of bodily harm by drivers…"—it then resolved, "The citizens of Montgomery are requesting that every citizen in Montgomery, regardless of race, color or creed, to refrain from riding buses owned and operated…"

This document supposedly was proof that the leaders of the MIA had gotten together; they had conspired to launch and support an illegal boycott as defined by the city statute. Peter Hall objected loudly and dismissively to its introduction, pointing out there was nothing to connect this document to Dr. King. "It is not signed by the defendant… It is purported to be a Resolution and nothing to show where it came from."

For many Americans, but especially throughout the South, this trial was the first time they were being exposed to Black lawyers in a courtroom. While Thurgood Marshall was emerging on the national scene, it was still not common and few people knew what to expect. The very popular radio and television comedy *Amos 'n' Andy*, a show in which Black men were portrayed as semiliterate hustlers, childlike innocents and con artists, featured a shyster lawyer named Algonquin J. Calhoun. This broad and insulting caricature was the primary image of Black attorneys known to most people.

Peter Hall was the antithesis of that buffoonish figure. A 1946 graduate of DePaul University's law school, Hall was tall, light-skinned and handsome. He was always fashionably dressed, had a pencil-thin mustache and bore a casual resemblance to Billy Eckstine. He walked with a slight limp, the result of having an artificial leg. At times he was known to enter the courtroom just a little bit late, making certain the jury noted his disability. Although he had been born and raised in Birmingham, he spoke without any trace of the South in his words. Looking at him, listening to him, it was a lot easier to picture him among the swells at Harlem's Savoy Ballroom than walking quietly to the back of an Alabama bus. There was no hesitation in his voice when he addressed the court, his demeanor conveying confidence and determination.

What Peter Hall knew, what Shores had taught him and Fred Gray and Billingsley and Langford, was that simply being a good lawyer was not good enough. The ground on which they were competing was not level; the law flowed downhill into the hands of the white establishment. They had to be better than their adversaries. The only advantage they had was that in most situations those adversaries were going to underestimate them.

Orzell Billingsley, who had been mentored by Hall, stood up and respectfully cited the law while also objecting to the introduction of the Resolution, explaining, "The proper procedure would be to lay the predicate before the witness is allowed to see the paper."

Gray sat quietly. As the youngest and least courtroom-experienced member of the defense team, his primary responsibility was to coordinate the defense case. "I wasn't that interested in being out there," he explains. "I wanted to be sure that these men who had the experience would have the opportunity to use it. As the local counsel in Montgomery and the person who had worked closely with Dr. King from the very beginning, I had to coordinate our activities and keep communications flowing between each of us. I don't believe any of us had ever worked on a team this large before; getting that many Black lawyers together in a state courtroom was very unusual. Keeping those channels open sometimes was a hard task.

"But it wasn't that important who was actually speaking for us. Robert Carter, for example, was sitting with us at the defense table and he wasn't allowed to say one word. But he would continually whisper advice. Bob Carter brought a different kind of experience to the defense. He was a typically sophisticated New York lawyer; he was very good, with a big ego, and wasn't shy about letting you know it."

Judge Carter agreed that the Resolution would not be admitted as evidence "unless connected up with King here." When Thetford tried to offer it as evidence, the judge repeated his instructions. "It has to be connected."

"Every conspirator would be liable for the acts of a fellow conspirator," Thetford insisted.

The judge reminded him, "A conspiracy hasn't been proved yet."

The solicitor tried a different approach, asking his witness, "Did this defendant tell you the Negroes would go back to riding the buses if their demands were met? Did he or didn't he?"

Bagley eventually testified, "He said if they got the demands that he had read over he thought that would satisfy the colored people."

Thetford told the court, "I think we have shown a conspiracy."

To the surprise of many people in that courtroom, Judge Carter disagreed. "I don't think a conspiracy has been shown yet."

Thetford's voice thinned as he began showing his frustration. He had actually been opposed to bringing these criminal indictments against the leaders of the boycott but had been practically forced into it by Jack Crenshaw, the bus company's increasingly belligerent attorney. Thetford had objected that rather than ending the boycott, criminal prosecutions carried relatively light penalties and would only strengthen the Black community's resolve. Thetford had recommended strongly that Crenshaw obtain an injunction against the MIA, showing the company was suffering irreparable damage due to an illegal boycott. This strategy would not have forced the state to defend segregation, but Crenshaw resisted, wanting to maintain the myth that the bus company was a neutral party, forced into these regulations by state law.

Like most everyone else watching the case, Thetford undoubt-edly expected this to be a one-day trial during which the pros-ecution would go through all the legal niceties required to get to the predictable ending. That's the way the system worked. That's the way it had always worked. But the defense lawyers, with unexpected cooperation from Judge Carter—perhaps un-accustomed to the national spotlight—were gumming it up. They were making it very difficult for him to prove legally what everybody already knew was reality: a wildly successful boycott was being controlled by the MIA and Reverend King was leading that organization.

Thetford kept trying, probing for the appropriate way to ask this question: "How does your traffic since December 5th com-pare with your traffic before December the 5th?"

Billingsley rose. "We would like to interpose an objection."

"Sustain the objection." Each small victory brought smiles to the packed courtroom. "How many white people ride the buses hasn't anything to do with this case."

Thetford asked the same question about "colored people." This time the witness was permitted to answer. "It is only a small percentage riding now that were riding before December the 5th. I would say maybe five or six percent, something like that."

"Do you know the reason for this?"

This time Lawyer Shores stood. "We object to the reason."

"Yes," agreed the judge. "It calls for a conclusion of the wit-ness."

"It is a fact," Thetford insisted. Clearly this was not proceed-ing as he had expected. "I asked him if he knows the cause of this condition."

"It is a conclusion of the witness," Carter responded. "If King entered into the cause of it I would let him testify."

Several minutes later he finally was able to get Bagley's testimony into the record. At a meeting in city hall with eight white people and eight members of the MIA, according to Bagley, King had said, "(T)he reason they wasn't riding, on account of what they was requesting; that they were tired of being treated with discourtesy, and also as being treated as second-class passengers when they was paying the same fare as any other passenger. Or something to that effect." Several other people in that meeting made similar statements, he continued, naming specifically Jo Ann Robinson. The legal definition of a conspiracy is "an agreement between two or more people to commit an illegal act." Until this moment Thetford had been unable to show King had conspired with any other defendant.

Peter Hall objected, again pointing out, "Jo Ann isn't charged with everything." Judge Carter told the defense that if the prosecution was unable to connect the various defendants, proving they had conspired, he would not consider this testimony.

The morning session of the first day ended when the defense chose not to cross-examine Bagley. He had done their case no harm. As the trial broke for lunch, reporters and photographers surrounded Dr. King, although he had sat silently throughout the morning. Reporters asked the obvious questions as the photographers snapped away. King didn't flinch, patiently answering each question in his slight drawl, repeating the points he had made at rallies. "Negroes in Montgomery are tired of the conditions they have experienced over a number of years... We are not just trying to improve Negro Montgomery but we are trying to improve the whole of Montgomery." The protest, he believed, "would continue, whatever the outcome of this trial."

Meanwhile, about one hundred miles north by US 82 West, a brief trial in Tuscaloosa had been gaveled to order about the same time as this one. An all-white jury took twenty minutes to convict a young Black soldier and his brother for assault with intent to murder. It started when Arthur Shores's client, Autherine Lucy, enrolled at the University of Alabama to take classes. Days later, when a riotous mob forced her out, a Black soldier named Arthur Washington with his younger brother John restrained and beat a white engineering student. That student suffered only minor bruises, but his parents had insisted the solicitor indict and try them for attempted murder. The jury had recommended a $500 fine and the maximum penalty, two to twenty years, but the judge instead sentenced the brothers to six months.

About the same time up in Fayette, Governor James Folsom was reassuring anxious Alabamians, who had been shaken by recent Supreme Court decisions, telling them he wanted to convene a special session of the legislature so that he might legally "be relieved of my obligation...to uphold provisions of the United States Constitution affecting racial segregation." The governor was hoping the state legislature would grant him authority to enforce provisions of the state's 1901 constitution that legalized segregation.

When the afternoon session began, assistant solicitor Robert Stewart began the questioning. Stewart was among the leading practitioners in the city, and it was well-known that he had been the personal attorney of legendary country singer Hank Williams. "Stewart was a very good lawyer," Gray remembers, "maybe even better than Thetford. And like all of the people we were dealing with, he was committed to the preservation of segregation."

Stewart called the Reverend A. W. Wilson, the pastor of the Holt Street Baptist Church, the largest of the Black churches in the city. There actually were two churches on that block: the Holt Street Baptist Church and the Holt Street Church of Christ, where Abraham and Nancy Gray had been worshipping since the mid-1920s. In addition to its main auditorium, the Holt Street Baptist Church had a large basement and upstairs area, it was surrounded by open spaces, and its many smaller meeting rooms already had loudspeakers in place. On the evening of December 5, 1955, more than five thousand people had attended the

DAN ABRAMS AND FRED GRAY WITH DAVID FISHER

first meeting of the Montgomery Improvement Association held there. The Reverend Wilson, who had made his large church a center for protest during his seventeen years there, was also a defendant, having been indicted by the grand jury as a member of the MIA's executive board. Calling him as a witness put him on the center spot; no one doubted Reverend Wilson would be telling the truth. But as the prosecution was to learn, the English language, in all of its nuances, provides plenty of hiding places for those clever enough to seek them.

Reverend Wilson readily admitted he was a member of the MIA, but testified he had not attended the afternoon meeting at which it had been organized and incorporated. Asked, "Will you state the names of the officers of the Montgomery Improvement Association... The president is who?", he replied directly, that was no secret. It was even on the stationery. "The Reverend M. L. King."

Stewart then guided him through the entire roll of officers. This one was the vice president? Yes. That one was treasurer? Yes. But while answering these basic questions, Reverend Wilson set the tone for other witnesses, whenever possible artfully avoiding giving Stewart the answer he wanted. Asked to confirm the members of the executive board, he explained, "Not being present at the election of the executive board, I wouldn't want to name the persons other than those (the officers) because I couldn't prove they had been duly elected."

"Will you just name the people with whom you did meet who purported to be the executive board whether they are properly elected or not."

The Reverend Wilson's tone suggested a deep desire to cooperate but an unfortunate inability to do so because, he explained, "I met with a number of persons whose names are not even on this list. I just don't know all the members of the board."

"I feel sure this is true," Stewart replied, a touch of sarcasm in his words.

"Yes, sir," Wilson agreed. It was almost possible to hear the smiles in the room.

Stewart then recited a list of names, asking the witness if he had met them at all or some of the MIA meetings: Reverend Abernathy? Yes. Reverend Hubbard? Yes. Reverend Glasco? Yes. Reverend J. W. Bonner? Yes. Rufus Lewis? "I don't know whether he is on the board or not." Reverend Binion? "He was in the meeting, but being a member of the board, I cannot establish that fact." Jo Ann Robinson? Yes. Rosa Parks? Yes. Thirty names. Forty names. Stewart using the repetition to try to establish his point: this was an organized effort that involved most of the leading members of the Black clergy and activists.

The solicitor then began asking about that first meeting, which was held at Wilson's church. It actually had been organized quickly to embrace the surprising success of the planned one-day boycott. The more than five thousand people who had packed the church and surrounding streets heard, according to the *Advertiser*, "a tornado of freedom oratory" from leaders like Dr. King, who told the assembly that the time had come to deal with "A paralysis that is crippling the spirit," a time "when people get tired of being trampled by the iron feet of oppression."

Many of the people in the crowd that night were seeing and hearing Martin Luther King for the first time. They had heard just a little bit about him, the new young preacher of the fashionable Dexter Avenue church and his attractive wife, but now they had to decide if he had the magic to lead them. "Work and fight until justice runs down like water," he had urged them. "Work together and stick together to gain justice on the buses of the city... If we are wrong," he continued, "justice is a lie.

"But we are not wrong."

That night King had knit together the disparate strands of a new civil rights movement. He had become their leader. And Solicitor Stewart wanted to show how that happened, how that organization had come together. "Who first got in touch with you and asked for the use of your church for a meeting of some type on December the 5th?"

"Nobody contacted me December the 5th," Wilson replied. "Somebody called on the phone and asked permission to hold a meeting at my church. Left it with the secretary. I left word to give permission to go ahead." He did not know who had made that request, he said.

African Americans had spent centuries, literally centuries, learning carefully how to avoid directly answering questions that might cause them harm. "Did you attend the meeting?" Stewart asked.

"I was at my church."

"In your best judgment, about how many people attended that meeting?"

"I couldn't judge."

A minute later Stewart asked, "Do you know who presided at that meeting?"

"I do not."

"At what stage of the meeting did you come in and take part in it?"

"I did not take any part."

Stewart was growing increasingly frustrated at his inability to get the simple, straightforward—and pretty obvious—answers he needed to make his case. This was not the way the legal system was supposed to work. He tried a different approach. "What position did that man who presided at the meeting take, standing in or around the pulpit or platform of the church?"

Wilson shook his head. "I wouldn't know that," he explained, "because I didn't know who was going to preside."

"Did you see this defendant, M. L. King, any that night?"

The truth lay in the no-man's-land separating the races of Montgomery. "Not that I recollect... I don't recollect who I saw that night."

"Did you hear any speeches at that mass meeting?"

"I spent the evening in my office."

For the solicitor, it must have felt like trying to punch mercury. "I thought you said you came in that night just before the meeting opened?"

"Just before the meeting opened."

Stewart then wondered why Reverend Wilson had testified before the grand jury "that you came in the meeting when the collection was being taken up."

"Not that I remember."

Wilson would not be shaken. "Do you recall seeing Reverend M. L. King at your church either before the meeting, during the meeting or immediately after the meeting that night?"

"I did not."

Reminiscent of a subdued church service, often after an answer that successfully avoided a specific answer, murmurs of approval would ripple through the spectators, causing Judge Carter to gavel the courtroom quiet. But Reverend Wilson's verbal dexterity continued. Did he know Reverend Alford? "I know two or three Alfords. I don't know which one this is referring to." Did he see Reverend French at the meeting? "It is possible I saw him." Could he name the officers of the Interdenominational Ministerial Alliance, the group that had made the arrangements for the mass meeting? "Not all of them."

Stewart persisted, though. "Do you know of a transportation committee active on behalf of the Montgomery Improvement Association, do you know of the existence of such committee?"

The fact that reports about this committee appeared in the newspaper every day did not affect Wilson. He simply would not be pinned down. "There was a group got up, I think," he acknowledged. "Whether you call it a committee or not, I don't know...

"Not being a member of it, I don't know its definite purpose." But in general, he told Stewart, its purpose was "To help people get back and forwards in work."

"Was there also a finance committee of the Montgomery Improvement Association active in helping?"

"I would think there would be," he agreed; that was logical, but no, sorry, he just did not know who served on that committee. This coy rhetorical maneuvering set the stage for what would become a two-pronged, and at times contradictory, defense. On the one hand, the defense wanted to put the city, the buses and segregation on trial by highlighting the shameful treatment of good, hardworking people based on the color of their skin. At the same time, in an effort to avoid crossing certain legal lines, the defense witnesses often feigned ignorance of the very efforts initiated to end that mistreatment.

Regardless, the almost all-Black courtroom was delighted as Reverend Wilson continued toying with the system that had for so long constrained all of them. And there was little that system could do to prevent it.

The defense team stayed mostly silent throughout this questioning, Fred Gray leaning forward with his hands clasped in front of him on the table, Arthur Shores leaning back with his head cradled in his hands, only occasionally objecting to make a procedural point, but just as likely as a reminder they were there and ready to pounce. Fred Gray recalls that they had talked to the witnesses but "we hadn't rehearsed them or even suggested how they should testify, but we did make sure they understood what our defense was. They understood to some degree that the prosecution wanted to put everything on Dr. King. That just wasn't accurate. In the final analysis this wasn't anything Dr. King started. He didn't create it; he just happened to be there at the time and had the ability to communicate our message. He wasn't the leader of the protest—he was its spokesman. The people appointed him to represent them. That was true and that was our defense, and these witnesses knew that.

"We told them to listen very carefully, make sure they understand the question before they try to answer it, do not volunteer any information, and remember our basic message: this was an entirely volunteer situation where nobody was forcing anybody to do anything and they could all make up their own mind as to what they did.

"So, without telling them what to say, we pretty much prepared them to testify. We just told them to use their good common sense."

At one point the prosecution offered a copy of the MIA Resolution into evidence. Lawyer Billingsley objected, "To the introduction of a photostatic copy of whatever it purports to be. Now, he said this is a photostatic copy. I don't know. Certainly it is a photostatic copy of whatever it purports to be. There must have been an original... We object because it is not shown that it is a true and original photostatic copy of whatever it purports to be, no foundation has been laid by the state for the introduction of that particular piece of paper into evidence."

The defense actually was not concerned about the document nor about whether this was an accurate copy. Everything in that Resolution had been published in the newspapers many times. There was nothing in it that would be especially harmful to their case. What Billingsley was doing was making a vital point: the defense was not going to allow this case to proceed with niceties and stipulations. The old ways of doing legal business were done.

His objection was overruled. The witness read the document and agreed that "It looks like what I heard (Dr. King) say." But Billingsley persisted, demanding the law be upheld. And, in this instance, the document "is not certified it is correct," as the law required, forcing the judge to "rule it out temporarily."

The judge interrupted Reverend Wilson's testimony to allow James Bagley to retake the stand. The original, Bagley said, was in the bus company office. Okay, Judge Carter told him, go get it.

When Reverend Wilson sat back down in the witness chair,

Stewart asked him the question that most concerned white Montgomery. "Do you recall whether or not Reverend M. L. King stated in substance that he or his organization were not out to change the segregation laws?"

Wilson's playful banter disappeared. "It has been the contention not to; we were not out to change any segregation laws…" Then he added, "…at that time."

The solicitor began asking about other meetings. Regularly scheduled meetings were being held each week in an effort to promote and demonstrate unity within the community, to share information and reinforce the commitment. "The general purpose was for education," Reverend Wilson told Stewart, "and to encourage people to display Christianity in their attitudes."

"In their attitude toward what?"

"Toward anybody."

There had been stories circulating in the city that many Black people who might have ridden the buses had been intimidated; there were claims that people had been threatened or even physically forced to honor the boycott. Stewart was hinting at that when he asked, "Did that attitude then have anything to do with the riding buses, or refraining from riding buses, or not?"

Wilson replied evenly, "This was a matter of their own conscience."

When Stewart pointed out that the subject of "nearly all the meetings" concerned "Negroes riding buses," Billingsley objected to that leading statement, complaining, "He is putting in his mouth what to say."

Sustained. Don't do it anymore, Judge Carter admonished.

Stewart did keep after it, though, perhaps hoping to find an applicable answer somewhere among his questions. Did Wilson attend the January 2 meeting at the Holt Street church? "It is possible, yes, sir." Did he recall who presided at that meeting? "No, I don't." What was the subject of Reverend Bonner's pep talk? "That is what I couldn't tell you."

"Did it have anything to do with riding the buses?"

Once again, Wilson found refuge in the mysteries of the language, responding, "I think you could hardly pledge any vital citizen from the situation that was in force."

"The situation then was what?"

That seemed obvious. "The fact that they were not riding the buses."

Stewart continued questioning Reverend Wilson into the later afternoon, finally getting him to admit that he had heard Martin Luther King speak at one of those meetings. "He made some remarks," the minister testified, about "general development and attitude of the people in following the leadership." Whose leadership? "The total ministry of Montgomery, I guess you would call it." What leadership? "The first place, not being violent." But mostly, explained Reverend Wilson, "I just cannot recollect what went on." Every person in that courtroom knew the truth, and the fact that Reverend Wilson refused to acknowledge it was their shared secret. These were people who had spent too many years listening to white people telling shaky versions of the truth in Alabama courtrooms to be surprised or offended by Wilson's testimony.

Wilson acknowledged that money had been collected at these meetings to be used by the Montgomery Improvement Association. Asked what those funds were used for, he replied, "To my best judgment, whatever it was needed for." The entire courtroom burst out in delighted laughter.

Finally it had come down to the MIA, the organization running the boycott on a daily basis, arranging rides for people, setting up car pools and taxi service, solving innumerable problems. Stewart asked casually, "What was the purpose of the Montgomery Improvement Association?"

Wilson responded with a direct and obvious answer, as if it should be clear to everyone: "To improve the general status of the colored people in Montgomery." Once again, the court-room erupted with laughter.

Stewart obviously had not learned his lesson through this long testimony, continuing to pursue Wilson into the maze. "General status in regard to what?"

The solicitor threw a fastball right down the middle of the plate. "Whatever improvements would be needed." The newspapers reported, again: the courtroom rocked with laughter.

After Stewart concluded his direct examination of Reverend Wilson, he recalled James Bagley. This time Bagley had brought with him a copy of the Resolution supposedly passed by the MIA at a meeting and mailed to his office. It was, he agreed, a duplicate of the photostatic copy. Judge Carter admitted it into evidence.

Fred Gray handled the cross-examination. That made sense; it was Gray who had handwritten the Resolutions. He remained seated at the table, asking questions in a friendly manner, as if just trying to clear up some minor misconceptions. Reverend Wilson was well respected in both the Black and white communities and Gray knew him reasonably well. There was little doubt the photostat was an exact copy, he agreed, but there was one thing bothering him; it was an exact copy of what, exactly? "At this particular meeting, wasn't an oral statement made instead of a written statement?"

"It is possible. I am not sure."

Gray clarified the issue. "As a matter of fact, there was no written Resolution presented…and if any statement was made at the time, it was a statement concerning three demands, and those statements were made orally, and this is written… As a matter of fact, the three demands are not contained in that document at all."

"As a matter of fact," Wilson now agreed, "I question whether or not it is the original."

"To refresh your recollection, isn't it a fact there were no written Resolutions made at that meeting?"

"Seems perhaps you are correct."

Still, in the same genial manner, he suggested, "This Resolution which has just been admitted into evidence is not the Resolution, if any was made, that was made at that particular meeting?"

"It doesn't contain the three proposals."

"It doesn't contain the three proposals," Gray repeated. "And the Resolution you adopted did contain them?"

"Whether or not it was made at the time, whether written or not, it did contain them."

Stewart next called Erna Ashley Dungee. Erna Dungee was the only female member of the MIA board. She also was the younger sister of Mahala Ashley Dickerson, Montgomery's first Black female attorney. Apparently, the prosecutor still believed he could use the leaders of the movement to make his case. One thing was well-known in the Black community: nobody told Erna Dungee what to do or say. She had a strong mind and she was going to speak it. It is probable Robert Stewart believed he was going to have an easier time with this witness, a woman, than Thetford had struggling through with Reverend Wilson. It is equally probable Erna Dungee had been preparing a lifetime for this day and was going to take hold of it.

Erna Dungee had been born poor in rural Alabama in 1909. After moving to Montgomery as a teenager, she got an education, eventually graduating from Alabama State, becoming a teacher, then marrying the respected Dr. A. C. Dungee. She was among the leading activists in the community. She had been a cofounder of the Women's Political Council, which had nurtured Montgomery's growing civil rights movement and had planted the seeds of the boycott. Although she was the secretary of the large Mount Zion church, she also served as the financial secretary of the MIA, making her responsible for the flow of money into and out of that organization.

She had attended the organizational meeting of the MIA. "Nobody" had asked her to be there, she testified. "I was at the church, I am secretary of the church and I was on my job." Asked about the specifics of that meeting, who was there, who spoke, her memory was vague. There had been so many meetings since then, so the details of what happened when had become blurred. She did remember that no Resolution had been read at the mass meeting on December 5. Well, wondered Stewart, "Could there have been another meeting you didn't attend?"

"I couldn't say."

Eventually he got around to the reason he had called her to the stand. A sizable amount of money had been donated to fuel the boycott. As it continued, donations had arrived from hundreds of individuals and organizations throughout the nation. At a rally in New Orleans, five thousand Black men and women had raised $3,000. Congressman Diggs had brought a $5,000 check from Detroit. In Cleveland, 2,100 people at a protest-prayer rally donated $3,301.64. Small donations arrived in the daily mail: a teenage girl sent a one-dollar bill. Erna Dungee had been responsible for making certain it was all recorded and used properly to keep the alternate means of transportation running. "Do you sign the checks?" Stewart asked.

"Yes, I do." Each check required three signatures, she replied, her own, E. D. Nixon and Reverend King.

After Stewart established that the funds were kept in several different banks, Peter Hall objected, claiming, "They know this has no part in this charge of conspiracy, what they do with the money or don't do with the money."

Judge Carter had to reach deeply into the law to find a reason to overrule the objection. "It is possible, if they are using the money for an illegal purpose, it could be. I am saying it could be... The law says in a conspiracy case you can go a long ways."

The solicitor then interrupted his own questioning to put an assistant cashier from the Alabama National Bank on the stand. Once again, Stewart tried to introduce photostats into evidence. But it appeared he had learned his lesson: he had to send the employee back to the bank to get the original documents.

With Mrs. Dungee back on the stand, he resumed his questioning about the MIA's finances. He didn't get much help from her. "Do you keep a running account in the checkbook so you know the balances in the bank?"

"I started it; but discontinued that method because it was too confusing."

"You have the stubs of the checkbook here?"

"We have the checkbooks," she replied pleasantly, "but we discontinued that method. I told you."

"Is there another way besides the account books?"

"Yes, sir, we have our accounts audited on the 27th of February."

"Have you a copy of that audit?"

"We discontinued that method of keeping books and don't enter the deposits in these checkbooks."

Judge Carter was correct, this was not vaudeville, but based on the amusement in the courtroom, it certainly had the elements of great comedy. Stewart was an experienced litigator, used to maintaining control; his voice betrayed his frustration and his questions became curt and at times derisive. Billingsley objected "to the manner of questioning the witness and the type of questions." The judge called the lawyers up to the bench for an off-the-record "argument," then overruled the objection.

Eventually both Stewart and Dungee added up all the deposits she had made into the Alabama National Bank. "According to my figuring," she said, "I got $30,713.80. Is that anywhere near right?"

"I got $29,763," Stewart responded. Close enough. What was all that money used for? he wondered.

The majority of the money, she responded, paid for gasoline.

"Who did you pay for gasoline?" he asked.

"Filling stations." Eight gas stations participated. Cars used by the MIA to transport people could go to those stations and sign for gasoline.

"Do you know what the gasoline was used for?" Stewart asked.

Erna Dungee didn't hesitate. "Naturally. The gasoline was apparently used in driving. Driving and taking people, I am sure."

Stewart forged ahead. "Taking what kind of people?"

That seemed obvious. "Well, people like colored people, I imagine."

"Colored people who don't want to ride the buses."

She would not be pushed into his answer, replying politely, "That is going further than I was going to say."

Through the afternoon Stewart showed her check after check, asking who signed it—Dr. King had signed some of them—and what they paid for. His questions finally got so tedious that Mrs. Dungee decided, "I am going to object to this. I am not going to add up all these checks."

The judge informed her that, as a witness, she did not have a choice.

Stewart finally changed gears; what other expenses had she paid with those checks? he asked.

"Driving." Among the popular radio comedy acts of the 1950s was Bob and Ray, whose mostly ad-libbed act consisted primarily of absurd deadpan interviews featuring a sincere man giving increasingly ridiculous answers to an oblivious interviewer. At times, this testimony might have been billed as Bob and Erna.

"What do you mean by driving expense? Was that the so-called car pool?" Robert Stewart asked.

"The persons drove cars and used the gas," Erna Dungee responded.

"Persons driving?"

"That drove the people."

"Several paid men?"

"That is all right."

"Who are they?"

"Persons who burned the gas."

Once again, Stewart droned through a long series of canceled checks, asking the witness what each of them was for. For example, "I now show you check number 133 payable to Johnson Printing Company in the amount of $19.78 and ask you what this is issued for?"

"This check could be for receipt books."

"For receipt books?"

"Yes, sir."

"What were the receipts used for?"

That certainly seemed obvious to Mrs. Dungee. "For writing receipts." For moneys received by the MIA, she added over the laughter.

Eventually the solicitor focused on one check signed by the defendant, Dr. King, casually hinting that perhaps some of the money was misused. "I show you check number 86 dated January 10, 1956, drawn to cash in the amount of $5,017.50, and ask if you can tell me what that check drawn to cash was for?"

There was no amusement in her response. "That was the matter of the transfer of some money."

"That check is endorsed by M. L. King Jr.?" It was. "That is the defendant, is it not?" It is. "So he received $5,017.50, as far as you know, according to that check?"

"This is a matter of transfer of some funds, though, but it wasn't for him."

Stewart cast a long aspersion. "The check reflects it, doesn't it, a cash amount paid to him."

"It wasn't paid to him," she corrected patiently. "He endorsed the check." Then she explained, "It was a matter of transferring $5,000 from the Alabama National Bank to another bank." That other bank was in Atlanta. Although Mrs. Dungee did not explain it, when donations from around the country began pouring in, a decision had been made to move funds out of Montgomery into a bank in Georgia to make certain Alabama authorities could not touch any of it.

"Do your books and records reflect that $5,017.50 was deposited in the Citizens Bank?"

"Not the $17," she admitted, "but the $5,000." What happened to that $17? Stewart asked. "Oh, well, that $17 paid the expense of money orders."

Another check, this one for $30, was payable to Eddie T. Posey "for use of the parking lot," she explained. "Evidently his place, Eddie Posey's parking lot." That was the monthly fee paid by the association to use that parking lot as a pickup and drop-off point.

Check number 208, a check for $900, was payable to attorneys Fred D. Gray and Charles Langford for their legal representation of the MIA from December through January, although Mrs. Dungee couldn't exactly tell him what those "general services" were.

Stewart just continued, check after check after check. This one for driving, that one for fueling, until they all ran together. By the time court adjourned for the night, the prosecution had spent the day establishing that Erna Ashley Dungee had written numerous checks that the organization known as the Montgomery Improvement Association had written in support of the boycott.

Tucked in a corner on its front page the following morning, below the headline reporting that a massive snowstorm had dumped 13.5 inches of snow on New York City and paralyzed the entire Eastern Seaboard, the *New York Times* informed readers that the trial had begun. "Mr. Thetford and his deputy, Robert Stewart, ran into heavy weather with the three witnesses called today."

The *Chicago Tribune* ran similar stories, although its coverage of the snowstorm that killed 162 people included a story that the weather bureau's new "mechanical brain, a million-dollar electronic computer" had failed miserably, reporting Saturday night that "the nation's capital would have a light snow and 'golf and gardening' would be in order Sunday afternoon."

The *Tribune*'s trial story appeared on page 5, but it did not include any suggestion that the confident prosecution had been about as wrong in its expectation of a quick and simple trial leading to an immediate conviction as the weather bureau had been—even without that mechanical brain.

CHAPTER FOUR

Sitting by Reverend King's side as the trial continued, Fred Gray held no illusions; this trial was not going to end segregation in Montgomery, Alabama. It was possible it wouldn't even change the racist bus policies. For Gray, this trial was simply another important step forward on the long, winding, dangerous stairway to equality.

Montgomery had spent a century institutionalizing the separation of the races. Black people were not allowed to hold public office; in fact, few of them could vote. In 1954, for example, Lowndes County, which was 60 percent Black, did not have a single Black voter—and to make sure those Black residents understood their position, they were not permitted to use the front door of the local courthouse. In the 1950s, the median income of Black men was slightly less than half that of white men. Other than teaching, the ministry, blue-collar labor and working as a domestic for a white family, few jobs were open to Black applicants.

The insults, the humiliations filtered into every aspect of life in Montgomery, literally from the hospital in which you were born to the cemetery in which you were buried. There were statues and plaques honoring Confederate heroes throughout the city, high schools and streets bore their names. The state officially celebrated Robert E. Lee's birthday, Confederate president Jefferson Davis's birthday and Confederate Memorial Day. Black children were not permitted to take books out of the main branch of the public library. In some shops, Black customers were not even permitted to try on clothes; if they wanted to buy a pair of shoes, they had to outline their foot on a brown paper bag and take that to the store.

Fred Gray, meanwhile, continued to put his faith in the law. Two days after the bombing at Dr. King's home, as the protest entered its third month but over a month before this trial began, Gray and Langford filed a federal lawsuit, *Browder v. Gayle*, in which they contended the city ordinances and the state statutes violated the Equal Protection Clause of the Fourteenth Amendment. They demanded that the city be enjoined from enforcing segregation on public buses, describing it as "a conspiracy to interfere with the civil and constitutional rights of the Negro citizens" of the city, utilizing "threats, violence, intimidation and harassment" to do so. Gray and Langford asked the court to declare those laws "null and void." Filing this lawsuit dramatically raised the stakes. This was no longer just an effort to secure seating on buses; it now was a direct attack on segregation. As the *Advertiser* reported, if successful, this case "would knock out separate facilities for Negroes and whites at bus and train depots and abolish segregation lines on all buses, trains, streetcars and other vehicles." It had become Montgomery's worst nightmare.

The goal of every lawyer is to get their case heard in the most hospitable legal setting. The intricacies of the American legal system often result in overlapping jurisdictions, allowing attorneys to go "forum shopping." Gray, Langford and Clifford Durr, an extraordinarily dedicated white Montgomery attorney who risked his life by joining the fight for civil rights, had been carefully planning this action for several weeks. They were hoping eventually to get to the Supreme Court—where the decision in *Brown v. Board of Education* might be extended to public transportation. It was a complicated legal maneuver, but filing for an injunction challenging the constitutionality of a state statute, and naming state officials, allowed them to bypass the federal court of appeals and instead ensured that the case would be heard by a three-judge US District Court panel with immediate review by the Supreme Court. It was like having the opportunity to take an express elevator to the top rather than having to stop on additional floors.

In their response, attorneys for the defendants tried to keep the case out of federal court, claiming that the plaintiffs should have used state courts to "adjudicate all matters" before turning to the federal government, that they suffered no irreparable injury and federal courts have "judicial knowledge that harmony between Negro and white races in this city depends on continued segregation."

Aurelia S. Browder, the named plaintiff in the case, was one of the five female plaintiffs who had been mistreated on the buses. Browder was a housewife and, like Rosa Parks and so many others, had lost patience waiting for equality. Warned by a relative that participating in this case could put her life in danger, she reportedly responded that she was ready "to die for something. If you live and you haven't stood for anything, you didn't live for anything either."

Among the other plaintiffs were Claudette Colvin, Mary Louise Smith, Susie McDonald and a woman named Jeanatta Reese. Ironically, Rosa Parks was not among them. "The reason I did not include Rosa Parks in this case," Gray recalls, "was because her criminal case was up on appeal and I didn't want that to be used as an excuse to delay the federal case. I wanted her case to go on to the state court and go well there, while we would have a clear course in the federal case. If we eventually lost the Parks case and had to pay a $10 fine, so be it, but as far as I was concerned, our real case, where the decision was going to be made, was in federal court. And we were the only such case at that time raising that issue." In addition to Mayor Gayle, the defendants included several members of the Board of Commissioners, the chief of police, the bus company and two bus drivers.

Almost immediately, plaintiff Jeanatta Reese withdrew from the Browder suit, supposedly because she had received threatening phone calls and been warned to do so by the veteran white police officer for whom she worked as a cook. Gray also received tremendous pressure from numerous public officials. He had been contacted by "numerous local, county, state and federal officials in all three branches of government" to quietly let this thing go away. It would create unnecessary turmoil in the city, he was told, "and give me the reputation of an agitator, which I actually took as a compliment," without really accomplishing anything of value, they warned. "Other people suggested I let the court pass the case over for a period of time so there would be no ruling on the existing segregation laws." While those officials didn't technically offer him a bribe, they did assure him that his career would be made if he dropped this action, that they would make sure "I had all the legal cases I could handle. They were capable of referring clients that would enable me to build a substantial practice."

Gray wasn't insulted by the offer; he was well aware that in the city people got along by going along. They were offering him membership in the elite group of people who made things happen. He just had no interest in being part of that club.

After those attempts to buy his cooperation failed, they attacked him legally. Gray had proved to be incredibly effective in directing the protest through the legal maze. As far as the city was concerned, he and King were the problem—stirring up the Black community. So in March, a Montgomery grand jury

MONTGOMERY COUNTY ARCHIVES

Twenty-five-year-old Fred Gray was arrested at the same time as Martin Luther King Jr., Rosa Parks and eighty-seven other participants in the bus protest. But in an effort to thwart his legal maneuvering, authorities instead arrested him on a false charge of barratry—committing legal fraud—a charge that could have led to his disbarment.

indicted Gray for barratry, the crime of encouraging a lawsuit simply for personal gain and profit. Suddenly, Jeanatta Reese claimed she had not retained him as her lawyer and was not aware that she was listed as a plaintiff in *Browder v. Gayle*. Gray was arrested and briefly held in jail. Reese, it turned out, had been in a terrible position and perhaps to save her job had made these claims. Knowing the pressure all the plaintiffs had been subjected to, Gray did not want to attack Reese publicly, but still felt he had to defend himself and, in the most polite terms, informed reporters her statement was "far from the truth."

According to Reese, the night her participation in the lawsuit was reported in the newspapers, she received several threatening phone calls, among them one from a police officer and another from an anonymous person who warned her to get out of town. When she arrived at work the following morning, her white employer told her "She was surprised" to see Reese's name on this lawsuit. Reese said she responded, "I'm surprised too. You know I don't want nothing to do with that mess."

Reese continued that she had initially gone to Gray's office to deal with an insurance issue, and while she was there he asked her if she had been treated fairly on buses. "I told him no," she said. "I had been pushed around and passed up a lot of times. He asked me if I would say that anywhere and I told him 'Sure...' He asked me if I wanted to sign and I said, 'Yeah, they treat us like horses.' So I hauled off and signed. He didn't say anything about a suit." Reese was permitted to withdraw her name from the lawsuit, which had no impact on it.

These charges were easily disproved; the meticulous Gray had recorded the conversations in which Reese had agreed to become part of the lawsuit, and he had the papers she had signed agreeing to participate in the case and photographs in which she had posed with the other plaintiffs for *Jet* magazine.

While theoretically Gray had little to be concerned about, in reality he knew how often and easily the law had been twisted and manipulated, turned into something ugly, in the defense of segregation. While he was meeting with widely respected federal judge Frank Johnson Jr. on a different case, Johnson casually reminded him that if any offense had been committed, the case was filed in a federal courthouse, on federal property, which meant neither the city nor state had any jurisdiction.

At the initial hearing, the prosecutor, the same William Thetford who led the prosecution of Dr. King, was forced to ask the court to dismiss the indictment, admitting he lacked jurisdiction. He was going to refer the case to the United States attorney, he said. It disappeared. Even though the charges eventually were dropped, this effort to harass him would hang over much of his legal career.

Fred Gray had become a difficult problem for Mayor Gayle and for segregationists. They couldn't bribe him, nor successfully invent a crime or infraction with which to charge him, so they tried a completely different tactic: as a minister of the Gospel, he had been given the draft classification 4-D, a religious exemption. Only days after Gray had filed *Browder,* his local all-white Selective Service board changed his status to 1-A, claiming he was not active in the ministry—even though he was assistant minister of the Holt Street Church of Christ—and ordered him to take his preinduction physical. It was a clever ploy: suddenly they were casting him as a draft dodger.

"My draft board didn't notify me, they hadn't asked any questions, they just changed my draft status," recalls Gray. "We all knew when we fought the system the system would fight back. These people were fighting for their tradition and their way of life and I had proven to be a danger to them."

But this particular effort to question his religious work was very personal to Fred Gray, who had even baptized neighborhood cats and dogs as an adolescent. "My whole life had revolved around the church. My grandfather, Reverend Thomas Jones, was a Methodist minister. Our minister at our home church, Holt Street Church of Christ, was from Tennessee, and he somehow arranged for me to attend the Nashville Christian Institute, a well-known prep school that trained Black Church of Christ ministers. I was one of the first students selected by Marshall Keeble, president of the school, to travel around the country preaching to raise money and recruit students for the school. While I was a student at Alabama State I had worked as the minister of Lanett Church of Christ in Lanett, Alabama. In law school at Western Reserve I was the assistant minister at East 100th Street Church of Christ in Cleveland, Ohio. And even after being admitted to the Alabama bar, I continued serving as an assistant minister at the Holt Street Church of Christ and later as minister of the Newtown Church of Christ. I had been preaching most of my life, and now the white system was claiming I was using my religious training to avoid the draft. I don't know why I was furious, but I guess I never got used to watching the system being used to punish people. Maybe that was one of the reasons I'd become a lawyer."

The entire Black community understood the vindictive nature of this effort, but there wasn't very much that could be done about it. Gray's appeal to his local draft board was rejected unanimously, by law blocking him from an appeal. Every aspect of it was legal, on paper, and it looked like they finally were going to get rid of him.

Both the Alabama and Montgomery County bar associations also decided to get involved. If Gray had made misstatements on his applications, he could be thrown out of those organizations as well.

He would be disbarred, essentially ending his career in the state. Montgomery City Lines attorney Jack Crenshaw wrote to the secretary of the Alabama state bar, requesting that organization open an investigation. "According to newspaper reports," his letter read, "Gray was deferred by his local draft board on the basis that he was a full-time minister of the Gospel. I understand this is contrary to the representation made in his application to the bar."

To release that application from Gray's file, the board of bar commissions had to approve. Only one attorney of the twenty-six state bar commissioners voted against releasing Gray's application.

"It has always been the duty and usually been the custom," noted that lone holdout, Charles Scott, "that in times of excitement and great hysteria lawyers have kept their feet on the ground and have been able to stem the tide created by people less accustomed to controversy." The bar association did investigate Crenshaw's claim but found no basis on which to discipline Gray.

But efforts to get rid of Gray and King continued. King was arrested for speeding and briefly put in jail. While Gray was waiting for a flight to Boston, where he was to speak at a rally, he was arrested for violation of a city statute by sitting in the airport's white section and refusing to move to the "colored area" when asked to do so. He was booked and fingerprinted, then released on bail. His trial, *City of Montgomery v. Fred Gray*, took place in the Recorder's Court and a judge quickly dismissed the charges.

So when the *State of Alabama v. Martin Luther King Jr.* resumed for a second day, in addition to this case, his growing number of clients demanding his attention, and the likelihood that he was about to be drafted, Fred Gray also was in the middle of planning his wedding to Bernice Hill, scheduled to take place on June 17.

His role as the legal director of the bus protest had made him a popular figure within the community and his wedding was going to be a major event. A lot more people than he and Bernice had intended to invite wanted to be there. More than two thousand invitations went into the mail. It was getting set to be the largest wedding ever held in Montgomery. There were a lot of people praying it would be a celebration of a great victory. Gray was not one of them: he was too much of a realist.

Early on the morning of March 20, Gray left the house he still shared with his mother on West Jeff Davis Avenue, wearing the red, white and blue tie he favored for most court appearances, and drove to the old courthouse. A small crowd had already gathered outside the building by the time he arrived. The white pillared courthouse had celebrated its centennial two years earlier, having opened in 1854, even before the Confederacy was formed. Although it had been extensively expanded in 1892 and continually updated to keep pace with technology, construction was about to begin on its replacement.

Among the reporters who were already at the courthouse that morning was thirty-one-year-old Keith Kyle, reporting on the boycott and trial for the prestigious British magazine *The*

The trial took place inside the majestic Montgomery County Courthouse, one of the last trials held here before it was demolished and replaced. The first county courthouse had been built on Court Square in 1822. This building was constructed in 1854 and enlarged fifty years later. For most of its history, Blacks were not permitted to enter through the front door.

Economist. Segregation had always survived easiest in the shadows; the less white people talked about it or thought about it, the less opposition to it there was and the easier it was for it to continue. This boycott, and specifically this trial, was bringing more attention to the situation than most white Montgomery residents believed necessary. This is the way things had always been there, and this is the way they are supposed to be. People from outside didn't need to be butting in. But as Kyle told the *Advertiser*'s city editor, Joe Azbell, the British were practically experts on the subject of racism: "Some provinces under the Union Jack have segregation as acute—if not more so—than the South's, but it is of a different nature... In Africa we have a tremendous racial problem which has all the complex features of the South's problem." But it is quite different, he continued,

DAN ABRAMS AND FRED GRAY WITH DAVID FISHER

because in those African nations "the white population is in
such a tiny minority."

Azbell then fueled every white Southerner's fears, reminding them of the Mau Mau uprising that had begun three years
earlier in Kenya. After white settlers had taken most of the
best farmlands, he wrote, Blacks had created a secret society,
the Mau Mau. Repeating wildly exaggerated stories from British propaganda, he reported it was "voodoo in ritual. (Initiates
were sworn to kill whites when commanded and were bathed
in fresh goat's blood moved about their head seven times.)... In
twelve months the Mau Mau had killed 1,000 whites, slashing
their heads off or burning them alive..."

Azbell, who described Kyle as looking like a young Sherlock
Holmes, noted that the young journalist had been sitting in the
front row of the courtroom for several days, scribbling notes,
"watching attentively as a scientist would observe an inoculated
guinea pig, attempting to discover for himself the mind of the
South." And, undoubtedly, spreading news about the success of
the bus boycott and its leader, Dr. King.

When Judge Carter gaveled the morning session to order,
prosecutor Stewart's first witness was the bank cashier, Stuart
Patton, who this time had presumably brought with him the
MIA's original bank records. When he presented photostats of
MIA checks, Stewart asked, "Tell me where the originals of
these checks would be?" He responded, "They would be in the
hands of the Montgomery Improvement Association."

Perhaps the best-known courtroom axiom is that an attorney
must never ask a question to which he does not already know
the answer. Stewart blundered into this when he asked, seemingly surprised, "The bank doesn't have them?"

"No, sir."

"You haven't turned them over to the state?"

"No, sir, we have not."

Stewart did his best to recover, telling his witness, "I show you a group of checks which have not been introduced in evidence, checks of the Montgomery Improvement Association, and ask if these checks also would have been returned to the depositor..."

With that, Erna Dungee once again took the stand and the Bob and Erna Show resumed: Bob asked straightforward questions, and to the delight of the spectators, Erna continued leading him on a merry and mostly fruitless chase. One by one, Stewart took her through all the checks she had written for the MIA, $24 check by $24 check by $24 check by $24 check, signature by signature, purpose by purpose; this was the courtroom equivalent of Muzak, the uninspired background music being played in the elevators of the new skyscrapers rising in cities throughout the country. Most of those checks, Mrs. Dungee explained, and then explained again, were payments "for transportation." Asked to identify still another batch, Mrs. Dungee stopped suddenly, a perplexed look on her face. Holding up a copy of a check, she said, "Here's one that doesn't have any signature on it."

"I wonder how that got through the bank?" Stewart said.

"The bank can probably tell you," she advised. The two checks with it, she continued, "has to do with transportation... People use their cars and there is the matter of wear and tear, and a matter of maintenance in a way for the use of their cars." Stewart did the math: it came to $4 a day.

Eventually he asked Dungee about the total balance in the Alabama National Bank account. "I don't have any balance," she told him. Asked for an approximation, she said flatly, "I have no idea."

Stewart continued, asking what the audit had calculated.

Erna Dungee was not going to be pushed. "I said I don't remember the figure, and the fact didn't materialize."

Stewart finally shifted gears. Mrs. Dungee acknowledged she had attended the first mass meeting, but told the solicitor that she did not know who presided at that meeting, she did not see Dr. King at that meeting, in fact, "I didn't see anyone at that time."

Stewart was incredulous. "You attended the meeting which there were some one thousand or more people but you saw no one?"

No one presiding, she corrected, adding she was sitting at the rear of the church. And if Dr. King had made a speech, "I don't recall that, definitely!" To the delight of the spectators, her memory remained faulty. "I attended so many meetings," she said, adding later, "I don't remember particularly these meetings. A lot of them I have attended, but who did this and that, I don't recall."

After more questioning she finally agreed that she had seen Dr. King at some of these meetings. "Did he, or did he not, talk about the bus boycott?" Stewart asked.

She considered that. "Well, we never talked about the bus boycott." Then what did they talk about at these meetings? "The protest."

"Did he, or not, talk about the bus protest at these meetings?"

He certainly did, but she couldn't remember exactly what he said about it. "It wasn't so impressed on my mind for as what." Then she admitted, "I am getting confused. That is as far as I could go."

But still, Stewart persisted. She testified that the headquarters of the MIA had been moved from the Montgomery Negro Baptist Center to the Citizens Club but could not recall how long it had been at the Baptist Center. "Was it a matter of days, weeks or months?" asked Stewart.

She agreed, "All three!"

No, she did not know how many people belonged to the MIA, she testified, yes, they did have membership cards but they paid no dues. Stewart finally got to his essential point: the MIA had been set up to run the illegal boycott. Its leaders had conspired together to defy the law. "Is the Montgomery Improvement Association performing any function other than support of the bus protest movement?"

"Well, I don't know directly," Mrs. Dungee admitted. "Indirectly, yes."

"Directly no?"

"Indirectly yes."

"Is that your answer?" Yes, it was. And indirectly what other functions did it perform?

She paused to consider that. "Well, I would say that its—the organization is made of an alliance to the various churches, for their Christmas and things given, projects to be helped." Whatever she meant by that, she was quite certain about it.

Stewart wondered, "You mean the ministers alliance?"

She did not. She knew exactly what she meant: "Oh no, you asked indirectly and I was answering you indirectly."

"Tell me what indirectly the Montgomery Improvement Association did for the benefit of people at Christmas."

"We give baskets, and so forth. Christmas contributions."

Courtroom lawyers also are taught the importance of ending testimony on a positive note for your case. Get what you need and walk away. Stewart did exactly that; cutting through all the confusing replies, he asked, "Has the Montgomery Improvement Association spent any money for anything except the bus protest?"

Erna Dungee had to admit, "I don't know of it spending any other money."

Arthur Shores's cross-examination consisted of a single question. "Do you recommend or approve payment of checks or just sign them?"

In other words, do you participate in policy-making decisions? "I sign checks. I write them, rather, and sign them."

Mrs. Dungee left the stand to the approval of the spectators.

The state's next witness would be the recording secretary of the MIA, Reverend Uriah J. Fields, the young, outspoken pastor of the Bell Street Baptist Church. Fields was a rising leader in the community, and at the first mass meeting he was given the

AP PHOTO/HORACE CORT

Legal actions to outlaw segregation on public transportation had begun more than a century earlier, but by 1955 every jurisdiction had the right to determine its own seating policy. The only thing all of them throughout the South had in common was that African Americans had to sit in the rear.

honor of reading the Scripture. He had been born in the hamlet of Sunflower, Alabama, one of sixteen children, served in the army during the Korean War and graduated from Alabama State. Reverend Fields had been one of the earliest and most persistent voices against "segregated buses." Almost two years earlier he had written in the *Advertiser*, "The Negro citizens of Montgomery are fed up with having to stand up on buses when there are vacant seats in the front. Especially buses going to and from areas which are predominantly inhabited by Negroes. These practices must be abolished. The Negro is not asking for anything special. He just wants what any other citizen wants."

From the very beginning of the boycott, Reverend Fields advocated a much stronger stance. Rather than accepting better treatment on segregated buses, he wanted to fully integrate the buses. In another letter to the *Advertiser*, he rejected efforts to compromise, criticizing leaders of the boycott for even suggesting it.

As often happens when businesses or organizations succeed and grow, there are conflicts as people vie for power. The MIA was no different. What had been created as a local organization with a specific objective had gained national attention and prestige. Dr. King, a relative newcomer to the city, was emerging as the spokesperson for a much broader movement. There were unhappy people, people who felt they were not receiving the credit they had earned and deserved. In fact, weeks after the conclusion of the trial, Reverend Fields would resign from the MIA, complaining publicly that certain people had become "too egotistical and interested in perpetuating themselves."

Reverend Fields's unhappiness with the leadership and his questions about the legal strategy were well-known. Perhaps that was why the prosecution was willing to risk putting him on the witness stand. He had been one of the founders of the organization. He knew all its secrets and could tie the defendant, Dr. King, to the conspiracy. Fields was a veteran and a college graduate; he ran a large important church. And as a minister, a man of the Lord, he was bound to tell the truth.

The prosecution called the Reverend Uriah Fields. He was well-dressed, sporting a thin mustache and the hint of a goatee that made him appear both distinguished and sophisticated. The problems for the prosecution began when they asked him to place his left hand on the Bible, raise his right hand and solemnly swear to tell the truth, the whole truth and nothing but the truth, so help me God, just as witnesses had done since the first English settlers arrived in America.

Reverend Fields politely declined.

CHAPTER FIVE

As its newly elected recording secretary, Reverend Uriah Fields had carefully kept the minutes of the afternoon organizational meeting of the Montgomery Improvement Association. The prosecution intended to tie him to his records, proving that the MIA had been organized to run the boycott and the defendant, Dr. King, was its president. It seemed like a simple task. They had the minutes, and the man who created them was on the witness stand. Their problems began when he refused to take the witnesses' oath. "I don't swear," he explained. "I follow my religious convictions to tell the truth, the whole truth and nothing but the truth."

The oath is a legal commitment to testify truthfully and, once taken, subjects a witness to potential harsh penalties for perjury. Its use in the courtroom can be traced back to at least the twelfth century, when the fear of eternal punishment was deemed sufficient to guarantee witnesses would testify honestly. The Bible warns people against taking oaths they cannot fulfill. Deuteronomy 23:21-23 commands "If you make a vow to the

Lord your God, you shall not delay fulfilling it, for the Lord your God will surely require it of you, and you will be guilty of sin. But if you refrained from vowing, you will not be guilty of sin. You shall be careful to do what has passed your lips, for you have voluntarily vowed to the Lord your God what you have promised with your mouth."

While a judge could charge someone for refusing to take the oath with contempt and put him in jail, Judge Carter accepted Reverend Fields's personal affirmation he would tell the truth. He had been the pastor of the Bell Street Baptist Church for about three years, he testified. He lived in Montgomery and was an officer of the Montgomery Improvement Association. According to those minutes, he'd been elected on December 5, 1955.

The difficulty continued when he was asked who called that meeting. "I don't know," he replied.

"Who invited you?"

"I don't know." Someone had called him, he recalled, but that person had not identified himself. The people who attended that meeting were members of the Interdenominational Ministerial Alliance, he agreed. When asked who presided at that meeting, he replied, "I think it is a reverent group."

"Did King preside?"

A yes or no question. "Not to my memory."

"Who stated the purpose of the meeting?"

Fields shook his head, then answered accurately, "According to my minutes, I don't have that information." Meaning it was not in those minutes. Fields had revealed his own strategy; he was going to stick like flypaper to the minutes.

Judge Carter interrupted, "Did you make those minutes?"

He had, he admitted. But his memory of what happened that day, he continued, was limited to what he had written down. "I cannot remember now things that were discussed any more than I have here. I cannot trust my memory." Nor, he knew, could he be found in contempt for having a bad memory.

Answering questions truthfully without answering them honestly is an art usually more within the purview of a seasoned lawyer rather than a pious witness. "What was the purpose of that meeting?" Stewart asked.

"The purpose isn't indicated on the minutes." But did he even know the reason the meeting was held? "I don't know exactly..." he replied. "No more than to say we are concerned about our people."

"What was the first order of business?"

Didn't need his notes for that. "Prayer."

"What was the next order of business?"

"Song, I believe."

"Who led the prayer?"

"That I don't know because my head was bowed, and just asked for a volunteer, someone to lead us in prayer." Following prayer and song, he acknowledged, officers and a board consisting of volunteers were elected.

Stewart continued to try to force Fields to directly respond to his questions. He had him read a portion of the minutes, then asked, perhaps with satisfaction, "That reflects what happened at the meeting, doesn't it?" He had quoted word for word from Fields's own notes.

But even then Fields was hesitant. "I wouldn't say that reflects; I would say that is one fact." But didn't that accurately reflect what happened? "Well, to some degree it does." According to those minutes, there also was a Resolution committee "appointed or elected" at that meeting, and among its members were Reverend Abernathy and Mr. Gray.

Mr. Gray? "Can you tell me whether or not the Mr. Gray there is Attorney Gray here at the counsel table, or some other person?"

"I don't know."

"Do you know Mr. Thomas Gray?" Attorney Fred Gray's activist brother. He did, but whether he was the Gray mentioned in the minutes was something Reverend Fields claimed he just did not recall. Also in the minutes, Stewart pointed out, was a mention that another committee was appointed or elected and "The President, Reverend M. L. King, Attorney Gray and Attorney Langford is on the committee." What committee was that? the prosecutor asked.

"My memory does not allow me to recall," he repeated, with perhaps exaggerated frustration about his supposedly failing memory. Referring to the printed minutes, he pointed out, "It just says, 'the committee.'" Stewart continued to question him about committee assignments until Fields finally claimed, "I see these things there and they don't make any sense to me now." Asked if the notation "Finance" referred to the finance committee, he responded, "I cannot recall to the best of my memory."

The next morning the *Advertiser* would describe Fields's testimony as "evasive," but every person in the courtroom knew exactly what Fields was doing with his always polite but complete and intentional disregard for the solicitor's questions. And the great majority loved him for it. In fact, the newspaper reported, after the session ended, members of the community boasted to each other, "Man, did you see Fields playing with them today?"

Fields, too, took obvious delight in sparring with Stewart. When asked if he remembered which committee voted to present the recommendations to the mass meeting on the fifth, he couldn't do that; he explained, "I always tell the truth, nothing but the truth, but I don't know whether I can trust my memory because I couldn't be definitely certain."

Reverend Fields was balancing skillfully on the edge of a legal cliff, carefully avoiding making any direct statements that could be proved false. Blacks were used to seeing certain white witnesses tell broad lies about them under oath, while the testimony of Black witnesses was often ignored. The pain of Emmett Till's murder and the almost instant acquittal of his accused killers was still resonating throughout Black America. During that trial, held only seven months earlier in Tallahatchie County, Mississippi, white witnesses had made claims that were widely disputed—but provided sufficient cover for the jury to find the defendants not guilty. With Uriah Fields's verbal dexterity, the fox finally was chasing the hounds.

"Were, or were not, those recommendations drawn up at this meeting and which you attended?" Stewart asked.

"Which meeting?"

"This one we're talking about."

"We have had so many I haven't a definite recollection of it."

"The recommendation that you are referring to in your minutes here, that recommendations to be presented to the citizens at the night meeting. What recommendation was that?"

"Evidently the committee was to prepare the recommendations."

"What committee?"

"I don't know. I couldn't say. Whichever committee it was to prepare the recommendations."

When Stewart asked, "Was, or was not, the matter of the bus boycott or bus protest discussed at the meeting?" Billingsley objected.

Judge Carter overruled. "He said 'was or was not.'"

But, Billingsley said, "It has not been established what 'it' was."

The court directed the witness to "Go ahead with your answer."

Reverend Fields shrugged. "I forgot the question."

After it was repeated, Fields looked history right in the eyes and said, once again, "I couldn't say beyond what is indicated here on this paper. No, sir. I just cannot remember. That is right."

Stewart wouldn't admit defeat. "What was the purpose of establishing these various committees?"

"Well, I would say the Resolution committee had some type

of Resolution to make. I would think so. What the discussion they had, though, I don't know."

Finally, finally, Stewart appealed to the court for assistance, complaining to Judge Carter, "It would help greatly if this witness would just give direct answers to the questions."

The judge admonished Fields, reminding him, "You objected to being sworn when you came up here; you promised to tell the truth, which means the same thing, and if you know, say so, and if you don't, say so."

Nothing changed. It was noted in the minutes that "the protest would be continued until conditions are improved." Asked what protest that referred to, Fields pointed out, "That is not indicated" in the minutes. "I cannot say if this refers to the bus or something else." Clearly playing to the spectators, he added, "Since I promised to tell the truth, the whole truth and nothing but the truth, I don't know. I am not sure of that. I can't say."

In desperation, Stewart reminded him that he was the secretary and that much of the minutes were in his handwriting. Fields acknowledged that "I am secretary," but unfortunately, he conceded, he was not a very good secretary, as "my multiplicity of duties makes it impossible for me to be an efficient secretary." And what might that multiplicity of duties be? "I have to keep in touch with my Creator." Perhaps speaking for every member of the community, he explained, "It takes a lot of prayer through times like these."

It's almost possible to hear the Amens rippling through the courtroom.

For the next hour, Stewart continued going through the minutes kept by Reverend Fields of the various meetings. Fields's lack of memory never faltered; his testimony was an unending recital of "I don't know," "I cannot recall," "it isn't in the minutes," "not to my recollection." But through all that clutter, Stewart did manage to eke out some evidence: at many of the meetings, according to Fields's notes, there were "Remarks by the president." And who was that president? he was asked. "Reverend King."

Listed among the speakers at the mass meeting on January 5, when the boycott was in full operation, was Reverend Fields. Stewart wondered what he spoke about. "Well, I talked about being spiritualized," he remembered. "I talked about living close to the Creator; and tried to have a better, improved life regardless of how and where you live, and he who lives by the soul shall perish by the soul… My talk was pertaining toward improving Montgomery…"

That finally was enough for Stewart, who asked Judge Carter to declare Reverend Fields a "hostile witness." That is the legal term for a witness called by one side whose testimony, rather than supporting their case, benefits the opposition. In a trial, there are two broad types of questions: direct and leading. A direct question allows a witness to answer it with a longer explanation, as Reverend Fields was doing. A leading question, which normally is limited to cross-examination, can suggest the answer or be used to challenge the witness, and often is answered with a simple yes or no. The judge has the discretion to declare a friendly witness hostile or sometimes adverse, giving the attorney far greater latitude in the scope of his questions.

But rather than agreeing to Stewart's request, an exasperated judge looked directly at Fields. "You are on the witness stand," he admonished. "Tell the truth. You know whether the bus situation was discussed, or not. Now—you tell the truth." Lying or making false statements under oath is a crime and can be punished with fines or even jail time. It is tough to prove, though, and rarely worth the effort for a prosecutor.

"I am telling the truth," Fields replied. "I tell the truth on all occasions."

"You know whether it was discussed, or was not. You went to all the meetings and heard the talk."

Fields's reply was the most honest answer he had given. "I was concerned about my people."

"We want the truth," Carter insisted, "whether it was discussed or not; not what they said, but was it mentioned?"

"Not to my recollection."

More than his answers, it is likely that Judge Carter and Stewart found Fields's attitude far more offensive. *Uppity* was the derisive word used by certain white Americans to describe it. Fields and Gray, Langford and King, all of the young educated Black men involved in this trial were harbingers of a future that Montgomery had vowed to resist. Fields wasn't only standing up to the white prosecutor, he was playing with him, a tactic in the past that had on occasion literally proved deadly. A lot of white people considered Black ministers and lawyers to be the troublemakers, the instigators. Thurgood Marshall, for example, had lost count of the number of times his life had been threatened. In addition to twice escaping lynch mobs, more than a decade earlier he had been stuffed into a car and driven down a lonely dirt road; his life was saved when white men in the car ahead of him turned back to help him.

When Stewart resumed his questioning, he asked, "At any other mass meeting you don't recall the bus situation discussed by someone, do you? One single person?"

Fields considered that. The spectators waited to see how Fields would respond to the judge's warning. Would he behave as a proper, docile witness? After a long pause, he replied, "Will you tell me what you mean by the bus situation?" In the gallery, spectators shared knowing smiles.

"The Montgomery bus boycott, the protest, whatever term you use."

Fields answered honestly, but it was not an answer to that question. "We have been concerned about our people making good citizens."

If this had been a jury trial, Stewart probably would have

taken a different path, but in this case, the verdict would be rendered by one man, by Judge Carter, and perhaps Stewart wanted to reinforce to the judge the fact that witnesses would not answer his questions. So he continued, stumbling into dangerous territory by asking the purpose of the mass meetings.

Fields's answer seemed to be as much a warning as a response. "I think that one of the purposes was to prevent any uprising for our race, and to keep peace in Montgomery, or bring peace to Montgomery."

Stewart would not let go, asking, "Bring peace to Montgomery or prevent any uprising in connection with what?"

"I have read pieces in the paper of a council being organized here," Fields replied, "the White Citizens Council, and we don't want any trouble here in Montgomery."

There wasn't a sound in the courtroom other than Stewart's voice as he asked, "Do I understand that these meetings were organized or held to combat the White Citizens Council?"

The reverend did not back down. "Not to combat it. Probably the white people might try to get our people into an uproar." The MIA, he admitted, had nothing to do with that council. "We have been concerned about our people here in Montgomery."

Stewart made one last attempt, having Reverend Fields read aloud some of his grand jury testimony, during which he is quoted as saying about the December 5 meeting, "I would say that, as the minutes indicate, they agreed to continue the protest until some favorable results had come our way."

Reverend Fields agreed. "That sounds like my talk." But that was as close as the prosecution could get to proving that the MIA had illegally conspired to start and manage the boycott. With that, Uriah Fields was excused.

While the trial was in session, during a press conference in Washington, President Eisenhower was asked by *New York Post* reporter Robert G. Spivack, "With regard to the situation in

Alabama, Mr. President, how do you feel about Negroes being brought to trial for refusing to ride the Montgomery buses?"

This question was loaded with enormous political consequences and the president did his best to avoid answering it, ironically responding with the same type of deft evasion that Fields had demonstrated. "Well, you are asking me, I think, to be more of a lawyer than I certainly am. But, as I understand it, there is a state law about boycotts, and it is under that kind of thing that these people are being brought to trial. I think that the statement I made last week on this whole subject represents all the views that I now have to make; and I do believe that it is incumbent on all the South to show some progress. That is what the Supreme Court asked for. And they turned it over to local district courts. I believe that we should not stagnate; but again, I plead for understanding, for really sympathetic consideration of a problem that is far larger both in its emotional and even in its physical aspects than most of us realize."

While Eisenhower clearly was trying to avoid saying anything that might cause political problems, the reporters persisted. The *New York Times*' Anthony Lewis asked if the president had any plans to actually do something about the issue. Did he intend "to mobilize religious and other leaders of the South to your point of view of moderation and progress on the segregation issue?"

Once again, Eisenhower said nothing but effectively disguised it as an answer. "Well... That is one thing Billy Graham teaches not only abroad, he teaches it among ourselves and, frankly, I do believe that the pulpits do have a very great responsibility here." Graham had emerged as America's leading evangelist; his television and radio programs and in-person "crusades" attracted an audience of millions—and included in his sermons was a plea for racial integration.

The president continued, "This is a very tough one, and people have to search their own hearts if we're going to a decent answer and keep going ahead. Now, let's don't try to think of this as a tremendous fight that is going to separate Americans and get ourselves into a nasty mess. Let's try to think of it of how we can make progress and keep it going and not stop it. Now that, I believe, the pulpits can help on."

By "pulpits," though, he was referring exclusively to white religious leaders. If the president had even heard of Reverend Martin Luther King at that point, he made no reference to him. His safe political position was the politically correct, go slow.

Alabama's governor, Big Jim Folsom, also spoke to reporters that day. "The problem of integration is not an immediate one," he said, referring specifically to public schools but generally to all aspects of society. "A lot of us won't be here when it comes." By that he meant it would not be a political problem for him, as "This is my last political office." But he did reassure Alabamians, "We are going to maintain segregation in this state."

Back in Montgomery, the prosecution called Rufus Lewis. Lewis and E. D. Nixon together essentially formed the engine of change for the Black community. While Nixon was a workingman, a union man without a formal education, Lewis was a graduate of Fisk University, a military veteran, a librarian, a teacher, for a time the football coach at Alabama State, and the owner of a popular social club. People used to say about them, "Mr. Nixon had the masses and Coach Lewis had the classes." Both of them understood that any progress depended on getting people out to vote and were leaders of registration efforts.

Both men also were founders of the MIA. Nixon was appointed treasurer, while Lewis was made head of the transportation committee. He was a good fit; because his wife co-owned a funeral home, he had instant access to the large automobiles and hearses operated by the several funeral homes in the community. Lewis had an almost impossible job; he had to arrange transportation for the almost forty thousand Black people who regularly used the buses—and he had to get that system up and running within a few days. Somehow, he had managed to do it, putting together a ragtag fleet of taxis, personal cars, business cars and just about anything else on four wheels, arranging central drop-off and pickup points, making certain he had drivers and the cars had fuel.

Rufus Lewis was arguably the most respected Black man in the city. By the time he sat down in the wooden witness chair, the makeshift system he had built was operating efficiently. To the chagrin of the local white establishment, Black people were getting where they needed to go when they needed to be there.

On the witness stand, though, Lewis had to tread carefully between taking pride in his accomplishment and essentially pretending it didn't exist. After going through the basic questions and establishing he served on the transportation committee, Stewart asked the purpose of the transportation committee.

"To get people to and from destinations."

"What kind of people?"

"People who are interested in riding and have no transportation."

After trying unsuccessfully to find out all the people who served with Lewis, the prosecutor asked, "What has the transportation committee done in reference to transportation?"

Lewis could barely believe the question. The answer seemed so obvious he repeated it as if to confirm he'd heard it correctly. "What has the transportation committee done in reference to transportation?"

"That's right."

He responded with the only possible answer. "We transported people." In response to Stewart's asking how the system had been set up and operated, he said, "We asked for people who would volunteer us their cars to transport people to various destinations (and we got) approximately two hundred... We established our pick-up of people so (the drivers) got paid for their car...a matter of $4 a day to people who did transport or used their car all day from approximately six o'clock in the morning until six and seven at night."

Stewart guided Lewis through the details, who got paid how much how often, which gas stations were used, where the pickup points were, including a place on McDonough. "What is that place called?" Stewart asked.

"A parking lot."

It took about a week to get the system operating, Lewis explained. It wasn't complicated. "People would gather (at a dispatch location), other people would go there and pick them up in their cars." It was all free; nobody paid for transportation. And while he reported regularly to the general meetings, he never discussed it with Reverend King. As for the communications, he continued, "We do have a phone… If there is a person who needs transportation and cannot get it otherwise that person will call and if we have an automobile we will send it for that person."

By taking Lewis through the mechanics of the operation, Stewart confirmed it was an established, well-organized effort. Those were important elements to prove that people had conspired to stay off the buses in violation of the city statute.

But Lewis was much less forthcoming about the defendant's involvement. When asked if King had attended the afternoon ministers' meeting, his memory clouded. He thought Dr. King was there, but he couldn't be certain. When asked about that meeting, he replied, sighing, "I don't know because I am confused on the dates."

Did Dr. King speak at that meeting?

"I don't recollect."

"What was said in general about the bus situation?"

"I couldn't say what was said now."

Judge Carter interrupted again. "He doesn't mean the exact words," he told Mr. Lewis, "but rather the substance of what was said. No person could remember exactly what was said away back there."

Lewis nodded in agreement, a habit of his. "It was a general discussion." By that point he had remembered that his memory was poor. Was the MIA organized or set up at that December 5 meeting? "I don't know." Were officers elected at that meeting? "I don't know." Did he recall discussing the Resolution to be presented at the mass meeting? "No."

The mass meeting was called, he testified, "To give information…to the people" about "the situation that exists in the bus protest." What situation? "The intimidations, the threats, things of that sort."

"And were those things discussed at the mass meeting at the Holt Street Baptist Church?"

"No. Not discussed," he said, then clarified, "They were presented."

Lewis danced carefully through several more questions about the MIA, but then, once again, Stewart asked a question to which he obviously did not know the answer. "As a member of the Executive Committee of the Montgomery Improvement Association, do you know of any function it has performed which is not directly related to the bus situation?"

Indeed he did. "There have been quite a number of collections of shoes gathered up mostly for the needy people of the community. That is one service that is done. And helping to uplift the citizens in our community. That is another. And in addition to shoes, clothes are gathered up." And who was in charge of those collections? "I am."

While there had been few objections, the judge had overruled almost all of them. Lawyer Billingsley objected after Stewart had read a long passage of Lewis's grand jury testimony, concluding by asking, "Isn't that true?"

"He doesn't even ask a question," Billingsley complained. "He just makes a statement and asks him if that isn't true."

After initially defending the question, Judge Carter decided, "If you objected to it on the ground it was so involved, that there were so many questions in one, I probably would rule with you."

Okay, Billingsley agreed. "We object to it on that ground—and the other ground!"

Stewart withdrew the question. After he completed his direct examination, Arthur Shores conducted the first real cross-examination. Shores's calm demeanor carried with it his decades of experience in hostile courtrooms. The defense intended to prove there was a valid reason for the boycott, which would make it legal under the statute. Shores began by showing the protest did not happen suddenly, but resulted from years of people being mistreated on the buses and the refusal of the city to take steps to remedy the situation. "I believe you stated your discussion at the meetings was along the lines of threats and intimidations you had received pertaining to the bus situation. Is that correct?" It was. "Had there been complaints generally to the association about mistreatment on the buses?" Yes. "Do you know of your own knowledge recourse had been made to the bus company and to the city commission to alleviate those conditions?"

"Yes, it had. I have been in several of the meetings with the city…several times before December 5th."

"To see if you could get some relief from this mistreatment?"

"Yes."

Shores also emphasized the fact that no one paid for transportation, and no one was paid for the use of their car.

Fred Gray enjoyed sitting quietly and watching Arthur Shores take control of a courtroom. It was like being back in law school, watching a gifted professor teaching by example. Shores went about his work with the ease of a surgeon, deftly cutting through the clutter to get to the salient point. And always with his low-key manner, treating every person—including his white adversaries—with unfailing respect, never allowing himself to let an emotion leak into his questions. Maybe Thurgood Marshall and Robert Carter were getting national attention, but Shores and several other men like him were working in the trenches of history, changing the world on an everyday basis.

Arthur Shores had been Gray's mentor and was one of five practicing lawyers who had submitted a character reference on his behalf. With Shores's guidance, Gray had become the youngest member of the very exclusive club of Black lawyers admitted to the Alabama bar, a small, tightly bound group that included Shores, Peter Hall, Langford and Billingsley that conferred often, sometimes enlisting the support, advice and participation of Thurgood Marshall and Robert Carter and sometimes including the white civil rights activist Clifford Durr. Sometimes together, sometimes just some of them, sometimes alone, they worked on a great variety of cases—all of them sharing the single objective, as Fred Gray had promised, to fight segregation anywhere and everywhere.

Shores and Lewis had spent their entire lives preparing for this testimony. Shores had been born in 1904, two years before Lewis, and the two men had grown up in segregated Alabama. But while they brought to the moment different living experiences, both men had fought the system to get college educations and then had spent their lives fighting ingrained racism. It was almost possible to feel the warmth and respect they had for each other.

When Shores completed his cross-examination and thanked the witness, Stewart began his redirect. It was as if a burst of cold air had blown over the courtroom. Stewart was all business; his job was to expose these people, to return the city to good order. "Do you know or do you not know approximately how many passengers your transportation committee has been transporting since early December?"

The correct answer was, everybody who needed a ride. An astonishing accomplishment, but instead Lewis replied, "No.

We don't keep records as to how many." Asked to estimate, he shrugged. "It wouldn't be too accurate. Several hundred. That is the best I can say."

Once again, Stewart tried to directly connect the MIA to the boycott, asking, logically, if they were "being transported in an effort to keep them from riding the buses?"

Lewis shook his head. "It is not to keep anybody from riding the buses; it is to give transportation to people who want it in preference to the buses."

As if to make sure he understood the response, Stewart inverted it. "For those people who don't want to ride the buses you have been furnishing transportation. Shall we put it that way?"

"Yes, sir."

A few moments later the solicitor asked if Reverend King had presented certain demands at a meeting with the City Commission. Billingsley objected, telling the judge that the use of the word *demands* calls for a conclusion. Stewart substituted the word *requests*; a small change but a significant difference. Black residents of the city had almost never been in a position to make demands of the city; Black people didn't make demands in Montgomery, Alabama, but they certainly had made numerous requests—and very few of them had been granted.

Lewis agreed that Dr. King had presented a list of "requests," but he did not remember what they included. Stewart reminded him: "Didn't he point out, request one, more courtesy from bus drivers… The second, seating of white and colored passengers from the front and rear respectively on first come, first served basis; and three, the employment of Negro bus drivers on predominantly Negro lines?"

Lewis agreed. "I think so." But he wasn't sure it took place at that meeting.

Stewart pounced, asking if those same demands had been presented at both the afternoon ministerial meeting and the mass meeting on the fifth.

Not at the afternoon meeting, Lewis replied. At that meeting, he clarified, "Conditions with reference to the bus situation were discussed, but I don't think these particular proposals were discussed." He shook his head. "I don't recall."

Stewart had managed to get some evidence of the connection between the MIA and the boycott into the trial record. Arthur Shores stood up to repair that damage with his follow-up re-cross examination. He went right at it: "Has your committee ever kept Negroes from riding buses?"

"No."

"Just left it up to the people?"

"Yes, sir." In other words, there was no coercion, no force, no threats, no intimidation. People had made their own decision not to ride the buses, all forty thousand of them.

"Whether they ride or not."

"Yes."

To demonstrate that the MIA had been established to "improve the community" in ways other than staying off the buses, he asked if the association had a committee on registration and voting. Yes, Lewis said, and "I happen to be cochairman of that committee."

In addition to that committee, "Do you know whether or not there has been a committee to establish a bank in connection to the Montgomery Improvement Association?"

"I wouldn't say establish a bank," Lewis said. "A bank in the area."

"Those are some of the official functions of the Montgomery Improvement Association for the improvement of Negroes generally?"

"Yes."

Now it was Stewart's turn to respond. "When was this committee on voting set up of which you were chairman?"

Only a few weeks earlier. Just like the banking committee. "As a matter of fact," he pointed out, "all three of the committees you testified about, the one on voting, the one in connection with setting up a bank and the one for distribution of shoes and clothing, were all set up after the grand jury returned this indictment, weren't they?"

In fact, that was true. "I don't think so," Lewis responded.

Stewart didn't pursue that; his question had included the information he wanted in the record. And then he tried to bring out that the MIA had aggressively maintained the boycott. "You say on cross-examination your committee hasn't urged the Negroes of Montgomery County not to ride the buses."

Rufus Lewis disagreed. "I didn't say they were not urged to ride the buses. I said we didn't interfere with or try to keep them from riding the buses." Once again, a few small words made a huge difference.

"Hasn't your committee been urging them not to ride the buses at all?"

"Our committee has been inquiring as to whether they wanted to ride the buses."

Stewart's voice was rising as he finally got to his pertinent question. "At those meetings you attended, haven't you heard various speeches to urge the citizens not to ride the buses until their demands had been met? Have you or have you not heard people urge the colored citizens not to ride the buses at those meetings?"

Lewis already had testified to that, so he had no difficulty in agreeing with that statement. With that "Yes," Rufus Lewis was excused to a smattering of applause from the gallery.

CHAPTER SIX

By the time Rufus Lewis stepped down from the witness stand, Montgomery had settled into the workday. To the casual observer, it seemed like an ordinary March morning. At Green's supermarket (formerly Silver's!) sirloin steak was selling for forty-five cents a pound and Grade A eggs were fifty-five cents a dozen; on TV *Burns and Allen* started at seven o'clock and *I Love Lucy* began at eight; *Holiday on Ice 1956* was opening at the Coliseum. For the more adventurous, "The beautiful exotic Sherry Lynn, direct from the Gypsy Room in Atlanta" was opening at The Flamingo nightclub on the same bill as "America's number 1 blackface comedian, Cotton Watts." At the Paramount, *The Last Hunt*, starring Robert Taylor and Stewart Granger, was playing "in color and CinemaScope" on a double bill with *Land of the Nile*, while at the Fairmount Drive-In, actress Terry Moore was costarring with Frank Lovejoy, Keenan Wynn and Lee Marvin in *Shack Out on 101*, a story of "Four Men and A Girl... They crashed every stop signal!" In the classifieds, a reward was being offered for a missing blue parakeet and John Boswell Dodge-Plymouth wanted to hire a "sober and reliable first class mechanic." There were births and deaths—comedian Fred Allen had collapsed on a Manhattan street and died—and social announcements—Mrs. Nora Hill had left the city on Sunday to visit her sister in St. Petersburg, Florida—and a letter from the editor of England's *Manchester Guardian* apologizing for "a colored student" who had claimed to be its correspondent at the trial.

But all of it was background to the bus boycott, which was economically devastating the city, and the fact that its Black population had risen up. The trial down at the circuit court-house was the focus of the city.

As the trial began, Mrs. Claire Mack had written indignantly to the *Montgomery Advertiser*. "I am, a housewife, (white)," her letter began, perhaps venting for her neighbors, "born and bred in the South. I am so fed up with the things the Northern news-papers have to say against the South. They have printed lies, insinuations and dirty wisecracks until my blood pressure rises every time I pick up a paper...

"Why does someone not tell them that we Southern whites are the only true friends the Negro has ever had in all this world?... We have given them jobs, financed their schools, boosted them and cheered them on their way to make something of themselves, shown pride in their success and now, thanks to us, they have a way of life equal to our own. They have comfortable, modern homes, fine cars, schools, theaters, television...

"We have given them everything in life but social equal-ity with our people. It is not the Negro who is oppressed and underprivileged—it is the white South. An attempt is being made to force integration upon us...it is unthinkable that our children should intermarry with another race. Nature did not mean it to be."

Personally, she continued, she had always spoken kindly to Negroes, only showing anger when they did not appreciate that kindness. She admitted this revolt had caused her to panic, because she felt, "ending bus segregation we knew meant only the first step toward school integration and that we cannot tolerate…"

They were being forced to fight back, she pleaded, because integration "is worse than death itself…"

This self-described "housewife" represented the majority of white Alabamians who were intently following this trial, fully aware of what was at stake. Like the rest of the South, Montgomery had created a two-tiered society that was working quite well for its white citizens. The city was growing rapidly; by the end of the decade, its population would have increased by 26 percent to 134,000 residents. It was the home of two major defense installations, which provided jobs for both races. "Blacks and whites generally got along," remembered Eddie Phillips, a white man who grew up there during this period. "When it came to racial injustice, the vast majority of whites simply chose not to think about it."

While there appeared to be racial peace, there certainly was not harmony. White residents mostly accepted white superiority as the consequence of nature and history. In fact, some Montgomery schools taught that slavery actually was a way of protecting Black people, because they did not have to be on their own and take care of themselves. And the city took great pride in its ability to navigate the rocky racial waters. Most people accepted that change was coming, but no major changes and certainly not very quickly. The prevailing attitude might be summed up by the fact that the city had hired its first four Black police officers in 1954, officers who would patrol Black sections and would not be permitted to make arrests outside that area. They were to be given radios to call white officers should it become necessary to arrest white people. Chief of police Ruppenthal had reassured anxious white residents, telling reporters that these new officers were "just n——s doing a n——'s job."

But that would change abruptly after the Supreme Court issued its ruling in *Brown*, which ended segregation in public
schools. That was too much too fast for many white Southerners. The quest for racial equality had suddenly intruded in their
lives. On March 22, for example, in the middle of the trial, in
addition to reporting on Eisenhower's press conference and Governor Folsom's response, the *Advertiser* included different stories
reporting that Florida governor Leroy Collins announced he was
calling a special session of the state legislature to legally prevent
"coerced integration"; that Oregon senator Richard Neuber-
ger was threatening to introduce a bill taking House seats away
from Southern states that prevent Black residents from voting;
that Tuskegee Institute was holding a celebration of its seventy-
fifth anniversary and founder Booker T. Washington's one hun-
dreth birthday. On its editorial page, obviously referring to the
Northern and Western journalists covering the trial, it printed
a column referring to a letter written by its editor, Grover C.
Hall Jr., to James Wechsler, editor of the then "ultraliberal" *New
York Post*, offering to "aid him in investigating and reporting
on racial clashes in New York and the North." In his column,
city editor Joe Azbell related the story of a young reporter for
the 1,500,000 circulation French newspaper *France-Soir* "who
arrived here early to bone up on the Negro bus boycott before
covering the trials" and who became terribly upset when he was
misquoted in an earlier edition of the *Advertiser* supposedly saying "in France people have gone to jail for just walking." And
finally it included the one-panel nationally syndicated cartoon
Hambone's Meditations, featuring a caricature of an older Black
man dispensing folk "wisdom," in this edition: "You cain' have
ev'rything right, *all* de time—ole sun a mighty good frien' in
de wintuh time but he *hard* on you in *July*!!!"

Every person in the city realized on some level that the life
they had known in the Reconstructed South was going to

change. So they followed this trial with excitement or trepidation, with pride or fear, but they did follow it.

As the next witness, John Oliver, a hardworking Black businessman, owner of John Oliver's Service Station and Garage, took the stand, the prosecution expanded its case. The third member of the solicitor's team, twenty-nine-year-old Maury Drane Smith, cleared his throat and began questioning Oliver. Smith was a native of the city, he was young and ambitious, a rapidly rising star on his way to success and prestige. After serving as an infantryman in World War II, he had graduated from the University of Alabama, where he also received his law degree. He might even have been Fred Gray's classmate there, had the university accepted Negroes. Appearing in a trial like this one, with all the visibility that came with it, could be an important step up for him.

He was going to use the Black owners or operators of service stations to demonstrate that while the boycott may have been thrown together quickly, it had evolved into a highly efficient organization. And someone had to be running it.

For a working man like John Oliver, being called to testify in this trial most likely was an unwelcome intrusion into his life. This boycott, this trial, was ripping open the city. Until now, it had been loosely held together. No good could possibly come to a man like him by being put down in the middle of it. He was just trying to run his garage, make a living. He wasn't used to being in the spotlight. Just like for Mr. Smith, participating in this trial carried with it all types of possibilities. The difference was that there was little gain in it for Oliver. There was no next step up, just the risk of saying the wrong thing, making problems for his neighbors, or his people.

He had been charging gas to the Montgomery Improvement Association, he testified in response to Smith's questions. Somebody, he didn't know who, had come out to the station "and wanted to know if I could give them gas at all times... I didn't pay much attention to them. I am out of the station most of the time; I am in the shop working… They just dropped in to see if I would charge gas when the cars in the pool stopped there, and if I would send them a bill they would send their check promptly."

They paid every two days, he continued, taking the court through the logistics. Stewart showed him a check for $48.69 and asked who had signed it. "M. L. King," the witness replied, "and E. D. Nixon and Erna Dungee." Who signed this check for $74.50? "M. L. King, E. D. Nixon and Dungee." This check for $75.11? This check for $74.87?

Peter Hall objected, pointing out the checks were already in evidence and, as Judge Carter explained when making one of his rare rulings for the defense, "The check shows on its face who signed it."

Undeterred, Smith continued plowing through the stack of checks. As he expected, he got the same answer every time—until he asked about a check issued on February 1 for $78.93. The witness surprised him; that check was payable to his brother, Ernest Oliver. "I cashed it. Made to my brother." Most of the other checks, Oliver continued, paid for gas, but some of them were for "Minor repair of an automobile in the pool."

Smith pounced. "What do you mean by car pool?"

"Well, that is what I asked them, what were the cars, and they said just give them gas for the cars when they come in."

The defense waived its cross-examination.

An effective trial lawyer, almost by definition, is an actor, able to elevate the mundane elements of their case into something far more meaningful and important than might otherwise be believed. That was the task facing Smith. Thetford had given him the unenviable but necessary task of making prosaic testimony, facts that served to reinforce the prosecution's claim that the MIA was a functioning conspiracy, seem a whole lot more significant than it actually was. Joe Foster, the manager of the Derby Auto Service Station, followed Oliver onto the stand.

Foster testified that he had opened an account for the MIA, but he didn't know exactly when that took place. "Maybe January or December. When it first started."

"When what first started?"

"Whatever it was, yes, sir."

"Bus protest or boycott?"

Foster shrugged. "Whatever it is." He also said he did not know, exactly, who had opened the account, explaining, "To the best of my knowledge it must have been a group of people or somebody that could have called on the telephone?... The first person called me and sounded like he was in a crowd or something."

His testimony basically was a repetition of Oliver's. People came in and got gas, the MIA paid him by check every two days or so. Smith's efforts to expand that testimony failed dismally. "What were the checks for?" he asked.

"For gasoline."

"All gasoline?"

"Gasoline that the individuals received and we were supposed to allow to them."

"What individuals?" Smith asked.

"The ones that got the gas." He did agree that it was the Montgomery Improvement Association that eventually paid for all the gasoline that had been charged.

The defense waived its cross-examination.

Hezekiah Nunn, "the sole owner of the Day Street Service Station, not the property," took the stand. His participation began when three men from the MIA had come to his station. "Would I sell them gas? I told them yes."

"Did they tell you how they would pay for it?"

"I had to know a little something about it," Mr. Nunn replied. "I told them I would if they would pay for it twice a week."

It wasn't very complicated: people came in, got gas and left. In return he got checks. "What were all these checks given for?"

"Was to pay for the gas."

"For what gas?"

"Gas I sold to the Montgomery Improvement Association."

The defense waived its cross-examination.

Mr. D. W. Williams, owner and operator of the D. W. Williams Gulf Service Station for the past nine years, went through the same questions and gave the same answers. "There wasn't no arrangement," he explained. "Reverend Powell just said he wanted me to let the cars come in and get gas, for me to take the number and let them have the gas... I didn't particularly try to identify them. They said they wanted the gas and I gave it to them."

Smith began going through another collection of checks, asking, "Who paid you those checks?"

It was obvious, Mr. Williams pointed out. "It has got Montgomery Improvement Association on there."

Smith just barged ahead. "What did they pay you for?"

"For gasoline."

"What kind of gasoline?"

Williams did not hesitate. "Gasoline that went into cars."

Even then, as spectators tried desperately to restrain their laughter, Smith continued. "Went into what cars?"

"Cars I just told you about, or trying to."

The defense waived its cross-examination.

Solicitor Thetford took over the prosecution, calling Detective K. Y. Jones. In his quest to break the boycott in January, Mayor Gayle announced that the three-member City Commission, representatives who had been elected for four-year terms, "was through pussyfooting around." Montgomery was governed by three men, two commissioners and the mayor. In addition to Mayor Gayle, the commissioners were police commissioner Clyde Sellers, a hard-core law-and-order segregationist, and Frank Parks, who was a member of the Masons, the Shriners and, people joked, any organization that would have him. The commissioners announced that they had joined the pro-segregation Central Alabama White Citizens Council (twelve thousand members in the Montgomery area)—and Commissioner Sellers had instructed his officers to bring the weight of the law down on the boycotters. The Montgomery Police Department began a pressure campaign, threatening people waiting at dispatch and pickup points to disperse or risk arrest for hitchhiking, loitering or vagrancy. Drivers were ticketed for minor offenses like stopping in a crosswalk, picking up people in unauthorized areas and driving too close to the sidewalk. Dr. King was arrested for speeding, allegedly racing at thirty miles an hour in a twenty-five-miles-an-hour zone. He was taken to the police station and booked. Fred Gray defended him at his trial, unsuccessfully appealing the guilty verdict and the $10 fine. Police officers regularly stopped MIA vehicles, checking licenses, insurance and their condition, eventually issuing hundreds of tickets and making sixty arrests.

Among the people who had been stopped and later arrested was Fred's brother Thomas Gray, who had been a volunteer driver since the beginning of the protest. What struck him at the time was how polite the police officers were; there was no sense of hostility, as if they were being forced to perform an unpleasant task. The volunteer drivers were not arrested at that time, but the police officers wrote down all their identifying information.

Detective Jones had played a role in this harassment, but Thetford simply wanted him to testify that this was an organized boycott effort, a conspiracy. His "investigation," he said, had begun January 11. "At that time," the solicitor asked, "were, or were not, any substantial number of Negroes of the City of Montgomery riding the buses?"

"No, sir." Police officers generally have a very specific way of testifying. That is part of their training. And unlike civilians, who might testify once in a lifetime, testifying is part of a police officer's job. They often become comfortable with it. When possible, they respond with succinct answers, generally in line with the prosecution's objective. Jones and his partner, Detective Jack Shows, had stopped and questioned a number of drivers, "right at the entrance to the parking lot behind the colored Y building... The place for them to come to get an automobile ride to the destination they were going."

At times, he said, there was a man in the parking lot directing the operation. "When a car pulled in he would call out, 'Anybody going south,' or 'north' or 'east' or 'west?' and the people going in that direction would get in the car. As they pulled out of the parking lot on to the street we stopped them."

He estimated that on an average day he had stopped about thirty cars. Thetford asked, "Did, or did not, any of them admit they were driving in furtherance of the boycott?"

"Yes, sir." Among them was William Johnson, in his 1953 Chevrolet, who told them, "he hauled two or three hours every day; that he started hauling in December, that he was getting four gallons of gas a day at the Day Street Service Station and that the Montgomery Improvement Association was paying for the gasoline."

Orzell Billingsley had been objecting to much of this testimony; this time he asked that the detective's testimony be stricken from the record "on the ground that it hasn't anything to do with this defendant here, M. L. King, or the Montgomery Improvement Association."

As expected, overruled. "He said so himself," Judge Carter explained. But then he connected the testimony he had heard thus far: "The defendant was president of the Montgomery Improvement Association and had discussed the bus protest or boycott, whatever it be. A prima facia case of conspiracy has been established, and that being so, I would hold that this testimony is relevant provided it is connected up as being an agent of the Montgomery Improvement Association."

Judge Carter had made a significant decision: the MIA had conspired to create and maintain the boycott of the city's bus system. Billingsley asked for "an exception," a legal phrase meaning that he did not agree with the judge's ruling. Like a baseball manager arguing with an umpire. While it has no bearing on the trial, it may become relevant during the appeal process, when judges on the next level review the trial transcript.

The defense had been taking exceptions to almost every one of the judge's rulings, so Billingsley finally suggested, "I would like to object to every one he says."

"You want the same objection to each of them?" He did. It was fine with the judge. "It is agreed that each of these questions are objected to, and overruled, by the Court. The objection being on the same ground as stated by the attorney representing the defendant in the prior objection, and an exception is given the defendant."

The defendant, Martin Luther King, at times seemed like an afterthought. He hadn't yet been asked a question or said a word in the trial, but he remained the center of attention. During each pause in the proceedings, reporters would descend on him, seeking a comment. His subdued responses were respectful but noncommittal. Day by day his reputation was growing, not only in the South, but throughout the entire country. A participant in the ministerial meeting on the afternoon of December 5 recalled that there had been a lot of discussion about leadership but no agreement on who that would be. Dr. King had arrived late. "When he entered the room, it was like someone had sent him. He was it."

That same feeling seemed to be spreading in Black communities across the country. As a reporter noted in a series of articles about Dr. King in the widely circulated Black newspaper the *Pittsburgh Courier*, "Handsome and well-poised, the Reverend Mr. King is five feet seven inches and weighs 159 pounds. There are moments when one feels he is about to break out in a bit of boyish wit, but he seems to change his mind before the first thought comes through. His calm is amazing. He seems constantly at peace with himself. He inspires confidence almost immediately."

In Montgomery's Black community, his church, the Dexter Avenue Baptist Church, was known as "One of those Baptist churches where you don't show your emotions." That description accurately reflected his courtroom demeanor. He continued to sit impassively, occasionally nodding in agreement, or leaning over and whispering something to Gray or another attorney, then focusing on the witness, showing no awareness that he had already taken the first tentative steps into history.

Solicitor Thetford continued questioning Detective Jones. The officer testified about the men he had stopped. Arbie E. Brooks, for example, told him "that he hauled every day...and when I asked him why he was hauling, and he said he wanted to help the movement here in Montgomery."

Other drivers he stopped told him they were transporting people that, in most cases, they did not know and their gas was being paid for by the MIA. Lawyer Peter Hall asked the judge, "Are you ruling the mere furnishing of gas indicates a Montgomery Improvement Association employee?"

Judge Carter looked at Thetford. "Does anything connect them in any way with the protest or boycott?"

Thetford replied, "By the driving of people."

Hall pressed his point. "We would like to understand whether or not that would indicate to Your Honor that if ever an individual was helping the Improvement Association, selling gas and using gas, and using none of the association gas—" In other words, would the owners of these service stations be considered part of this conspiracy by contracting with the MIA to sell gasoline to drivers?

Judge Carter had boxed himself in. "Indirectly that would

be," he replied. "That would be my ruling if he would do anything that would help the protest."

Hall had his legal teeth into him and wouldn't let go. "It would be the same if he paid for it?"

Judge Carter tried to explain. "If he was helping in the furtherance of it and paying the bills, and he was engaged in picking up people, he would be just as much involved as those who charged their gas and had it paid by the association. One of them said he was given four gallons of gas a day."

"There is no evidence he was working for the Montgomery Improvement Association."

Carter tried to find a reasonable explanation for his decision, explaining, "It depends on the facts. I am taking it from the evidence that is in (the record). You cannot use an isolated case..." Minutes later he ended the morning session for lunch.

When court resumed in the afternoon, Thetford asked Detective Jones about the various drivers he had stopped and questioned. There was no question about the legality of these stops, as every Black citizen knew—in many cases, from their own experience—the law could be sufficiently bent to cover the actions white officials were taking against Black people. The boycott was illegal under the 1921 statute; therefore, police officers had a right to investigate. Detective Jones, for example, stopped Burl Mack Everhart as he exited the parking lot being used as a pickup point. "Did he have a load? Did he, or did he not, have passengers?"

"He had four colored females and one colored male."

"Did you ask him if he knew any of them?"

"He said he knew two of them." Thetford led him through a series of encounters with different drivers. "He knew two" of them. "He didn't know any of them."

"He knew two."

"I paid for my own gas."

"Fletcher Smith, who owns and operates the College Hill Service Station, was furnishing the gasoline."

Detective Jones testified he saw Mr. S. P. McBride coming out of the parking lot three times on February 4, although he stopped him only once. McBride did not know any of his passengers—but "He told me he was buying his own gas."

The seventh most popular TV show the week of the trial was *Dragnet*, which had been in the top ten almost every week since its debut in 1951. It starred Jack Webb, who introduced himself at the beginning of every episode, "My name is Friday. I'm a cop." Sergeant Joe Friday was a no-nonsense LA police officer. *Dragnet* was television's first popular police procedural, presented as a semidocumentary, with many episodes based loosely on actual crimes. Webb's Friday was a by-the-book cop who demanded of the people he questioned, "All we want are the facts, ma'am." Police officers around the country patterned themselves after the stern, direct, dispassionate no-frills character created by the former marine Webb. That was the image they wanted to project: cool and controlled. Jones might have been one of them, sitting tall in the witness stand, looking directly at Thetford and responding with crisp, curt answers. Just the facts.

Thetford's questions and the detective's answers were repeated with the grace and regularity of a jackhammer: "Where did you stop him?"

"Coming out of the parking lot at Monroe and McDonough."

"Did he have any passengers in his car?"

"Yes, sir, he had two (or three or four) colored passengers in his car."

"Did you ask him whether he knew any of them?"

"He knew two (or none or three) of them."

"Did you have any conversations with him as to how long he had been hauling in this car pool?"

"Yes, sir. Since December (or when he could, or he didn't remember exactly when, or two or three every day since weeks ago)."

His investigation was not without challenges. At 5:30 a.m. one morning, Jones told the solicitor, he and his partner had arrived at the Holt Street Baptist Church, and "When we first got there, there were two Negro women there, and they were standing next to the church sign out in front, and then they left there and went in a house across the street...a few more came up, and they went into the house and we never did see anybody pull up in an automobile, and we left." They then drove to a dispatch area at Mobile Road and Oak Street, "and there was a pretty good crowd of people standing in front of the church, and automobiles were pulling up, picking up, loading up passengers and going on." He spoke with several of those drivers, he said.

Thetford asked, "Now, did anyone, or any of them you talked to, ever tell you they were paying, they were being paid by the passengers?" No, they had not. "Did you ask any of them?"

"Yes. I asked all of them." They all denied they were charging passengers or being paid.

Several questions later Thetford completed his direct examination. Then Arthur Shores began his own no-frills cross-examination. "I believe you testified you are a City Detective of the City of Montgomery, Alabama?"

"That is right." He had been on the police force about seven and a half years, he said. He had been a detective about three and a half years. "Do you have a regular assigned job?"

"No."

Short and direct, establishing his own staccato. "What are your working hours?"

"My schedule doesn't call for certain hours. Whenever needed. We work all hours."

"You work all hours?"

"That is right."

"Did you have any special jobs during January and February of this year?"

"No." He had begun investigating "this protest or boycott" on January 11 and sometimes worked "from six in the morning until sometimes as late as one o'clock the next morning."

Shores's voice never wavered; he spoke in natural tones that never got louder or softer with inflection or implied disbelief. Just the other facts. "Who authorized you to make this investigation?"

"We were assigned to the solicitor's office."

"You were assigned to the solicitor's office?" That's interesting. "Did you work for the state or the City of Montgomery?"

"I am paid by the City of Montgomery."

"You are paid by the City of Montgomery… Then you worked for the City of Montgomery, is that right?"

"This is right."

"Were you assigned by your superior officer of the city to work under the solicitor's office?"

"That is right."

"Who is your immediate superior officer?"

"Lieutenant Lacey."

"Lieutenant Lacey?"

"That is right."

"When did he assign you to work under the Solicitor's direction?"

"January the 10th. He didn't assign me."

'Did the Commissioner authorize this?'"

"I don't know."

After several more establishing questions, without determining exactly who had assigned Detective Jones to the solicitor's office, Shores began questioning him about his investigation. On the twenty-third, he wondered, "Do you recall, what time would you say you first noticed a car coming out of the parking lot?"

"Around four o'clock in the afternoon…"

"Is that a public parking lot?"

"As far as I know it is, yes."

"And numerous cars park there during the day, or during the time you made your investigation you found several cars?" He had. "Did you stop every car coming out of this parking lot?"

"No."

The thrust of Shores's questions was becoming clear. "How did you determine which car to stop?"

"The cars that were loaded inside the parking lot…"

"Weren't all cars loaded inside the parking lot?"

On *Dragnet*, Sergeant Friday was almost never corrected on the witness stand. "That is right."

Shores reinforced his point. "I didn't quite understand you. You say you stopped only cars loading inside the parking lot?"

"Loaded by the dispatcher, whoever he was." They had spoken to the dispatcher, Jones said, Mose Whaley Richburge, who told them he was loading the vehicles. "We asked him what his duties were and he told us helping load the cars."

"It wasn't any different from other parking lots to have attendants there to assist individuals in parking and coming out of the parking lot?"

"That is right."

"Do you know whether or not this man was one of the assistant attendants there?"

"I presume that it was."

"You presume that he was one of the assistants working there to park and assist cars in coming out?"

"That is right."

"What did Mr. Thetford tell you to do when you were assigned to his office by your superior to work under his direction?"

"He told us he wanted an investigation of the boycott made."

"Wanted you to investigate what now?"

"The boycott."

"Investigate the boycott?"

"That is right." He had been told to "check automobiles which were hauling." Among the other assignments he was given, Detective Jones testified, was "checking the banks."

Shores responded with just enough surprise to infer this was important news. "Checking the what?"

"Checking the banks... Get all the checks in the bank account of the Montgomery Improvement Association and photostat them."

"Were you authorized by the Montgomery Improvement Association to investigate its account or have its account opened up to you?"

"We were authorized by the solicitor," the detective replied, just a bit more defensively.

Shores sometimes would pause before asking his next question, as if considering the previous response. "You were authorized by the solicitor?... Did you get a court order?"

"We got a solicitor's subpoena."

"You got a solicitor's subpoena... On whom did you serve that subpoena?"

"Mr. Flowers at the Alabama National Bank."

"Now," Lawyer Shores asked, as he began tying together the bits of Detective Jones's testimony, "what kind of order, if any, did you have to stop and investigate cars as they came out of the parking lot?"

"We had orders to check particular licenses, see whose automobiles they were, and what the drivers' names and addresses were."

"And you were employed by the City of Montgomery?"

"That is right."

"Had those persons violated, or committed any crime, violated any city ordinance or State law in your presence?" It became obvious where Shores was heading.

"By that you mean drunk?"

"Drunk or any other violation."

"Not unless it would be in violation of public law."

"Did you arrest anybody?"

"No."

"During all your investigations," he wondered, emphasizing the "all," "you didn't arrest anyone?"

"No."

"*All* the persons you stopped and questioned?"

"No, sir. Didn't arrest the drivers of the automobiles."

"Not any in the automobiles?"

Detective Jones's cool was wavering slightly. "Not any in the automobiles?" he repeated.

"Yes."

"No."

The police officers did make one arrest, Jones recalled. Richburge, the dispatcher.

"What offense did you charge him with?"

"Vagrancy."

With a hint of disbelief, Shores asked, "You all charged him with vagrancy?"

"That is right."

"Was he convicted?"

"No."

"He wasn't convicted?"

"That is right." They made one other arrest. "We arrested one for being drunk."

"Was he driving his car in connection with the boycott?"

"Not that I know of."

Shores then reached his point. "Were all of the persons whom you stopped and questioned colored or Negroes in connection with this boycott, as you call it?"

"Yes."

"Did you stop any white persons in connection with the boycott?"

"No."

"Nor arrested any white person in connection with the boycott?"

"No."

"You found no violation of the law in connection with the boycott?"

"No traffic..."

Thetford finally objected on the grounds Shores was asking the witness to make a conclusion. Judge Carter let Shores conclude his cross-examination. "Did you arrest them?"

"No." Shores let that hang in the air, then said he was done.

Shores had made some headway in showing that the police had targeted, even harassed, Montgomery Black residents, including some not even involved in the boycott. But as a legal matter, if there was a boycott and Dr. King had led it, the defense would need to show "just cause or legal excuse" to justify it. That could be accomplished less with the police officers enforcing the law and more with the largely autonomous bus drivers actually administering segregation on a daily basis.

The prosecution was preparing to put them front and center.

CHAPTER SEVEN

On the night of December 5, 1955, the newly elected president of the Montgomery Improvement Association, Dr. Martin Luther King, made the biggest speech of his career. Speaking without notes to the estimated five thousand people gathered in and around the Holt Street church—most of whom were rooted in the tradition of rousing speakers from the pulpit—he brought them a new message, a new and daring strategy to fight for their rights: their weapon would be love.

"We are here, we are here this evening because we're tired now. And I want to say we are not here advocating violence. We have never done that... My friends, don't let anybody make us feel that we are to be compared in our actions with the Ku Klux Klan or with the White Citizens Council. There will be no crosses burned at any bus stops in Montgomery. There will be no white persons pulled out of their homes and taken out to some distant road and murdered. There will be nobody among us who will stand up and defy the Constitution of this nation..."

Dr. Martin Luther King Jr., here addressing the mass rally at the Holt Street church, neither created nor organized the bus protest. But as the Montgomery Improvement Association (MIA)'s compromise choice to act as its spokesperson, he first received national publicity. And when the city put him on trial, he emerged as the leader of the embryonic civil rights movement.

Throughout his speech, it was reported, King's emphasis was on peaceful action, orderly protest and Christian unity, and he urged those gathered there not to be frightened "off your right to protest," and to continue "to work and fight until justice runs down like water."

According to *Advertiser* columnist Joe Azbell, "The meeting was much like an old-fashioned revival with loud applause added. It proved beyond any doubt that there was a discipline among Negroes that many whites had doubted. It was almost a military discipline combined with emotion."

Martin Luther King had learned nonviolent passive resistance by reading about Gandhi, who had successfully used that tactic to lead India to its freedom. It was in Gandhi's "emphasis

on love and nonviolence that I discovered the method for social reform that I had been seeking... I came to feel this was the
only morally and practically sound method open to oppressed
people in their struggle for freedom." Many argued that turning the other cheek resulted in getting hit in both cheeks. The
MIA had only reluctantly adopted it.

An essential aspect of the prosecution's case was that King's
doctrine of love had not worked, that at least some Black people were staying off the buses not just by choice, but because
they had been intimidated by both threats and actual violence
from the MIA and the Black community. In addition to being
an important part of Thetford's legal strategy, it also was an attack on Dr. King's credibility and the entire concept of passive
resistance. So the solicitor sought to publicly discredit the perception that this was a nonviolent movement, that in fact the
boycotters had resorted to force. As part of this campaign, police
commissioner Sellers had told reporters that many Blacks "had
been threatened with physical violence" from "goon squads."

Now Thetford would try to prove it in the courtroom. He
began that effort by calling several bus drivers. Mr. George Henderson was first. Like every one of the bus drivers the company
employed since 1938, Henderson was white. He told Thetford
that he had been driving for the Montgomery City Lines for
thirteen years. On the morning of December 6, he said, he was
driving back to the garage after his last trip. The bus was empty
as it drove through "a ninety-eight percent colored" neighborhood.

"Now," Thetford asked, "did anything unusual happen to
you at this time?"

"Very unusual, yes, sir."

"What happened to you?"

"I was shot at six times. Yes, sir."

"Shot at six times?" So much for passive resistance.

"Yes, sir." Two of those shots hit his bus "two or three feet behind me… One came through the window above my head and the other through the top of the bus." The shots missed his head, he continued, by "a couple of feet."

"Could you tell how far away these shots came from; did you see the flash?"

"Yes, I did," he said firmly. "I could see this house they came from which was close to the street. I would say twenty-five to fifty feet… It was a large caliber, thirty-eight to forty-five, I would say." It most likely was a pistol, he added, "because a shotgun mostly don't shoot six times."

"Did you stop your bus?"

"No, sir, I didn't. I didn't see anybody and I didn't have any protection at all." He reported it to both the police department and his employer.

In his booming voice, Peter Hall loudly demanded that this testimony be excluded, as "It isn't connected up with this defendant or with any alleged conspiracy… This witness hasn't testified who shot at him, whether white, brown, or who, and has no place in this record…and if not connected up with this defendant it is incompetent." Incompetent, in this usage, meaning it is irrelevant or immaterial, that it has no bearing on this case.

"Overruled." And so they would have to address it on cross-examination. Once again, Arthur Shores had only a few basic questions, poking holes in the testimony. "Did you see the person who fired the shots?"

"I did not."

Perhaps it had nothing to do with the boycott, he suggested, wondering if Mr. Henderson knew "whether or not it was a person who tried to get a ride…into town; could it have been somebody you passed up who wanted a ride in?"

"I couldn't give any reason for it."

Maybe it was an enemy "taking a shot at you?"

"If I have one, I don't know it."

"Do you know whether white or colored shot at you?"

"I don't."

"Was there anything to indicate that it was white or colored?"

"No, sir, no more than it came out of a house where colored people live… Either out of a house or off the porch."

"Did you see it?"

"Flashes of the gun, yes."

"Was your car moving or standing still?"

"Moving."

"Did you look back to the house from which you say the shots were fired?"

"I did not. If I went back down I couldn't tell for sure where it came from."

"Don't know whether he was shooting at you, or shooting at somebody else?"

"I couldn't say."

Shores thanked the witness and Thetford reemphasized the only thing that mattered: someone was shooting at his bus. "Hit your bus twice?"

"Twice. Yes, sir."

Bus driver Henry A. Burke was working the night shift on December 7, 1955, when suddenly, he testified, at about seven o'clock "Someone shot the bus…on Jeff Davis between Holt and Cleveland."

"Is that a predominantly white section or predominantly colored section?" Thetford asked.

"Colored." Also on the bus were his wife and two small children, when he saw "one flash," but heard "three reports. In other words, there were three different shots there and I guess the one I saw was the last one. I wasn't thinking about anything like that, you know, and when this happened I kind of looked towards the sound of it." He did not know where the shots came from. The shot came within two feet of hitting him, he guessed.

"How close did it come to hit your wife?"

"Well, if she had moved over it probably would have hit her because she was sitting on the...right and it came from the left."

Ironically, it turned out, Burke no longer drove for the bus company. In response to the drop in ridership caused by the boycott, several bus routes had been canceled and many people, including him, had been laid off.

The next witness, M. O. Beasley, was a former driver who had also been laid off, but on the afternoon of December 9 he was a passenger taking Sheldon Moseley's bus to Washington Park. "Did anything unusual happen on your ride?" Thetford asked.

"Just got shot is all." He had been sitting on the first side seat, right up in the front of the bus. There were no other passengers. "A colored fellow just got off at the corner of Oak and Jeff Davis," when "just one" shot was fired. "I saw the house," Mr. Beasley said. "As I glanced out I saw the door close, and we pulled on down, I guess, four or five or six houses and stopped. In the meantime all the houses was closed. We called the police and when we got back up there everybody had closed and locked their doors. We decided he had gone to another house. One old colored woman came out and said she heard the shot, and one girl came out and said she didn't hear it."

"Did the bullet hit the bus?"

"Yes, sir."

"How close did it come to you?"

"The paper said it was about five inches... I didn't measure it. It come close enough."

Like the other drivers, Beasley did not see the shooter. The bus was moving slowly, he guessed about fifteen miles an hour. "Now," Thetford asked, "is that a predominantly white or a predominantly colored neighborhood?"

"A colored."

As before, the defense asked to exclude the testimony because it had not been connected to Dr. King.

As before, Judge Carter overruled that objection.

The man who was driving that bus, Sheldon E. Moseley, took the stand and reiterated Beasley's testimony. "The bus was shot at about two-forty (in the afternoon)" in the "colored section." He did not see the gun flash, but "I just figured it come out of one of those houses. I just imagined that." The bullet hit his bus "Just about middle ways of the fourth window, I believe it was. Just behind on his side facing the driver which Mr. Beasley was sitting in."

Once again, the defense motion to exclude this testimony was overruled.

Driver D. S. Johnson's bus was struck "Third glass from the driver's seat." The only people on the bus at that time were Johnson and his son. He had been on his regular route but no longer was driving it because "That route had been discontinued."

And the defense motion to exclude this testimony was overruled.

Bus driver J. B. Gardner had a slightly different experience. On December 6, "I was coming into town...and as I crossed Union something hit the back of the bus on the left side. There was a rock, brick or something. It broke the glass...

"And the next trip...as I crossed Union, coming up and passed the Housing Project...this gun fired twice. Heard the gun fire and hit the glass beyond the door coming back from the front of the bus...and it hit this crosspiece the glass fits in, I reckon about two inches beyond." Fortunately, he said, those shots did not come close to hitting anyone because "mostly they were away from the front of the bus. I didn't have any colored on there."

Same objection.

Overruled.

Thetford was accomplishing his objective, proving that at the beginning of the boycott violent actions had been taken to warn people their lives were at stake if they rode the buses. Former bus driver C. A. Bedsole had quit his job, he said, after a window had been broken by a brick. He saw the people who had thrown it. "I don't know them... There was three young men... They were colored." When he stopped the bus, "They ran... When they throwed the rock I was just passing them, and when they throwed the rock they ran and took off. Two policemen followed them, and they jumped out of their car to catch them, but they didn't."

After Hall's objection was overruled, Shores cross-examined this witness. "Other than being able to identify or to say these men were colored, were there any other ways you knew who these men were?"

"No, sir."

"Could you tell which of the three men threw the brick?"

"No, I couldn't."

"Do you know whether either one of them threw the brick?"

"Well, they were standing on the corner and as I was beginning to turn I just looked into the mirror and noticed them kind of looking mean, and this happened to the back of the bus, that is when I stopped and got out."

"You said they were young boys or men?"

"Yes, sir."

The prosecution put two more bus drivers on the stand, each of them telling their own version of what was essentially the same story. On December 10, A. E. Beasley was a passenger on a bus when "something hit the bus and broke the glass out... cracked it, in the back of the bus." No, sir, he said, he did not see anyone throw anything, but the neighborhood in which it happened was "colored."

Objection.

Overruled.

A curious Shores asked, "All you know is you heard something hitting the bus you were riding in?"

"Couldn't see it," he agreed.

C. N. Courtney had been driving the bus on which Beasley had been riding. When he heard a noise "like something hitting a piece of glass," he stopped his bus and got out. He found a "little broken place in the glass."

Objection.

Finally. "I believe the Court would have to rule that out. I don't think there is enough evidence here to know what happened. Most anything could have happened to it." He looked at Peter Hall. "I am ruling with you."

"Thank you, Judge," Hall replied, and perhaps he meant it.

In addition to presenting evidence the buses had been attacked, the prosecution also intended to prove that some Black people were prevented from riding the buses. On the first day of the boycott, December 5, for example, the *Advertiser* reported in its page 1 story that there had been one arrest. Police officers had jailed nineteen-year-old Fred Daniel for disorderly conduct. The arresting patrolman said, "Daniel had grabbed a Negro woman by the arm about 7:15 a.m. at the intersection of Hall and Thurman and pulled her away from a City Lines bus she was attempting to board."

While the implication was clear, as it turned out later that story was false. The Black newspaper *Alabama Citizen* reported that all charges against Daniel—a student at Alabama State, a member of Reverend Ralph Abernathy's First Baptist Church and a news delivery person for the *Montgomery Advertiser*—had been dropped after the woman he supposedly grabbed testified during his trial that she was not trying to catch the bus. According to the *Citizen*, "Reports had circulated that Negro passengers seeking to ride the bus had been molested, intimidated, threatened and beaten," although apparently Daniel was assisting her in crossing the street.

But the claim that many Blacks honored the boycott out of fear was firmly established. The prosecution began its effort to prove it was true by calling Willie Carter, who worked "Out here at Maxwell Field," he said. Airplanes had been flying out of the historic Maxwell Air Force Base since the Wright brothers opened one of the world's first flying schools there in 1910; it had become a major Army Air Forces pilot training base during World War II, and it remained one of the city's largest employers.

It was just a coincidence that the judge and the witness shared a last name. No one paid it much mind. Carter was a pretty common name in Alabama. But it also was possible the two men shared their roots. There were slave-owning Carters who could trace their heritage in that state back more than a century, and in many cases their slaves had taken the surname of their masters. But if there was any connection no one was aware of it.

What did remain from that time, though, was their place in the community hierarchy. Judge Carter was a sophisticated, educated, well-respected, worldly man; he was welcome anywhere he chose to go, from the country club to the restaurants. Banks sought out his business and he lived in a fine neighborhood. Willie Carter had been brought up subservient; he had learned early on to take his seat at the back of the bus without disturbing the white passengers. He had been roughly educated, and while on paper he had his freedom, there still were limitations on what he might do with it. Banks would not extend credit, and he could live only in certain areas. If he did go to the country club or likely a restaurant, he would have been there to serve the judge and his friends.

The solicitor asked directly, "Have you, or have you not, been threatened about riding the Montgomery City Lines buses?"

He asked, "Do you mean about being assaulted?"

"That is right."

"Well, I have…the date of it I couldn't judge, whether it was or not, but I will say a little better than a month ago. I couldn't tell you right the date or anything because I didn't keep up with it."

"Do you know who threatened you?"

"Henry Dee… He picked me up on May Street. In other words, I was coming to the Field on the bus, see, and some of my friends saw me. One of these guys worked where I was… I was going into the place and one of my friends was in the car with him. I was going to catch the bus. So that man, he said he wanted to see me…"

"What did he tell you?"

"Well, he didn't have very much to say. He said, 'You know, the boys going to whip you about riding the bus.' So I didn't know what to say. So he said, 'If you stay off the bus the boys won't whip you.' And I says, 'I don't think they will whip me.' He said, 'Don't you tell me they won't whip you.'"

The pressure on working men and women like Willie Carter to join the boycott was immense. Not everybody supported it. Many of these people were uneducated; they were mostly blue-collar workers and domestics, going to work every day, trying to make a living. They had learned how to survive as second-class citizens in segregated America. Some good, some bad, but they got along, is how they might have described it. They accepted reality. They had come up in this system and nothing they had ever seen would make them believe things would ever change, even behind all those good words. Not in Montgomery, Alabama. In Montgomery, white folks had all the power and they were not about to give it up. Life was hard enough already; staying off the buses would make it even harder. It wasn't a matter of courage, it was just common sense. The entire community depended on those buses. They flowed through the community as naturally as water in the Alabama River. It was easy for the ministers to make all those promises, but Willie Carter still had to put food on his family's table every night. Staying off the buses put that at risk. Maybe too much risk for people like Willie Carter, who didn't want trouble looking for him; he just wanted to pay his dime and go to his job.

Solicitor Thetford asked his witness to repeat what he had just said. The courtroom was completely silent as he continued. Every person sitting there had been forced to make this same decision. "He said, 'Don't you tell me they won't whip you.' I said, 'Maybe I can beat them to it and they won't whip me.' He said, 'You need your neck broke. I want to get a good look at you anyhow, see what you look like.' I didn't know why he just went ahead and talked like that. And finally he told me, 'You all stay off the bus.'"

"Stay off the bus?"

"Yes, sir."

"Have you stayed off the bus since then?"

"Well, I rid the bus one more time."

Peter Hall objected once again. As compelling as this testimony was, there was no evidence to connect it to the defendant. Judge Carter decided that he needed to know who this Henry Dee was before making a ruling. Thetford asked his witness, "Who is Henry Dee?"

"I don't know him."

"White or colored?"

"He is colored."

"How old a fellow is he?"

"What I mean by that, I just don't know his age."

"How old does he appear to be?"

"Looks like to me, I imagine thirty, something like that."

"Do you know where he works?"

Willie Carter shook his head. "No, sir, I don't know where he works. I do know where he stays."

"Where does he live?"

"I don't know the number. He stays on May Street right next to a little store."

"How long have you known him, to your knowledge?"

"What I mean to say, that morning I rid with him for the first time. I had saw him, not talk to him."

Thetford clarified Carter's response: "You didn't know him before that morning?"

"No, sir."

Judge Carter asked the witness how he "had come to ride with Dee."

"Well, the boys told me. I was telling them I rid the bus. That was the beginning of it. I think they had stopped it out there and I had to get to the job the best way I could. I told them, 'I need that bus.' We was talking about it that morning, see? And that is how he knowed it, sir?"

The judge wondered if this Henry Dee had urged Carter to attend the mass meeting? When Carter said he hadn't said anything like that, the judge told Thetford, "I believe I will exclude it unless he is connected up with it, either going to the meetings or belonging to some organization."

Thetford tried again to find that connection, but failed. The judge decided, "The Court is still of the opinion it isn't connected up." He looked at Willie Carter and told him, "All right. Come down."

The next witness was Ernest Smith, who had to face a different kind of pressure. Smith worked in the courthouse, so he truly was caught between worlds. In fact, in his role as a janitor, he had cleaned the very courtroom in which they were sitting.

And unlike the great majority of Black people in the city, he had not stopped riding the buses. "Still riding?" Thetford asked, perhaps with a friendly smile.

"Yes, sir."

"Ever have any trouble riding the buses?"

He sure had, he replied, right down at the Old Post Office. To his best recollection, "It happened, I guess, about a week after it started."

"What kind of trouble did you have?"

"I went to step up on the bus and a man standing there just pulled me back and told me I wasn't going to get on. I got down and turned around—and knocked him down. I got back on the bus and when it turned the corner he was still laying down there."

"Tried to pull you off the bus?" Thetford asked.

"Yes, sir. Caught hold of this jumper, this jacket."

Thetford held tight to this testimony. "Tell us again what took place."

"I turned around and knocked him down and got back on the bus and the driver went on, leaving him laying there."

"He was still laying there when you left?"

"Yes, sir."

The spectators laughed out loud when the solicitor then asked, "Has anybody bothered you about riding the buses?"

"Not since," Mr. Smith replied.

"Since that ride?"

"Yes, sir. I don't have any car and things like this ain't going to change me."

Peter Hall made his same objection that had caused the testimony of the prior witness to be excluded, that the solicitor had not proved any connection to Dr. King. Judge Carter asked the witness, "You were getting on a bus?"

"Yes, sir. Figuring to get on."

Without any explanation, Judge Carter decided, "I believe I will let this in." When Hall wondered about this, the judge repeated, "He testified as he was getting on the bus this man reached up and caught his coat tail and pulled him back... What did he tell you?"

The witness replied, "You aren't going to ride no bus."

Carter looked directly at Hall. "Overrule your objection."

The courtroom was mostly shaded from the slanting rays of the afternoon sun. It had been built many years earlier, before it might be cooled by overhead fans and then air-conditioning, so it had been situated to keep the hottest part of the day from pouring directly through the windows. As a result, the subtle shift from the warm natural light of the morning to the cold whiteness of the fluorescent lights made the March afternoon feel somber and gloomy as Arthur Shores began his cross-examination.

The large courtroom overflowed with African American spectators every day of the trial. With the exception of journalists from around the world, so few whites attended that they were mostly seated in the jury box.

"You are Ernest Smith?" he began. "You work in the court-house?"

"Yes, sir."

"How long have you worked here?" he asked.

"Over three months at the courthouse." Before that, he continued, he had been doing construction, building houses for Moody and Pickett. A job he had held for several years.

"How did you get this job here?"

"Mr. Shaffer got it, told me to come to the courthouse." The defense was attempting to show this was a witness with an agenda, to keep his job.

The one-punch fight took place, Mr. Smith repeated, "A week after the boycott started."

"Do you know when it started?" Shores asked.

"No," the witness admitted.

"In your best judgment, did it start in 1956, or 1955, 1954 or when?"

"It was last year."

Any competent trial lawyer will try to expose or confuse a hostile witness as a way of mitigating damaging testimony. But doing this to Smith might have been painful for Shores, who was fully aware of the woeful lack of education in many parts of the Black community. There was no joy in embarrassing the man, but his testimony was potentially very harmful to this case. "Was it in the spring of the year, the fall of the year?"

Smith said easily, "Kind of in the spring like." It was clear the witness did not know when the boycott had begun.

"And you started work here soon after the boycott; isn't that what you said?"

"Started working here three months before Christmas."

"Three months before Christmas?"

"As near as I can get at it now."

"The boycott started in the spring?"

"That is right."

"Who did you tell somebody tried to pull you off the bus?"

"My boss man... Mr. Shaffer."

"Mr. Shaffer works in the courthouse?" Shores asked, making the obvious point.

"He is the boss man here. He bosses the men here." Ernest Smith agreed he worked directly under Shaffer. "I fire the gas boiler down at the jail, send the heat over here."

Shores then began carving his story, beginning by asking if Mr. Smith had spoken with Mr. Thetford after being subpoenaed. "Who?" The solicitor. "I sure haven't."

Pointing at Thetford, Shores asked, "You know him, don't you?"

"I know his face, sure, and I know him when I see him, because I ain't been working here that long."

As for the person who pulled him off the bus, "Was it a young man or an old man?"

"Kind of old fellow, stout fellow."

"Kind of old fellow, stout fellow," Shores repeated, then asked, "Was he about as old as you?"

"About my age," Smith agreed.

"How large was he?"

"About as heavy as I am."

"Could you identify him any other way?"

Smith frowned. "I ain't never seen him before. I don't know him."

"Was there anybody else standing around?"

"Nobody but me and him."

"Did anybody else see this when you got on?"

"When I got on, no, not but me and the driver."

As Shores finished, Hall once again made his fruitless objection, pointing out there was no obvious connection between this episode and Dr. King.

Overrruled.

A woman named Beatrice Jackson came next. She had not joined the boycott, and had continued riding the buses. In February, she testified, she had been accosted by a man she recognized, although she did not know his name. She was coming home from work at six o'clock Sunday evening and got off the bus on Fifth Street. And then, she said, "This man came up to me and said, 'I caught you riding and if I catch you again I am going to have to cut your damn throat.' I said, 'No, you won't.' He said, 'If I catch you riding again I am going to cut your damn throat.' I said, 'If you don't let me alone I am going to phone it to the Mayor...' and that is when he hit me."

"How many times did he hit you?"

"A couple of times," she replied, then held up a bandaged finger, "and cut me on that finger."

"What did he cut you with?"

"A knife... I didn't know his name. I cannot recall his right name. They call him Skeet. He had a trial in the Courthouse. They have his name down there."

When she had concluded her direct testimony, Hall moved to exclude her testimony, complaining "these actions...were perpetrated by some person she didn't know, and haven't been connected to the defendant in any way."

Overruled.

Fred Gray greeted the witness politely as he began the cross-examination, then asked, "Are you working at present?"

"Yes, I is. I was working nearly all the time." She had been working for Mr. Z. P. Anderson, in the family's turn-of-the-century house at 1595 Gilmer Avenue, for five years.

He just wanted to clear up a few things. While she had testified she was going home, "On the night of January 26th, didn't you go to your home...?"

"No, I didn't."

Gray then mentioned several names, asking if she knew them. She did not. "The man who followed you off the bus, you say they call him Skeet?"

"That is right." That was the only name by which she knew him.

"Is Skeet married?"

"I haven't heard of him being married. I don't know whether he is married or not."

"Has he ever been to your house?" Lawyer Gray, it appeared, was hinting there was more to this story than had thus far been brought out, asking questions with the confidence of a driver who knew exactly where he was going but did not yet want to share that destination with his passengers.

There was an unspoken expectation for Black attorneys, especially in Southern courtrooms. They did not enjoy the freedom to express emotions common with their white counterparts. They couldn't show anger or mock white witnesses in particular. "Not that I would have," Gray explains. "I was still learning what was expected of me in a courtroom, and the men I was working with in this case were good teachers. Generally, I always tried to establish a rapport with a witness. I wanted to let them know I was not trying to embarrass them; I was just trying to do my job. They had some information that I needed to elicit to help me with my case and help the court reach a just decision. I tried to show respect for a witness, I promised I would be as courteous as possible, and in return, I would ask the witness to be as truthful as possible, and together we could get to the truth.

"In this situation, someone had given us some information about this 'Skeet,' and I was trying to square it with her testimony. That's why I asked if he had ever been to her house."

"No, sir, he ain't...no, sir," she replied to Gray. And while she had never seen him before the night of the twenty-sixth, she had seen him since. "I seen him Saturday evening... On Hall Street. I was coming to town."

"Still don't know his name?"

"No."

"Will you describe him to the court, please. What does he look like?"

"I don't know."

"You said there was a trial. It was the result of this incident that happened to you; is that right?"

"Yes, sir, it was."

"What did you tell the judge at the time?"

"I don't know what I told him, has been so long." Gray's polite implication was becoming clear. Beatrice Jackson had a selective memory.

"It has been so long you don't know?"

"No."

"You don't know what you told the court?"

"I don't know," she insisted.

"What did this man do to you?"

"I told him what he done to me."

"Tell us again."

When she hesitated, Judge Carter said, "Go ahead and tell it."

"I said he told me, 'You think you are so damn smart, if I see you riding on the bus again I am going to cut your damn throat.'"

Gray asked if he had said anything else. "There was nothing else." She did not respond to that threat. She also did not tell her sister, with whom she lived, about this confrontation. In fact, even after the trial, her sister knew nothing about it.

Gray asked a second time, "Has this man ever been in your house?"

"No," she repeated.

Gray asked several more questions that indicated he had far more knowledge of this case: Did this happen near your house? Had she ever worked for Mayor Gayle? Did she have a criminal record?

Finally he began to reveal the source of his knowledge, asking, "Would you know the man you had arrested…if he walked into this courtroom?" When she replied she would, the defense asked for a brief recess, explaining, "I think we can have this man here."

When court resumed several minutes later, Gray admitted the defense had a problem. "Thomas Carter, who we have reason to believe was the person who was involved in this incident, is one of our witnesses and he has been served but we cannot locate him at present." He asked the court to excuse the witness subject to being recalled when they found still another Carter. "That was a discouraging moment," Gray remembers. "The information we had was not what we believed it to be. I did the best thing possible in that circumstance. I got the witness off the stand as quickly as I could."

The witness was excused.

The *Pittsburgh Courier* reported the next day that "throughout their testimony both Mr. Smith and Miss Jackson sneered and snorted at the defense attorneys."

Regardless of their legal significance, these witnesses had shown a fissure, no matter how small, within the Black community about the boycott. After all, these were still Black witnesses testifying for the white prosecutors and generally sticking to their accounts, despite tough and effective questions from Black defense attorneys trying to save a Black minister from a possible jail sentence.

This was, however, still testimony about the protest more broadly rather than the specific role of the defendant, "Mr. Martin L. King." That was about to change.

CHAPTER EIGHT

Joe Azbell, the white city editor and columnist for the *Montgomery Advertiser*, was the next witness called by the solicitor. Azbell might well have been the most influential journalist in the city. As an editor and reporter who covered stories and conducted interviews as well as writing a regular column, Joe Azbell straddled the fence between fact and opinion. The twenty-seven-year-old Azbell was well respected and trusted by both Black and white communities. In fact, two years before the trial he had been awarded an honorary degree by the all-Black Selma University for his work in helping Black children get the polio vaccine, and when Dr. King's home was bombed, he was the first to show up at the scene. Yet he would eventually write speeches for segregationist governor and presidential candidate George Wallace. Azbell also could relate to certain struggles of the Black community; as a teenager he had run away from his rural Texas home and hitchhiked across the country, surviving by doing menial labor, from picking cotton to selling newspapers. E. D. Nixon trusted Azbell enough to secretly hand him the copy of the mimeographed leaflet that the *Advertiser* ran on its front page, successfully informing the entire community about the boycott.

The media had played a vital role in the protest. The leading Black journalists in the country, led by the *Minneapolis Tribune*'s Carl T. Rowan, covered the protest and trial extensively. "It was not at all uncommon for Black leaders to try to establish good relationships with the media," Fred Gray points out. "During the bus protest I did the same thing with a young broadcaster named Frank McGee, then the news director of WSFA-TV, the local NBC affiliate. He called me one day and introduced himself, and told me he was sympathetic to what was going on, and that he was in a position where we could be of help to each other. We developed a mutual trust, we spoke reasonably often; he called or came to the office with questions, knowing that I would give an honest answer and if we had something we wanted made public I might contact him. He was very helpful to us in making this local protest a national story, and in turn the work he did in Montgomery led eventually to him becoming a network correspondent and host of the *Today Show*."

Azbell walked to the front of the courtroom, raised his right hand and swore to tell the truth. The fact that a journalist could be compelled to testify was the result of more than two centuries of precedent, although certain questions remained since a journalist's refusal to disclose certain information, including about sources, was among the murkiest of legal privileges.

The youngish-looking journalist wore thick dark glasses, his somewhat curly hair cut in the popular flattop fashion. Assistant solicitor Robert Stewart began by establishing the fact that Joe Azbell had been the paper's city editor for five years and had been covering the bus boycott since its inception. On December 5, Azbell told the court, "I went to the area that you all call Washington Park, and Capitol Heights and Abraham's Vineyard and came down to the White Dog area and went through Peacock Park to Court Square." He had visited those places, he explained, "Because they were predominantly Negroes" and he wanted "to determine the effect of the protest."

"Tell us what you observed in those places you went to."

He described the December morning that some people later would call the beginning of the civil rights movement. "Early in the morning, it was early dawn, but wasn't quite dawn, we went to Court Square first. Standing on the First National Bank corner there was a cluster of Negro men. I came up to the bus shed, parked my car and the first bus rode in. A lone Negro man passed by the bus as I got on and stood in front of it—he went on past it—and a white man came and got on the bus. A young Negro girl about nineteen years was standing there waiting for another bus. And she was the only Negro at the bus shed.

"On the corner of the Exchange Hotel, the First National Bank and Klein's corner, and National Shirt Shops, other Negroes in clusters were standing there apparently watching. There was an automobile there at the bus shed point. This automobile was driven by a white man at that time, and he picked up three Negroes and took them somewhere—I don't know where...

"And as the bright day began they came in rapidly. I stayed there about twenty, thirty minutes—and Negroes were all around the corners and cars were coming along and picking them up as if there was a migration of Negro people. They were hanging around on every corner, came up one by one, two by two, some came from that direction and some were going in another direction.

"The buses were empty except for a few white passengers... When we went to Washington Park we found most of those Negroes early that morning were walking and singing to themselves, 'We are not riding the buses,' and making a lot of hell. And we passed several pickup trucks with Negroes in the back singing 'We are not riding the buses.' On two or three

DON CRAVENS/GETTY IMAGES

As in many Southern cities, the Black community was heavily dependent on public tran-sit, and as a result, those bus companies relied on Black riders to survive. The possibil-ity that more than forty thousand people could go about their daily business without the buses for a year seemed impossible. But with ingenuity, sacrifice and determination, a viable alternative transportation system was created and prospered.

occasions we saw possibly two or three Negroes on the buses after we returned to town, but the majority of the buses were vacant."

In his travels that day, he continued, he saw signs and plac-ards, although, "I cannot recall the exact wording. It was not a legible hand. Something like, 'Don't ride the buses today be-cause of our cause,' 'to break our cause.'" They were not signed by any person or organization.

Stewart then asked him if he had attended the mass meeting the night of the fifth. Yes, he said, he had. Years later he would describe that night as "probably, in my lifetime, the most fired-up, enthusiastic gathering of human beings I had ever seen... I've never heard singing like that... They were on fire for free-dom. They were on fire that at last this was going to be lifted off them and I recognized that. There was a spirit that no one could ever capture again. And then King stood up...but they were peaceful...they were passive, and they called for law and order...

"...and Jesus was there. It was a Jesus meeting."

But he was far more subdued in his testimony. Although there was no assigned section for journalists at that mass meeting, he told the court, he was able to see the platform. "Who presided at the meeting?" Stewart asked.

Azbell reiterated the testimony of previous witnesses. "There was no presiding officer as such. I couldn't determine if this man presided or the other presided."

Obviously, this was not the answer the prosecution wanted; they wanted to put Martin Luther King front and center. So Stewart expanded his question. "Could you tell me who sat on the platform?".

"I knew the people," Azbell responded, "some of the people that sat on the platform, and heard different ones introduced at the meeting, and a lot of people were not introduced. None of their names were called at that meeting, as I recall." Still, no Dr. King.

"Name any of those who were known to you."

"Well, the Reverend Hubbard was there. Almost all the Negro ministers in the city. I wouldn't know all of their names. I know Reverend Abernathy and Reverend Hubbard and Reverend Glasco. There were so many people crowded around I couldn't see who was on the speaker's platform as far as Negro ministers were concerned." Still, no Dr. King.

Stewart tried a different approach. "Who spoke there?"

"Several different people. About twenty different speakers. None of them were introduced by name as such. I believe the Reverend Fields spoke, and Reverend Abernathy spoke, and Dr. King, and many others. The people introduced, Rosa Parks was introduced, Fred Daniels was introduced. It was a rather combined interest of the entire crowd. It wasn't any one particular person, but it appeared to be a group of people taking charge of the ceremonies."

Finally, at least a passing mention of the defendant—he was there—but it quickly was negated by Azbell's claim he was not in charge. The solicitor asked what was discussed at that meeting. "I'm going to say all that I heard that evening," the witness said. "The subject matter as such, it began with the Negroes declared, did they desire to choose to get all of their democratic rights as American citizens, did they desire to choose to get the rights which they had under the democracy, and they had been denied these rights, and they don't retreat one inch in their program to secure those democratic rights.

"Those are the principle subjects of the speeches, the things I remember they said: They discussed the bus protest or boycott... they discussed the cases... They introduced Rosa Parks and explained that she was an outstanding citizen of the community and she had been denied her rights by being arrested, and she had been convicted and she had been fined...

"Then various speeches told how they had been mistreated at one time or another by Montgomery City Lines drivers, and those people had grievances, and that the time had come for those people to do something about the grievances which they have had over a period of years."

In asking his next question, Stewart used a phrase that was just beginning to enter the American lexicon; while few people had heard it used before, within a few years it would become a political flashpoint. "Was there any affirmative action taken at that mass meeting?"

During the John Kennedy administration "affirmative action" would be used to describe the controversial policy of taking firm and directed steps to try to accelerate racial equality. It would be implemented across all sectors, including education, business and the social structure. Firms bidding for government contracts, for example, would have to stipulate they would hire a certain percentage of Black workers. In education it meant changing admission policies to ensure that the student population would become more diversified.

Affirmative action in Stewart's question meant taking specific actions to force change rather than letting events follow their natural course. The phrase itself was relatively new. Ironically, as the city statute used to prosecute the boycotters initially grew out of a labor dispute, this phrase also was meant to be applied to union workers. It appeared for the first time in the National Labor Relations Act of 1935, which established the National Labor Relations Board and for the first time granted protection to workers. It penalized employers proved to be violating its provisions, requiring them "...to take such affirmative action including reinstatement of employees with or without back pay..."

"Yes, sir," Joe Azbell agreed, there had been affirmative action taken at that meeting. A lot of affirmative action. "A resolution was introduced, which was read...which I would call an affirmative action. There were so many affirmative actions—there was a tumult of excitement for everything that was said. They read the Resolution, which said that Montgomery Negroes; let me say it as I recall it."

Stewart handed him a copy of the Resolution, asking if this was the document to which he was referring.

It was. "This Resolution was read over the loudspeaker inside and outside. And it is very difficult to picturize that shouting, clapping type of audience...and then, after the Resolution was read and the shouting died down, there was a speaker, and then there was a preacher that led them in prayer." And finally, "Reverend King came on the platform and he was urged to appear at that time as a speaker. As I recall his words, and I want to be fair, he said no Negro in Montgomery would be intimidated, and no intimidation methods would be used; that every Negro who was there could let his conscience be his guide whether he wanted to ride the buses or not, as I recall it."

Ignoring that, Stewart asked firmly, "Was there, or not, affirmative action taken to continue the boycott, or protest?"

There was.

Arthur Shores began the cross-examination. The relationship between the few Black attorneys in Alabama and the white press was mostly cool. Mostly, Fred Gray recalled, they kept a distance between them. They were used to being misquoted or seeing only portions of their comments in the newspapers. But they viewed Azbell a bit differently and Shores decided to use him to refute the prosecution's earlier witnesses. "During your investigation and your duties as a newspaper editor and reporter, did you at any time see any evidence or hear any comments as to any violence or intimidation in any of the number of meetings you attended?" he asked.

In several meetings or events, Azbell was the only white reporter in attendance. "I have never been intimidated in any of them," he said firmly. "I have been to about six of them. I have been asked one time to leave, but I wasn't intimidated."

Shores clarified that he was asking a general question, rather than about his own experience. "Did any of the speakers or any person there urge any violence or intimidation?"

"This one episode," Azbell continued, "...if I may explain this; if this is what you are talking about. At every particular point I have been in this thing, I was a white man. In many instances the only white man covering the story... The incidence which I refer to is at the time the Reverend King's house was bombed. And at that particular instance there was a crowd of Negroes there and this crowd of Negroes got out of hand, and I was there in that group, and Dr. King came from his house on the porch, he came out to the steps and asked the crowd not to become violent, not to get unruly, don't get out of hand, don't ever use weapons, continue the things we are doing, give up any idea of retaliation or any idea of intimidation. I was never intimidated at any of the meetings I was at."

Henry Parker, the white pastor of the First Baptist Church of Montgomery, as opposed to Ralph Abernathy's First Baptist Church, was called next. Mayor Gayle had appointed Reverend Parker to the committee negotiating with MIA representatives "to bring about a settlement of the boycott and to end it." At that time the committee met, the objectives of the MIA were to force specific changes in the transit system rather than broadly attacking segregation. They still were willing to accept the seats at the back of the bus. The community was just beginning to appreciate the potential of its economic power, while the city still believed it could end the boycott with minor modifications.

"The committee was composed of sixteen people," he told the court; "there were eight white and eight colored." Among the "colored" he continued, "The Negro brethren Luther King was on the committee, Lawyer Gray, D. Caffey, Lawyer Langford..."

D. Caffey, as he was known, just "D," was perhaps Montgomery's most influential Black businessman, particularly because he was respected by both the Black and white communities. Among his several businesses were a restaurant, a service station and the nightclub/banquet hall in which Fred and Bernice Gray were married. It was Caffey who had posted the bonds for many of the eighty-nine people arrested for the protest.

The committee held two long meetings, both of them lasting almost half a day. "Now," Solicitor Thetford asked, "who acted as spokesman for the colored group?"

"King and Gray were the main speakers," Reverend Parker replied. The committee had begun its work by discussing the MIA's three demands. "Number 1 was the matter of courtesy by the drivers of the buses. Number 2 was the matter of seating arrangements on the buses, first come, first served basis. And number 3 was the matter of Negro drivers, operators for the buses...

"Perhaps the first one was the one in which a concession was made. They were perhaps more in agreement on the matter of courtesy; that there had been discourtesy on the part of the

AUTHOR COLLECTION—FRED D. GRAY

As many as two thousand people attended the "Protest Wedding" of Fred and Bernice Hill on June 17, 1956. After Bernice's untimely death in 1997, Gray created the Tuskegee Human and Civil Rights Multicultural Center to honor her as well as the victims of the infamous Tuskegee Syphilis Study, whom he had defended.

operator at times, and certainly improvement was in order there...they were pretty well agreed on that point."

That demand was easily resolved. Seating was more complex. The MIA representatives demanded a "seating arrangement on the basis of first come, first served, with the Negroes going to the back of the bus and the whites beginning in the front of the bus and—" here was the key point "—no one would relinquish a seat under any circumstances."

Placing the blame for the failure of these negotiations where the city felt it belonged, Thetford asked, "In all the discussions with your committee, was there any change ever offered by the colored members of the colored committee in that seating arrangement?"

"Not in the committee meetings, no, sir." There was little discussion of hiring Black drivers, he said, because "This matter of seating, which seemed to be the main thing, and on that we spent most of our time." When it became obvious this committee could not find "a satisfactory settlement of the existing controversy," the meeting broke up and made a final report. "I have never had a request to call the committee together again."

In other words, Thetford repeated, "You have had no further requests on the part of the colored for a meeting and haven't had any further talks about it."

And finally, what was the involvement of the Montgomery Improvement Association in these discussions? "As I recall it, Mr. King and Mr. Gray, the lawyer, made a statement they were members of the Montgomery Improvement Association and, therefore, they were speaking for the colored people of Montgomery, and therefore for that reason they were not in a position really to bargain. The demands were made and they said these were the demands of the people."

"In other words, they took the attitude…the Montgomery Improvement Association represented all the colored people in Montgomery, or substantially all of them, and they represented the Montgomery Improvement Association?"

"That was the impression I got."

After the court adjourned for the day, Gray and Langford returned to their office to prepare for the next day, when the defense would begin presenting its case, as well as continue the necessary work on other cases. Dr. King had said very little during the proceedings. This was the first full trial of his career, and at times he seemed more of an interested observer than a defendant. He asked few questions, offered an occasional suggestion and generally supported the decisions being made by his team.

But outside the courtroom, the *Alabama Tribune* reported, the Black community was following the trial "word for word. They know their leaders…" but especially Dr. King, whose "stature grows bigger and bigger under abuse, and after the bombing of his home, during each hour of his trial (he) has told them to tell the truth, the whole truth and nothing but the truth. He seems eager to get on the stand to set the pattern."

Speaking to reporters, followers and coconspirators outside the courthouse, Reverend King said, "We believe we are right. The truth can't hurt us… We were tired of getting second-class treatment in exchange for first-class fares. We wanted a dime's worth of ride for a dime. We kept begging for it. They kept refusing it."

Weeks earlier, the *New York Times* had published an eight-page special section entitled "Report on the South: The Integration Issue." A survey conducted by the newspaper confirmed "Most white Southerners want to deal with the problems of integration by legal means. They usually disavow violence… Generally, white Southerners seem more troubled, confused and resentful than rebellious. They are troubled by the demand that they make radical change in their settled and preferred social patterns."

While Southern Negroes, according to this survey, "Want the rights vouchsafed to them in the highest court in the land."

Many Southerners also were resentful that civil rights was perceived by smug Northerners to be a regional problem rather than a national issue. The reality was quite different; Black Americans in all areas of the country faced discrimination in almost every part of society every day. To make that point on the second day of the trial, the *Advertiser* printed a letter from a former Alabamian living in Chicago, P. M. Wilson, who referred to the Windy City as "The Negro capital of the U.S." Among the "truths" Wilson had discovered was that "Segregation is practiced right here in Chicago, even more so than in Alabama…

Where I work Negroes are not allowed to use the same washing facilities or locker room. I understand it was tried but did not work out... Any Negro who has white friends lives better down there. If you could see some of the firetraps and holes they live in here you would say so too. Even the worst of the 'cotton cabins' are better by far... Most yankees are perfectly willing to take the Negro's money but will shun him socially...

"I don't know what the answer or solution to the question is—but I hate to see my state the whipping boy for something that goes on all over." The fact that there was discrimination in the North wasn't a secret; but it wasn't practiced as openly or with the same level of legal protection.

When the trial resumed on the third morning, the solicitor called Detective Jack Shows. Shows was an eight-year veteran who had been working with Detective Jones when the boycott began. He had attended a rally at the First Baptist Church the night of January 30. He was standing outside the church and heard the proceedings through speakers. "Did you hear Reverend King speak at that meeting," Thetford asked, "or hear him introduced as a speaker?"

"Someone introduced Reverend King and someone appeared, but I couldn't say who it was made a speech."

When the solicitor asked Detective Shows if he remembered what was said, Peter Hall stood and objected, asking, "You didn't see the person introduced or the person who introduced him or the person who spoke, did you?" He had not.

The prosecution argued that King was introduced and King was known to have spoken that night, therefore the speaker must have been Dr. King. Hall corrected him, "There is evidence some Reverend King spoke at some meetings."

The law does not recognize just logic. Close often doesn't count in courtrooms. During a trial nothing can be inferred; it must be proved. As Judge Carter ruled, perhaps a bit inconsistent with some of his previous decisions, "You have to connect

BETTMANN ARCHIVE/GETTY IMAGES

An entire alternative transportation system, capable of meeting the needs of forty thousand people, was organized and began functioning within days. To circumvent laws against operating a private company, new vehicles were purchased and registered to local churches.

Reverend King as being one of the speakers at the church. You just have someone was introduced and somebody spoke."

Thetford admitted he could not tie them together, and the witness was dismissed. He then recalled James H. Bagley, the manager of the bus line, to determine the success of the still-ongoing boycott. Bagley was a large man who sometimes looked as if he were carrying the entire economic weight of the boycott on his back. When the boycott began in December, Bagley told Thetford in a soft voice belying his size, "we had four routes that a large majority of the passengers were colored."

"Are those routes operating today?"

"No, sir... We took them off on account of the buses being shot into and bricks thrown into the windows to frighten any passengers riding."

The point made, Thetford had no additional questions.

Like so many other people both Black and white, James

Bagley had been caught in the middle of this crisis. Whatever his personal beliefs, he lacked the power to make any meaningful changes—even if he had wanted to do so. But as the public face of the bus company, he received hundreds of letters of both support and criticism from around the nation. Just as the MIA received donations from supporters, many of the letters Bagley received also included money, from a dime bus fare to as much as $40. Typical of the mail he received was a note from someone in North Carolina, who urged him, "Please, please don't let the n——s have their way about riding your cars. If you give into them the whole South will go black. I believe if you hold out, they will all eventually come crawling back to the buses."

Arthur Shores stood tall and began his cross-examination of Bagley with a challenge. "You don't know who threw the bricks?"

"No, sir."

"You don't know whether white or colored threw them, do you?"

"I don't know."

Shores had him on the run. "Don't know who shot into the buses?"

"I don't know."

"As a matter of fact," he said, "the bus was shot into a white neighborhood, was it not?"

Bagley tried to recover. "Right at the edge of where the white and colored live."

In the twenty years Bagley had managed the bus lines, Shores wondered, "Have you had numerous meetings with (Negroes)?"

Bagley was hesitant. "Well, I wouldn't say numerous meetings. For the twenty-year period I think you could call them very few for that length of time." Those meetings covered a variety of purposes, he recalled. "I had meetings where they were asking for some special consideration of the routes, and also to thank me for what I had done to correct what they had previously asked for."

Some people also made complaints, he admitted. There had been meetings in 1954 and 1955 to try to resolve some of those problems. Eventually, though, it came down to seating. Shores presented a rough sketch of a bus, indicating the seats to the witness. It is possible, looking at it, that it reminded some observers of the same type of rough drawing showing the lower deck of a slave ship. "Can you explain the policy of the bus company with respect to seating arrangements in the buses for white and Negro?"

The city ordinance, Chapter 6, Section 10, read: "Every person operating bus lines in the city shall provide equal but separate accommodations for white people and Negroes on his buses, by requiring the employees in charge thereof to assign passenger seats on the vehicles under their charge in such manner as to separate the white people from the Negroes, where there are both white and Negroes on the same car; provided, however, that Negro nurses having in charge white children or sick or infirm white persons, may be assigned seats among white people. Nothing in this section shall be construed as prohibiting the operators of such bus lines from separating the races by means of separate vehicles if they see fit."

Section 11 laid out how the law could be enforced: "Any employee in charge of a bus operated in the city shall have the powers of a police officer of the city while in actual charge of the bus, for the purpose of carrying out the provisions of the preceding section, and it shall be unlawful for any passenger to refuse or fail to take a seat among those assigned to the race to which he belongs, at the request of any such employee in charge, if there is such a seat vacant."

"You see," Bagley said, pointing at the drawing, "the colored people have been required to seat from the rear to the front, reserving—now, this is on predominantly colored lines—that would save ten seats up front, reserving seats for white people. And the same would apply to whites, if they got on this bus in a predominantly white section, they could seat back, and then would require them to save the number of seats for colored people... There would be ten seats saved for colored people."

Bagley made the seating system sound reasonable. And, he continued, in predominantly colored areas, ten seats were reserved for white passengers.

"Now," Shores asked in a quizzical tone, "in the event the bus becomes crowded, as they usually do in the colored area, and those white seats were not taken, were Negro people allowed to use any of those seats?"

Bagley indicated the seats in the middle of the bus. "Well, they would let them use these." He pointed to the seats in the middle. "And when you go on out in the colored section, why then they could sit in this area up here." He indicated the seats near the front of the bus.

Almost as if he was trying to figure out a complicated mathematical formula, Shores wondered, "Was there an agreement or understanding with the City Commission to reserve certain seats for whites for the buses going into some sections irrespective of whether the bus was crowded, or not, that Negroes wouldn't be allowed to use those seats?"

He was beginning to ease into the Rosa Parks situation. But Bagley resisted, claiming, "There was no agreement to that effect because they would go up there if you allowed them to sit down." Certain drivers, in fact, were known to let people sit in empty seats anywhere on the bus—until a white person boarded and needed a seat.

Shores tried to clarify the policy: "For the purpose of the record, do you mean to tell us in the rear of the bus Negroes were allowed to use ten seats?"

"Seats for ten people," Bagley explained, "and we held them front seats for ten people."

Clear enough, and then Shores indicated the larger number of seats in the middle of the bus. "This section in between, how was that utilized?"

"That is utilized first come, first served."

Shores wanted to make sure he understood. "On the routes predominantly colored, whites would—seats for ten persons would be reserved for whites, the seats in front, and in the back the last ten seats reserved for Negroes... The others first come, first served?"

"That is right."

The lawyer paused and considered that. Under further questioning, Bagley acknowledged he had attended two or three meetings at Mayor Gayle's behest to try to work out transportation problems. "At your first meeting with this group of Negroes and whites...was there any suggestion made about seating arrangements?"

"The colored people requested they would seat from rear to front and white people from front to rear on a first come, first served basis."

Bagley had been set up so smoothly he still didn't recognize the trap. "Now, that hadn't been the practice and policy prior to this meeting?"

"No," he admitted, "that wasn't the practice prior to this meeting."

A murmur of recognition rolled through the courtroom. "Then did I understand you to say—again I ask you—in predominantly Negro areas did Negroes ever begin sitting in the rear forward and white from the front backwards on the basis of first come, first served?"

"No."

A confused Judge Carter interrupted. "Let me see if I got that straight. In predominantly white areas the last ten seats were reserved for colored people…and in predominantly Negro sections the front ten seats were reserved for white people; is that right?" That was correct. "And then if the white people didn't need them, or, vice versa, the colored people didn't need them in those particular areas, they could have stayed there when anybody came on; is that right?"

"That is right."

Lost in this perfectly civilized conversation was the reality of segregation. That it remained legal to deprive American citizens of their constitutionally guaranteed equal rights because of the color of their skin. There was no discussion of right or wrong, no attempt to find a larger justice; they were arguing nuances of the existing law.

Arthur Shores had spent his entire career listening in courtrooms as white attorneys defended these laws, and he did so without allowing anger to inflame his words. He went about his business in a matter-of-fact manner, using the laws established by the system to protect the system, to try to change that system.

He had boxed Bagley into an uncomfortable position. "This was the policy of the company you just explained—was that the policy of the company?"

"Well, it was set up by the Commission so to comply with the laws and regulations of the company."

"Which laws and regulations?"

"The State laws and city ordinances… It is the policy of the company to abide by State laws and city ordinances according to our franchise we have to operate the buses." Essentially, he was claiming, the bus company had no options; in order to keep its franchise to run buses in the city, it had to adhere to existing regulations.

"Do Negroes have to get up when they have occupied the seats first; has it been the policy where Negroes were occupying seats, if they had occupied some of these seats in the middle—"

he indicated those seats on the sketch "—or toward the front, and which were not occupied when they boarded the bus?"

Rosa Parks, for instance.

Judge Carter asked Shores to clarify his question using the predominantly white and predominantly colored examples, so Shores slimmed it down to his real question: "Is it the policy in predominantly colored areas where Negroes are seated to require them to get up and give seats to white citizens?"

"No," Bagley replied, once again sending sighs and whispers through the spectator section. "That wouldn't be the policy if they are seated."

"You don't ride the buses yourself—" that was a statement disguised as a question "—and you don't know whether your bus drivers would require that?"

Bagley was intent on protecting the company. "Well, things can happen against the company's policy out there over the ten years that wouldn't meet the approval of the company." He then figuratively threw his bus drivers under their buses: "You will have some men that will violate the rules of the company that wouldn't be the policy of the company."

But hadn't he received complaints from Black passengers about that behavior? "Well, yes," he admitted. "I have had complaints from people, drivers being discourteous toward white and toward colored."

Toward white?

Shores nailed Bagley to history. "Do you know anything about the case of Rosa Parks?"

"I was present when…"

Shores cut him off. "Did the driver make a report?"

He had filed a report, and Bagley had read it. Her arrest had taken place on the Cleveland Avenue line, one of the four predominantly Negro lines. "Did the report of the driver indicate the seat where Mrs. Parks was sitting?" He did not recall the precise seat. "Do you recall whether she was sitting in the first ten seats, or in the middle of the bus, or in the rear of the bus?"

He didn't know, he told the court. "Not right now I don't know."

"Do you know whether she was required to get up?"

"The report stated she was."

Bagley was trying desperately to avoid any involvement in the Rosa Parks case. "Was Rosa Parks arrested for not getting up out of her seat?"

"I was told that she was." But not by him, he had nothing to do with that. "I didn't see it when she was arrested."

The report said the driver had called the police because she would not get up. "To give her seat to a white person?" Shores suggested.

"I didn't say that," Bagley snapped defensively. "He said to move to a section that he instructed her to move to."

Thetford asked only one question in his recross examination. "You testified on cross-examination you had received complaints from both white and colored people in regard to bus service and the actions of bus drivers. During the last five years, what proportion as between white and colored would be white complaints and what proportion would be colored complaints?"

"Well, it would run about fifty-fifty."

Shores began his own recross examination by introducing a new subject. "What is the company's policy on hiring Negro drivers?"

Bagley gave a technically accurate answer. "Well, we have had no policy, no set policy to say all-white should be employed." It was left unsaid that there also was no policy or regulation prohibiting hiring Black drivers—like so many other aspects of life in the city, it was just accepted that this was the way things are done.

Shores then asked the witness if he had the reports on several incidents, including Claudette Colvin. Those reports were in his office, he responded. So the witness was excused to retrieve those reports. "A matter of refreshing his recollection," Shores explained.

The prosecution then called to the stand the mayor of Montgomery, William Gayle. Perhaps the last thing any politician wants to do is sit in a witness chair and answer questions under oath, particularly in a case as politically and emotionally charged as this one. Even a misinterpreted response could be devastating. So this witness, with this much influence, would not have been called without his assent. Mayor Gayle obviously felt he needed to defend his city.

CHAPTER NINE

Mayor William Armistad "Tacky" Gayle was not Montgomery's mayor in any traditional fashion; the city was governed by an elected three-man commission, the so-called "city fathers" who shared powers equally. But because he administered city hall, he was referred to as the mayor.

"Tacky" Gayle, everyone called him Tacky although no one seemed to know why, had graduated from the University of Alabama, won a Bronze Star in the Army Air Forces during World War II and later rose to the rank of Brigadier General in the state's National Guard. He was an upstanding citizen who had first been elected Montgomery's public works commissioner in 1935, a position he held for sixteen years, and in 1951, with the strong support of the limited number of Black voters, he was elected mayor.

He had enjoyed considerable approval in the Black community, which considered him moderate, but generally fair and sympathetic within the bounds of the possible. It was during his administration that the city appointed its first Black police officers, several parks were built in Black neighborhoods and he had encouraged small changes on bus routes. But as the boycott progressed, he instituted increasingly more aggressive actions against protesters and whatever support he'd once enjoyed among Black residents had diminished. By the time the eighty-nine participants in the boycott were arrested, the last remnants of goodwill were completely gone. Fred Gray had reinforced that point when he named Gayle the defendant in his federal lawsuit, *Browder v. Gayle.* "Gayle was no different than so many other white politicians," Gray explains. "He was quite comfortable with the situation the way it was. He did whatever he felt was necessary to maintain segregation in the city, but face-to-face he was always cordial. I'm sure he was well-aware that while there weren't enough Black voters to elect Black leaders, there were enough to make the difference in an election. We had several meetings at city hall during which we had an opportunity to make our point; the people there listened politely to us and then did absolutely nothing about it."

Tacky Gayle's political career was at stake when he took the witness stand. He was riding the racial seesaw; as his popularity in the Black community plummeted, his approval among whites—who strongly favored his resistance to the boycott—went up. His objective on the stand was to solidify that support.

Gayle was a solidly built, heavyset man; his receding hairline, businesslike glasses and dominant nose gave him a vague resemblance to FDR. He was, he told Thetford as his testimony began, "Mayor and President of the Montgomery Board of Commissioners," which gave him the title of "Mayor of the City of Montgomery."

The solicitor began by establishing the relationship between the city and the bus company. Montgomery City Lines had run the bus system under a franchise first granted to that company in 1935. It had been renewed in 1955 for an additional ten years.

Then he asked, "Have you, or have you not, had any conferences or conversations with anyone in connection with this boycott?"

"Yes, sir," he said, his voice filling the room as if to demonstrate he had nothing to hide, "directly and indirectly, the City Commission had over twenty-some odd conferences." The first conference had been held at noon on December 8. "The conference started off by calling it to order, and asked the committee who would be spokesman, and Lawyer Gray said he would start it off and at that time he read the Resolution." This was the Resolution that Gray had written in collaboration with Robinson and Abernathy. Gayle had received an unsigned copy of it in the mail; he did not know who sent it, as "It arrived in a blank envelope."

"I will ask you this. Was the defendant, Reverend King, present when this Resolution was shown?"

"Yes, sir, he was present." No doubt about that. "I asked whom was going to speak for the group and Attorney Gray said he wanted to read this, he had something to say before Reverend King got up, and Reverend King came up and stood at the table by us and presented the three propositions which have been before the Commission ever since..."

"Was, or was not, the sense of the propositions to the City Commissioners or bus company was if these propositions or demands were met the boycott would be over; is that what you are telling us?"

"I don't think he guaranteed the boycott would be over, but that was the things they wanted us to agree on and he would go back and talk to his group... He represented a group. He had been selected by a group to speak for them." He repeated the three demands: courtesy, equity in seating and hiring colored drivers. Although the meeting lasted several hours, "Nothing came out of it."

The next meeting was held on December 17. "Was the defendant present at that meeting?"

"Yes, sir, he was there." No doubt about that. "...the white group from labor, and P.T.A. and furniture stores and merchants association, the Ministerial Association, and we called Reverend King who got his group together and we met there in the morning... After that meeting," he explained, "then the Commission appointed the white group and the colored group... Reverend King objected to both groups, white and colored groups."

"Why did he object to them, what did he say?"

"He said we hadn't checked up on them about the protest, and we hadn't done so. We were going to divide them evenly, and we picked eight white and eight colored so one group couldn't override the other and be one half for both groups." What could possibly be more fair than that, he seemed to be saying. We appointed an equal number of people on either side.

These groups met several times and were unable to make progress. "We got a final report from the white committee but not from the colored committee." The next offer from the MIA had come on January 9. Gayle testified, "The Reverend King said he had a small group of Negroes he would like to meet with the Commission... Lawyer Gray then presented the Resolution...and they had, however, modified in this the seating arrangement..." Again, nothing at all came out of those meetings.

Then Gayle began discussing the controversial meeting with the three Black ministers who were not associated with the MIA and did not represent the boycotters. "On the twenty-first we met with three ministers we were notified wanted to talk to us at the Chamber of Commerce. And we arrived at an agreement there at this meeting, and it was read to these ministers three times..."

This meeting had been a blatant attempt to create confusion in the Black community by announcing that an agreement to end the boycott had been reached with three ministers. The city even had issued a press release carried by the Associated Press claiming that the boycott had ended. The respected Black journalist Carl Rowan had called Dr. King to find out if this was true. King responded that he knew nothing about it, suggesting that the mayor wanted it to appear that there were two factions within the Negro community; "That we're split up, divided, to confuse the people into thinking that the leader did this." The terms of this supposed agreement fulfilled none of the MIA's demands, instead only promising to give serious consideration to the situation.

A day later, on January 22, the AP corrected its initial story, reporting, "Mr. King said tonight that [an agreement with] his group had not been reached. He added that he did not believe the Negroes were ready 'to go back on the buses.'"

To cover the city's tracks, although the mayor did not explain it that way, "it was agreed at this meeting the City Commission would not announce or tell the names of the three colored ministers who met with us, and we felt that it was a suggestion we all agreed upon, and then we did that. We just decided it was best we never mention their names. They asked us not to.

"And then Reverend Benjamin F. Mosely repudiated the statement and said it hadn't been made. But we have never mentioned the other two names and I will not mention the other two names now."

The members of the defense team sat silently, stiffly, displaying no emotion. The rancor within the community about the city's blatant effort to convince these three men to betray the movement had not abated. Gayle's attempt to blame this on those men only intensified the anger. It was obvious to everyone in the courtroom that Shores could barely wait for his opportunity to cross-examine this witness.

"Beginning of January 26th," Gayle continued, "I met with Governor Folsom representing the City Commission, with the full consent of the City Commission." Dr. King was not at that meeting, but "Governor Folsom sent a message to Reverend King...and Reverend King was understood to be in accord with the agreement between Governor Folsom and myself. Colonel Lylery put Reverend King on the telephone and I repeated what we had agreed on, and he said that was agreeable to him." It was Gayle's understanding, he continued, that this proposal would be drawn up and presented to the MIA.

"What happened to that proposal, was that proposal presented?"

"I got a copy of a letter through the mail saying it was turned down." That was the city's last meeting "with the colored groups."

And so the boycott continued.

Whatever was stirring in his heart, Arthur Shores was unfailingly polite in his questions. "How long did you say you have been Mayor of Montgomery?" he began his cross-examination. Getting the mayor of the city on the witness stand, testifying under oath, was a rare opportunity.

Five years, Gayle said, although he had been on the commission since 1935.

During his time as mayor, Shores wondered, "Have you had prior to December of 1955 any delegations to visit you of Negroes to visit you with respect to certain grievances?"

"I think the first one was back in about January of 1954." He wasn't certain.

"Do you recall one in November 1953 by the Negro Women's Political Council?" That was Jo Ann Robinson and her people. Mayor Gayle did not recall that meeting, although he did acknowledge that "Jo Ann Robinson has been there a number of times... I remember the way she acted on some of them all right." However, he did recall a meeting in 1954 during which "They talked about buses passing them up, and stopping every other block and not letting them in the front door."

"Letting them go around to the back door?" Shores asked helpfully.

"That is right. I am not sure whether the seating arrangement came up. I am not sure about that. I am positive about those two."

"That is before Reverend King came to Montgomery?" The meaning was obvious. The movement already was in progress prior to Dr. King's arrival in the city.

"I never saw Reverend King before December 8th," the mayor admitted.

Gayle had some difficulty remembering precisely when specific meetings took place, although he did recall a June 1954 meeting to discuss what Shores referred to as "the bus situation." "Discussion of abuses" is the way Gayle described it. "I don't know whether the seating arrangement was discussed at that time, but the front door again, them coming in the front door again. At each of those meetings the City Commission pointed out the city ordinances and the state laws and they were read at each one of those conferences." The law is the law is the law, he meant, and the city fathers were helpless to do anything about it. This was an excuse that so much of the South stood behind: we have to respect the law. He continued, "At that June 1st meeting I would like to say further that Jo Ann Robinson or some other woman called me several days after that, said they would just show me, they were going in the front door and sitting wherever they pleased."

He recalled another meeting in June 1955. "I was at a conference there. I sent our city lawyer, Mr. Walter Knabe, and Jack Crenshaw (the attorney for City Lines) and I think Lawyer Gray was at that one…and now the seating arrangement seems to be the main trouble."

When the boycott began, Shores pointed out, Mayor Gayle mentioned appointing a committee that included the president of the local CIO (a powerful association of industrial unions) and representatives of the retail merchants, the furniture dealers and ministers. Apparently, Mayor Gayle forgot one additional appointee. Shores asked, "Was there a member of the White Citizens Council?"

White Citizens Councils, organizations described by Dr. King as "a modern Ku Klux Klan," had been formed throughout the South in response to the Supreme Court decision to integrate public schools. Unlike the KKK, it was a public organization, and its membership consisted mostly of middle- and upper-class white people. While some of these local organizations resorted to violence and threats, like the Montgomery chapter, they generally used economic and social means to protect segregation. Mayor Gayle had announced he was joining the Montgomery WCC in January, telling journalist Joe Azbell, "I think every right-thinking white person in Montgomery, Alabama, and the South should do the same. We must make certain that Negroes are not allowed to force their demands on us."

The White Citizens Council was openly leading the fight against integration. At a mass rally held at the Alabama Coliseum on February 10, a rally at which vicious racist handbills had been distributed, a huge crowd of eleven thousand people rewarded Mayor Gayle with a standing ovation as he vowed to continue the fight.

Dr. King had asked President Eisenhower to investigate the WCC after his home was bombed and figures were hung in effigy, but assistant attorney general Warren Olney III, a civil rights advocate, responded, "(W)ith respect to alleged threats and violence directed against Negro citizens of Montgomery, including the bombings of certain homes... The information concerning the alleged violence, the activities of the White Citizens Council and the local officers, does not appear to indicate violations of federal criminal statutes."

But Mayor Gayle wanted the council represented in his meetings with the MIA. They "called upon a fellow named Johnson. He didn't show up so the committee wanted Luther Ingalls to be there and we rounded him up so they could go ahead with their business."

"Was he one of the organizers of the White Citizens Council?"

"I couldn't tell you that." Not, "I don't know."

"He is a member of the White Citizens Council?"

"Yes, I understand he is."

Without a tremble in his voice, Shores asked, "You are a member of the White Citizens Council?"

Gayle answered unapologetically, "I am, yes." He had joined in late January. When challenged, reported the *Pittsburgh Courier*, Gayle appeared "flushed," but then added that it was a perfectly legal organization, and "I wouldn't join anything unlawful."

"Do you know whether the other Commissioners, to your knowledge, are members?"

"Yes, they are members, they said they are."

Shores skipped to several different topics, finally asking, "I believe you said at one of the meetings the colored delegation made certain requests...with respect to better and more courteous treatment on the buses, better accommodations so far as seating arrangements are concerned...and employment of some Negro drivers on predominantly Negro buses? Did you consider those requests?"

The city was helpless to respond, he pleaded. It was the law. "We considered we had nothing to do with the operation or employment of anybody, or the organization or establishment of the Lines and the seating. We considered every one of them, and you couldn't have a seating arrangement that would violate the City Ordinances and also the State act."

"Did you consider the requests excessive?"

Here, again: "Sure. They couldn't be allowed by law. Seating arrangements couldn't be allowed by law." He repeated the general request, first come, first served, Blacks rear to front, whites front to rear.

"Would that violate any law?" Shores asked.

"In my understanding of existing laws, it would, according to the City and State act."

"Do you know the policy of the bus company? Hasn't it been the policy of the bus company to begin seating Negroes from the back?"

"The policy of the bus company should be the same as the law. That is what we expect them to carry out, the law."

The mayor seemed more confident with each answer. If any white citizen of Montgomery thought he was too soft on Montgomery's Black residents, he was refuting that in this testimony. And Shores helped him do so, knowing that every word was going into the record and would be part of the appeal. He asked Gayle if he knew how the policy of the bus company differed in Black and white routes. "Well, it is flexible," Gayle admitted. "Take the Woodley route as an example. On Woodley Road in the morning colored people are riding the buses, probably all of them riding are colored people. When it gets out there to the end of it all the cooks and the rest of them have gotten off, and they come back to the city with white people going to town to work. And in the afternoon it is just the reverse; majority of colored people going in town and white people coming out of town. Under the agreement the colored people were guaranteed to have ten seats in the rear and ten seats for whites in front, and the middle seats were on a first come, first served basis."

"And either party occupy the middle seats first come, first served?"

"That is right."

That sounded familiar. "Wasn't that the request they made?"

"No." Gayle was firm about that. No. "The request they made was first come, first served from the back to the front of the bus, no reservation for white or colored."

Shores tried to clarify that. "Would there be any difference between colored occupying seats in the back and moving to the front and whites occupying seats in front and moving to the back?"

"Yes," the mayor said, "be a whole lot of difference."

Shores again tried to clarify that. "Will you point out that difference?"

"Without ten seats up front reserved for whites they would go in and fill them up; and after they got all of them filled in the rear they could sit in those ten seats. The same proposition as to the colored, ten seats reserved for colored. If the front of the bus was filled up the white people couldn't sit back there. That is their suggestion. This proposal we made, equal facilities for whites and colored, we feel this is a fair proposal."

One more time Shores tried to unravel Gayle's knotted reasoning. "Do you understand the law to mean if buses don't carry ten seats for whites, even though no whites ride, would violate the law?"

Gayle agreed, but pointed out, "The same thing with the colored. If you haven't any colored. It would be a violation of the law as to both white and colored."

Shores snuck in a comment disguised as a question, certainly knowing it would not be allowed. "Would you consider it uncitizen-like conduct for citizens to refuse to patronize a concern like that?"

Objection!

"Does Beatrice Jackson work for you?" Shores moved on. Jackson was the Black woman who testified earlier that she had been prevented from boarding a bus.

Gayle began to show his irritation, snapping, "I have told you fellows twice she don't work for me."

Billingsley leaped to his feet, objecting to the manner in which the mayor had responded. The dismissive tone with which Blacks were used to being addressed by whites theoretically was not permitted in a courtroom. Judge Carter agreed. "Yes," he said. "Let us go ahead."

Technically, the mayor was being truthful. "Do you know Beatrice Jackson?" He did. "Does she work for anyone in your family?"

"Works for my mother-in-law, not me." Gotcha.

"When you announced your own bus policy, was it your opinion that would help solve the bus situation?"

With an edge of defiance sharpening his response, Gayle defended his actions. "I want to tell you that we have done everything in the world to help solve it. Every suggestion we make to your people, your people would refuse. There was nothing else we could do. We have tried to do everything."

And then, for the first, and perhaps only, time, Arthur Shores injected his personal feelings. "Do you feel your joining the White Citizens Council helped solve the bus protest?"

Objection!

With that, Shores was done. The defense recalled James Bagley to conclude his cross-examination. He had brought back with him the report about the Claudette Colvin case. "To refresh your recollection," Shores said. The report had been made by a bus driver named Robert W. Cleere. "Had colored passenger ejected from bus," the report read. "I was outbound to Highland Gardens on Commerce Street; I had white passengers standing; I asked a colored girl to move to the back, she refused to move; I called the police and they came and asked her to move, and she still refused; so they picked her up and carried her from the bus. They put her in a police car and carried her away."

Another similar incident was reported by bus driver J. S. Reynolds, who had ejected "a colored passenger," eighteen-year-old Mary Louise Smith, the previous October. Smith was a maid who earned $2 a day. She had worked for a white woman for a week and was owed $11, which the woman had refused to pay. Smith had taken the bus to that woman's home—and was returning angry and empty-handed when a white woman boarded the bus and told the driver she wanted Smith's seat. Mary Smith was ordered to move. She refused, pointing out she was sitting behind the sign indicating the Black section and telling Reynolds, "I am not going to move anywhere." She was arrested, tried and fined $9—and based on that arrest, she became one of the plaintiffs in *Browder v. Gayle*. "I was inbound to town from Highland Avenue," Reynolds wrote. "I saw a colored woman sitting in the middle of the bus. I asked her to move to the rear of the bus to give some room for white passengers; she refused to move; I called the police and he asked her to move, and she refused to move. He told her if she refused to move that she was under arrest, asked her to come get off the bus or he would use force. She got off and he put her in jail. She was the only colored passenger on the bus."

"Now the report on Mrs. Parks," Shores continued, "what is the date of that?"

"'December the 1st, 1955... J. F. Blake,'" Bagley read, oblivious to the fact that this was the incident that would change the world. "'I was outbound on Cleveland Avenue on Montgomery Street; I was stopped at the Empire Theatre loading passengers; I had asked some colored people to move back so I could make room for some white passengers; three moved back and one refused to move. I asked her to move again and she refused. I told her if she wouldn't move that I would have to call the police; and she told me to call them, that she wasn't going to move. She refused to move for the police, so they took her off.'"

Shores had one final question. "Have you any similar reports where white people were arrested for refusing to move?"

"Yes, sir. I have some reports from white people, that white people had to be removed from the buses, some disorderly conduct, and some for refusing to move up from the section. And it is on the police record where we have done that."

While the reasons at least some white passengers had been arrested were not explained, it appears at least some of them were trying to show solidarity with the Black community by taking seats in the back of the bus and refusing to move out of them when ordered to do so.

In each of these incidents, it was a woman who was arrested. It was ironic that while women in 1950s white America were expected mostly to stay at home and be supportive of their husbands—and had limited legal rights—in the Black community women took the leadership role in the fight. "The first major speech I was invited to give came from the Ten Times One is Ten Club (the first Black women's club in Alabama) to celebrate its 67th anniversary in October 1954," Fred Gray remembers. "I told them at that time they needed to be prepared to file lawsuits to desegregate everything. This was just a month before Rosa Parks was arrested." Among the early leaders of the quest for equal rights were strong women, among them Jo Ann Robinson, Rosa Parks and Johnnie Carr. Johnnie Rebecca Carr, an activist who eventually followed Dr. King as president of the Montgomery Improvement Association, suggested the reason for that. Drawing on the lessons of the past, she once explained, "If black men came out, they would have been crucified. The women had more freedom, so to speak. And maybe the women had a little more courage, too." It also was true that white mobs rarely hung or killed Black women.

With that, Solicitor Thetford announced that the state had finished presenting its case. Fred Gray stood to make a motion that Judge Carter declare a summary judgment, a decision to throw out the case, for Dr. King. To win that motion, the defense had to demonstrate that, even viewing the evidence in the most favorable light to the prosecution, there was no legal pathway for prosecutors to win the case. While no one believed Carter would do so, this motion would serve as the basis for appeal, assuming—as everybody did—that Martin Luther King would be convicted.

Among other claims, Gray contended that the State had not sufficiently proved its case, that there was no evidence of a criminal conspiracy. "That the State has made no showing that the defendant, or any person with whom he is alleged to have worked in concert, performed any illegal activities in support of any unlawful purpose…" Fred Gray had been practicing law for a little longer than one year and at this moment was standing in the public spotlight.

The defense also claimed the protections of "Section 1 of the Fourteenth Amendment to the United States Constitution," giving them the basis for appealing the decision to a federal court, and following a road map created by NAACP lawyers like Marshall and Carter "…in that the statute as applied to this defendant, constitutes a violation of freedom of speech, freedom of assembly, freedom of religion and the right to petition for redress of grievances, and it constitutes a violation of life, liberty and property without due process of law…and denies to him equal protection of the laws."

In his lengthy presentation, according to the *Alabama Journal*, "Defense attorney Fred D. Gray of Montgomery argued that the state had completely failed to prove that King had violated Alabama's anti-boycott law which prohibits a conspiracy or agreement to hinder the operation of a lawful business 'without just cause or legal excuse…'

"The Negro lawyer said that whatever action Negroes took in refusing to ride the segregated buses was taken among themselves and that they made no effort to stop the bus company from operating its business." And, Gray had argued, even if the State had proved there was a conspiracy, Thetford's team had failed to show that the boycotters did not have sufficient reason to boycott the buses after trying for several years—without any success—to modify the harsh treatment Blacks received on public transit.

Gray also attacked the solicitor's case. He dismissed the two Black witnesses who testified they had been threatened for riding the buses, testimony the *Pittsburgh Courier* described as "distasteful," suggesting they might well have believed their jobs were at stake; Ernest Smith was a county employee who actually cleaned the courtroom in which the trial was being held. "It is quite likely he would testify this way," Gray said, and Beatrice Jackson? Beatrice Jackson, who had derisively sneered her way through her testimony? She was employed by Mayor Gayle's relative. No one could possibly be surprised at her attitude or her claims.

Judge Carter listened attentively to Gray's long argument and, seconds after he was done, lightly banged his gavel and denied the motion.

Gray did not respond; he nodded respectfully and sat down. "I was not surprised by that decision," Gray remembers. "None of us were. Most times you make motions like that you can anticipate what the result will be. This witness was employed by the mayor's mother-in-law, so we expected her testimony to be consistent with whatever the mayor wanted her to testify to. If we allowed ourselves to get upset or angry about each small setback, we never would achieve our goal."

Gray also did not have the luxury of time to salve his emotions. In addition to his involvement in this trial, he and Charles Langford were now deeply embroiled in the federal lawsuit that directly attacked Montgomery's segregated transit system in *Browder v. Gayle*.

A favorable ruling in that case could eliminate the need for a boycott at all. According to the *Advertiser*, this suit threatened the entire system; "In the event the U.S. court ruled the city and state laws unconstitutional, it would knock out separate facilities for Negroes and whites at bus and train depots and abolish segregation lines on all buses, streetcars and other vehicles." The hearing in front of the three-judge panel was scheduled for early May and the pretrial work was already in full motion.

As the defense prepared to present its side in the King case, crosses were still smoldering on the University of Alabama campus to protest the admission of a Black student, and Alabama governor Folsom was appealing to the state legislature to convene a constitutional convention to review and determine the state's segregation policies.

The defense intended to put twenty-eight witnesses on the stand—including Dr. Martin Luther King. By the time they had concluded, as one journalist would write, it was enough "to make a white man ashamed of his race."

CHAPTER TEN

"Negro Montgomery," reported the *Alabama Tribune*, "at last got a chance to 'testify' to the wrongs it has suffered—from way, way back." This was to be that first, long-awaited day. And while this was taking place in a compact, aging courtroom in the heart of Dixie, the stories that were heard there might just as easily been told about many cities, both South and North, throughout the country. The defense case would be both a legal and moral one. As a legal matter, the defense would seek to prove that the mistreatment on the buses served as a valid "legal excuse" for a protest. But knowing their legal chances were slim, at the least they intended to publicly expose those indignities once and for all.

The defense had interviewed many dozens of people before settling on its witnesses. They wanted to present a cross section of the community, including men and women, educated and uneducated, young and old, rich and poor, to demonstrate that the only thing that all of these people had in common was the color of their skin. "I interviewed every one of them," Gray remembers. "Usually Shores or Orzell or other members of the team would come down to Montgomery and we would meet with people who had volunteered to testify in my office. We looked for people who had experienced the kind of problems that fit into our strategy and could describe those incidents in detail. There was no shortage of that. These people wanted to help and they did help.

"For some of them, it was not an easy decision. In some instances they had never before stood up to a white person. By testifying, they were bringing attention to themselves, those people who had jobs in the white community were risking them—and some people did lose those jobs because they testified."

Lawyer Langford began the defense case by calling Thelma Williams Glass to the stand. The dignified Professor Glass taught history, geography, English "and common sense," according to her former student at Alabama State University, Fred Gray. She also was a founding member of the Women's Political Council. "Mrs. Glass was my first college teacher," Gray remembers. "Alabama State was on a quarterly basis and I kind of rushed through my high school exams and enrolled there in December of 1947. Mrs. Glass ended up teaching me in English, history and geography, and then became our senior class adviser. Normally I would have examined her, which would have been fitting, but Charles Langford's two sisters were working with Mrs. Glass in the Political Council and they wanted to be sure that Charles played a role in the case, so we decided that he would examine her."

A prim, articulate, "smartly attired" (according to the *Tribune*) woman, Thelma Glass was called first to set the tone for the defense. "And she did," Gray recalls. "I insisted she be our lead witness because she had the ability to set the stage for what we wanted to show," Gray said. "We also felt it was appropriate to begin with a woman, because they had been disproportionally verbally abused by bus drivers, and it was the women in our

community who did so much of the work creating the movement." Glass had lived in Montgomery since 1947, she said, and
had helped create the Women's Political Council two years later.
It was formed "to promote good citizenship," she explained. "In
the first place, the Women's Political Council naturally is concerned with women's activities... We enter into political and
civic problems, particularly those relating to Negroes. In the
second place, we encourage women to become registered voters, to pay poll tax and vote...

"Most activities are proposed and designed to acquaint women
with current problems... Problems relating to the buses have
recently been part of our program."

Asked by Langford what the council had done to accomplish
its goals, she explained, "We have been trying for the past six
years, we have had various committees from the Women's Political Council who have made appeals to the City Commissioners." Her group had met "numerous times" with city and bus
company officials. Since the first meeting in November 1953,
they had focused on six specific problems: "Negroes had to stand
over empty seats when no whites are riding requesting them not
to occupy those seats where they are unoccupied; Negroes pay
fares at the front door, got off and go to the rear door to board
the bus, when fares are paid at the front passengers should get on
at the front. There is danger of a passenger being struck without the driver knowing it and there have been instances where
persons have paid their fares and the bus had driven off and left
them standing. Buses stop in sections occupied by whites at every
corner, but in sections occupied by Negroes they stop at every
other block, since all pay the same fare the buses should stop at
every corner in all communities."

The larger point Glass was making was that the Black community had been trying to reach a compromise with the city,
without any success, for more than two years before the boycott
began. The council turned over to the commission "names and

dates, the names of buses, the bus lines and specific experiences…
from people who complained against the bus company."

Stewart asked only a few questions in his cross-examination,
serving mainly to show the prosecution's lack of preparation.
"Are you a member of the Montgomery Improvement Association?"

"I am not."

"Have you attended any of the mass meetings held by the
Montgomery Improvement Association in connection with this
boycott?"

"I'm sorry," she apologized, perhaps facetiously, "I haven't
been able to get there at the time of any meetings. I work late."

Before releasing the witness, Judge Carter had a few of his
own questions: "Was there anything done about any of the requests you all made, or complaints you made to the Montgomery City Commission?"

"…The only consideration has been given, buses start and
stop at each block rather than every few blocks."

Most importantly, "How about the arrangement on the
buses?"

"Well, that is still going on, unfortunately."

The next witness was Sadie Brooks. It was obvious that the
defense team had decided to put Thelma Glass and Sadie Brooks
out front to show the white world, this is who we are. This is
what you don't know about our community. Sadie Brooks had
quietly been a leader in the fight for equal rights for more than
two decades. Soon after arriving in Montgomery, she had joined
the City Federation, a group of Black women's clubs. "The City
Federation is about fifty-eight years old," she told the court. "It
originated out of the National Association of Colored Women's
Clubs." The NACWC had been founded in 1896 in Washington, DC, by a group of women, among them Harriet Tubman,
to demonstrate to "an ignorant and suspicious world that our
aims and interests are identical with those of all good aspiring

women." Montgomery's Ten Times One is Ten Club had been part of that first union of Black women's clubs.

Sadie Brooks had been a member of the federation for twenty years. During that time, she replied to Langford, she had attended several meetings with the City Commissioners. "Have you been to the City Commission for the purpose of discourtesy?" he asked.

"Yes, I have... The first time, I believe, was when there was a discussion of raising the folks' rates. I believe that was 1952 we went down." At that meeting, she continued, "We made a statement that since Negroes did most of the riding on them they should have a little more consideration...(and) it would be nice for them to just let us ride on a first come, first served basis... And then, of course, we explained about the seating for Negroes and women with babies in their arms and carrying packages had to just stand over seats holding the packages with nobody in them. Of course, all of the members of the Commission smiled and didn't know about these seats. And a lawyer—I believe it was a lawyer—somebody, rose up and explained to us about these ten vacant seats that were reserved for white passengers... or what discussion, if any, concerning courtesy?"

At these meetings, Langford asked, "What did you specifically raise as far as discourteous treatment?"

Sadie Brooks considered that before responding. Her experiences were not unique. For twenty years she had been humiliated and frustrated and had been forced to contain her anger. Now, given the opportunity to tell the world outside Montgomery about it, she chose her words carefully. "There was a lot of discussion, and some of them said people were abused on the buses, and people making complaints buses passed by early in the morning and they had to stand in the cold and wait for the other bus while there were seats in the bus that were unoccupied. And I think some of them said the conductors or motormen took their fare and then started to get in the back door and in some cases they were not interested to know whether they got in, or not. And several instances they didn't allow you to sit across the aisle from another white person, and you had to get up. And I had that happen to me on one occasion; I was asked to get up and move because someone was sitting opposite me."

She began to discuss other indignities. In 1949, for example, she boarded the Cleveland Avenue bus. "On this occasion, when you get on with a dollar some of them will make change for you—but this driver didn't feel like changing the dollar I had in my hand, and just as I was getting off someone handed me the right change. On another occasion a man got on with a dollar, he didn't have change, and the argument persisted until the bus got outside the center of town. And this bus driver then whipped a gun out of his pocket and drove the man off the bus because he didn't have change for a dollar."

The courtroom was silent. It was likely almost every Black man or woman in that room had seen or been involved in some type of similar situation and was reliving it in their mind.

There was no cross-examination. Rufus Lewis was recalled.

Charles Langford asked Lewis if he was a member of the Citizens Coordination Committee, just as he had asked Sadie Brooks about the City Federation. He was, Lewis said, explaining that the organization had been founded three and a half years earlier for the purpose of "Helping the Negro citizenry of the city." And, like Brooks, he had represented that organization in several meetings with the bus company and commissioners long before the Montgomery Improvement Association had been formed, long before Martin Luther King had arrived in the city.

One of those meetings, he remembered, took place to discuss "the Claudette Colvin situation, where she was arrested for not getting up…"

"What was the condition that brought about that arrest?"

Simple. "She was asked to get up out of her seat."

The prosecution objected to that. He wasn't there when Colvin was arrested; therefore, it is hearsay.

Sustained.

He was, however, present at the meeting with the bus company and the commission to discuss it. There, he remembered, "The request was to alleviate or make better plans for Negro passengers to be accommodated on the buses." There were several subsequent meetings, during which they had "the same type of discussion...the same seating conditions, the same overcrowding situation, the same asking of people to get out of their seats."

"When you mentioned asking people to get up out of their seats," Langford asked, "who were they? White people?" Muted, knowing laughter rose from the spectators. One thing for certain: it was not white people.

"I mean asking Negroes to get up."

"To leave their seats?"

"To let white citizens sit down."

Lewis was excused and Judge Carter called for a brief recess. As the reporters at the "Negro press table" waited for the trial to resume, they continued a debate that had been going on for three days. A small watercooler had been placed on the corner of the judge's bench. A container of paper cups was next to it. The reporters had wondered if that cooler was filled with "white" or "colored" water? Were they legally permitted to drink water from that cooler? There was no sign posted to tell them. As the trial proceeded, and the overcrowded courtroom got warmer and warmer into the late morning, the question of the watercooler's designation had loomed larger and larger. One of the reporters finally offered a solution, whispering to Evelyn Cunningham, covering the trial for the *Courier*, "Let's boycott the watercooler!"

Eventually someone suggested they take the question to the NAACP's representative, lawyer Robert Carter. After considering it, Carter walked purposefully over to the watercooler, filled a cup with water, seemingly settling the issue, and turned to walk to his seat. Before he got back to the table, a muscular white bailiff had moved over a few steps and took up a position near the cooler. "Now this is the real test," another reporter said. "Who's gonna go up and get a drink of water?" No one volunteered; the question remained officially unanswered.

When the trial went back into session, Orzell Billingsley asked Mrs. Georgia Theresa Gilmore to take the stand. Mrs. Gilmore, a cook, was a large woman; the *Courier* described her as "a 223-pound mother of six children." To the many who would think of Black Americans in stereotypes, she may have reminded them of the radio and TV character Beulah, a Black housekeeper and cook, played on television from 1950 to 1953 by Ethel Waters, also a large Black woman. In this sitcom, Beulah was "The queen of the kitchen," who dispensed sage advice and solved problems her sweet white employers struggled with. *Beulah* and *Amos 'n' Andy* were the only shows on which Black Americans appeared, and served to reinforce the reassuring white image of the happy Black man and woman.

Georgia Gilmore was no sweet, amiable Beulah. In fact, she was far more representative of the tough, resilient women who were leading the movement. While she was described in newspapers as "spirited" and "plucky," a woman with a "swaggering" personality, the Reverend Thomas Jordan was more direct. "She didn't take any junk from anybody. It didn't matter who you were. Even the white police officers let her be. She wasn't a mean person, but like it was with many black people, there was this perception that she might be dangerous. The word was, 'Don't mess with Georgia Gilmore, she might cut you.' But Lord that woman could cook."

When the boycott began, Gilmore was working as a cook at the National Lunch Company, a downtown Montgomery lunch counter. She organized a group of women to essentially cater and help fund the protest movement, selling meals out of their homes and at protest meetings, with profits going to support the MIA. Because the meals were prepared in several locations, the group became known as the Club from Nowhere. At the regular meetings of the MIA, she would march proudly down the center aisle singing loudly, then depositing hundreds of dollars in small bills and coins in the collection plate. Eventually her kitchen table became a safe meeting place for Dr. King and other leaders, who knew they could talk openly there without fear of the FBI or local law enforcement listening.

Billingsley began by asking her about her background. She had come to Montgomery in 1920, she said in a loud, clear voice, and had been riding the city buses since then. "At that time I did all my riding on the buses, they were my sole transportation because I didn't own any car or motor vehicle whatsoever."

"When did you stop riding the buses?" Billingsley asked.

She answered firmly, "October of 1955." Weeks before the boycott began. "The last of October 1955 was a Friday afternoon. Between the hours of three and five o'clock I was on the corner of Court and Montgomery Street… This particular Oak Park bus came up to the corner. I don't know the driver's name. I would know him if I saw him; he is tall and has red skin, this bus driver is tall, red hair, and has freckles and wears glasses.

"He is a very nasty bus driver.

"This particular time the bus was pretty near full of colored people, only two white people on the bus. I put my money in the cash box and then he told me to get off. He shouted that I had to get on in the back. I told him I was already on the bus and I couldn't see why I had to get off. A lot of colored people were in the middle aisle almost halfway to the front, couldn't he let me stand there… He said, 'I told you to get off and go around and get in the back door.' I have a rather high temper and I figured, I have never been in any trouble whatsoever in my life, I was always taught that two wrongs don't make a right."

Stewart objected, although it was not clear what their objection was. Judge Carter responded, "All right," perhaps meaning Mrs. Gilmore should continue.

"I'm just telling you," she said to the assistant solicitor. "So I got off the front door and went around the side of the bus to get in the back door and when I reached the back door and was about to get on he shut the back door and pulled off, and I didn't even ride the bus after paying my fare. So I decided right then and there I wasn't going to ride buses any more… I don't know anything about the other incidences that have happened, and I was upset within myself, for I was so aggravated with the driver I didn't want to raise any fuss. And so I haven't ridden the buses because I really don't have to ride them. The taxi takes me in the morning…and walk home…"

Billingsley then asked a question he was to repeat throughout the remainder of the trial. It was almost a clarion call to show personal pride. "You are a member of the Negro race, are you?"

"I am," she said firmly. A few whispered "Amens" were heard from the spectators.

"Believe you said the bus driver was nasty to you?"

"Well, I didn't mean going around to the back door. What he said, 'N——r, get out that door and go around to the back door!' I resented his tone because I had already paid my fare. When I paid my fare and they got the money they don't know Negro money from white money. The Negro money and the white money goes in the same box."

This time the "Amens" were louder, and there were many more of them.

Mrs. Gilmore recalled several other "unpleasant experiences… Many times I have been standing without any white people on the bus and have taken seats, and when the driver sees you he says, 'You have to move because those seats aren't for Negroes…'"

"Have you ever heard any Negroes at all call the drivers any names?"

"No, never have."

"Have you heard the drivers call the Negroes any names?"

"I have."

"What are some of the names you've heard?" Billingsley asked.

The courtroom was silent. "'Black bastard,'" she said loudly, "and 'back up n——r, you ain't got no damn business up here, get back where you belong.'"

Hearing that derogatory term, the slur that would in future years become known as "the N word," was neither surprising nor shocking to the people in that courtroom. They knew that word, they understood the meanness, the contempt it expressed. They had heard it their whole lives, they had lived with it, always meant as an insult. The word itself in the English language derived from Latin *niger*, meaning the color black, and originally referred to a dark-skinned person. It appeared in print for the first time in 1574. It took almost two centuries, until the middle of the eighteenth century, for it to become a derogatory word. It was spelled several different ways, but always when used by a white person was intended to be offensive.

But even at the time of the trial, its use in testimony created a dilemma for newspaper editors. How should they publish that testimony? The *Alabama Tribune*, for example, used dots when quoting "Officials were polite. Bus drivers kept on calling Negro women 'n.....s,'" but the *Advertiser* spelled out the entire word. "The witnesses said the drivers had habitually referred to them as 'n——s...and other derogatory wordage.'" The *New York Times* avoided the problem by not including any testimony in its coverage.

And while some Blacks also used it, even then it was controversial within the community. During the trial, Tuscaloosa's *Alabama Citizen* published a one-panel cartoon entitled *Do's And Don'ts*, in which a Black man is telling a younger Black man, "You sure are one lucky N——." Below it was the admonition, "Stop Calling Yourself The Naughty Words, Others Will Too."

When Billingsley asked the witness if she knew other people who had been mistreated, she said she certainly did. "My mother, and she is deceased now.

"She was an old person and it was hard for her to get in and out of the bus except the front door. The bus was crowded that evening with people coming home from work. She went to the front door to get on the bus, and this bus driver was mean and surly, and when she asked him if she could get in the front door, he said she would have to go around and get in the back door, and she said she couldn't get in, the steps were too high. He said she couldn't go in the front door. He said, 'You damn n——s are all alike, you don't want to do what you are told. If I had my way I would kill off every n——r person.' And she always said, 'You cannot ride, you are riding among maniacs,' and she said…"

"We object to what she said," Stewart interrupted.

Sustained.

Perhaps more to herself than the court, Georgia Gilmore said aloud, "Makes me mad to think about it."

"I will ask this question," Billingsley continued. "I believe you said you haven't boarded the buses since October 1955?" That was correct. "As a result of the experiences you had on the buses in 1955 you quit riding the buses?"

"That is right." It had nothing at all to do with the boycott.

But just to reinforce that point, Billingsley asked, "Do you know any Negroes who stopped riding buses prior to December 5th?"

"Quite a few."

Billingsley had no more questions and the prosecution saw no gain in keeping her on the stand. But she was rolling, and seemed reluctant to step down, offering, "Y'all can ask me some more questions if you want to!" Like many of the other people who testified, Gilmore knew she was risking her job when she volunteered to take the stand. In fact, "Tiny," as Dr. King called her, was fired by the National Lunch Company days after testi-fying. Dr. King immediately suggested, "All these years you've worked for somebody else, now it's time you worked for your-self." He gave her money to buy big industrial pots and pans and such, allowing her to open an in-home restaurant that became legendary in the city.

Pullman porter Richard S. Jordan was called next. Fred Gray knew Jordan very well. Among his several jobs while in college, Gray had managed a newspaper circulation office and Rich-ard Jordan Jr. had been one of his carriers. Jordan had been among the eighty-nine men and women arrested and booked for participation in the boycott conspiracy. In his mug shot he is sitting sternly and staring directly into the camera, dressed impeccably in a light suit and tie, his dark hair closely cropped, two pens tucked into his breast pocket. Jordan had been a resi-dent of Montgomery for twenty-six years, he testified, and for much of that time had used the buses—and the streetcars—at least twice a day.

No more. He had stopped riding the previous November, he said.

"You are a member of the Negro race, are you?" This was not a facetious nor flippant comment. The defense team was well aware that any appeal would be based on the trial tran-scripts, and trial transcripts are color-blind. It was necessary to make certain the record accurately identified the race of each witness. The defense was claiming that these people had been discriminated against because they were Black, so they had to get that into the record. This was true in all civil rights cases.

Loudly, clearly, defiantly, Jordan announced, "I am a member of the Negro race, the Montgomery Improvement Association, registered voter and taxpayer and a member of the Dexter Av-enue Baptist Church." And, like seemingly every Black man or woman in Montgomery, he had "many, many unpleasant experiences" riding the buses. The first one, he began, took place in 1937 when...

The solicitor objected to going back that far. When Judge Carter agreed, Orzell Billingsley complained, "Negro seating arrangements have existed since the buses were put on."

Ten years, the judge ruled, no longer than ten years. That was not a problem for Jordan. "Ten years ago my wife was expecting a baby—now ten years old, and we had to ride the buses. Dr. Leslie was her doctor. The driver would yell out at Negroes to get back in the bus, and swear out in public, 'damn, dumb Negro.' And in a few minutes he was going through the same routine again, and race and swear and slam on the brakes...and many, many times my wife would say she was afraid with him..."

Inherent in Jordan's testimony was the reality that there was little a Black man could do to protect his wife from that abuse. Every Black man in the community had experienced that sort of racial emasculation. And so these incidents got stuck in their memory, always raising that same helpless feeling.

That day, Jordan continued, after waiting three hours to see the doctor, they got on the bus to go home. It was slightly after one o'clock "and quite a number of white ladies work at the state capitol crowded on the bus and left two places. My wife wasn't feeling good from the treatment at the doctor's and we just sat there. The bus driver looked back and said, 'N——r, give up that seat back there.' We occupied two seats back from the front of the bus, probably the first seat. About that time my wife said, 'Does he mean I am supposed to move back?'

"She looked at me and I looked out the window. The bus driver said, 'You better give up that seat back there, n——r,' which I resented very much."

"What did you resent," Billingsley asked. "Did you resent the fact he asked you to move, or resent the fact he called you a n——r?"

"I resented both."

His most recent experience had taken place the previous November. He was coming home from working a four-day trip to New York. He was taking the South Jackson bus home "and I was asked by the bus driver to give up my seat, and I looked out the window, so he looked a second time and said, 'I am talking to you back there.' I still looked out the window. Then the bus driver pushed through the crowd of people and said, 'It is time you paid attention to what I said to you.' So I didn't say a word because I heard it wasn't any help calling the bus company, neither going to the City Commission...so I took my bag and what packages I had and got off...and got a taxi to go home..."

He also had seen other passengers verbally abused, often referring to Black passengers as boy, girl or n——r. "Most of them use that word you're talking about?" Billingsley asked.

"If any of them don't, I haven't been able to find out. It is so common." And, he added, that dissatisfaction was not limited to the buses. "All the Negro citizens in the City of Montgomery were constantly talking about the bus condition, barber shops, beauty parlors, grocery stores, street corners, anywhere you see a Negro in Montgomery he is dissatisfied about the condition we put up with."

This time the assistant solicitor had a few questions, trying to attack Jordan's credibility. "You are a member of the defendant's church?"

"Dexter Avenue Baptist Church," he agreed.

"Of which Reverend King is pastor; is that right?"

"I think so."

"You know so."

Jordan smiled as he replied, "I think everybody knows he is pastor of that church."

Judge Carter clearly did not like this seemingly cavalier attitude. He admonished, "Let me put you straight. You are on the witness stand to answer any questions asked you."

"Yes," Jordan agreed, turning his head to look up at the judge,

"I am." In some situations, the judge or attorneys for either side might have asked for an off-the-record bench conference, a private conversation between the participants, to discuss an element in the trial. One reason for doing that is to prevent a jury from hearing the discussion. But as there was no jury—and the fact that the defense wanted every word on the record for their appeal—there were very few such meetings. In this case, Judge Carter obviously thought Jordan was too blatant in his attempt to avoid answering legitimate questions and chastised him directly for it.

Stewart continued, "You are a member of the Montgomery Improvement Association?"

"I am."

"You are one of those under indictment as a result of activities in the bus boycott?"

Jordan described his participation in the boycott differently. "Active in a Christian movement."

"You are one of those under indictment."

He finally admitted, "Yes, I am under indictment."

After the trial, Dr. King would express admiration for the extraordinary dignity with which people, many of them uneducated, told their stories. Among those people, certainly, was Della Perkins, the next witness, who said she had stopped riding the buses on December 3. "I was riding the bus on the way home," she explained. "I went off from work and I got on the bus...went in the front door and I was standing over two seats. The bus driver said, 'Get back, child.' I said to him, 'What did I do?' He said, 'I told you to get back, you talk fresh, you ugly black apes.' That is what he said."

"What happened then?"

"I asked him for my money and I told him I would get off."

"Did he give you your money back?"

"No, sir, he didn't."

"Did you get off the bus?"

"Yes, sir, I did."

She had other stories to tell. "Can you state the time and place?" Billingsley asked.

"Yes, sir, I can state it."

"Can you state the time and place?"

"I remember the approximate month, February, 1952... There were a lot of children on the bus. Me and a little girl were sitting on the same seat on the right side... She asked me to help her pull the cord to get off. The cord was up high for the girl opposite me to pull the cord... When I pulled the cord he said, 'Don't you pull the cord if you don't have to get off.' I said I would pull it when I got to my stop...

"I said, 'Please give me my money and I will get off...' He didn't. When I got up to get off some of the people asked me not to get off."

"These were Negro people you are talking about?"

"No, sir... White people."

"What happened as relates to the white people?" Billingsley asked.

"What happened as relates to the white people?" Della Perkins repeated. Yes. "They asked me not to get off the bus. Then the bus driver told me to get off the bus."

She also remembered hearing bus drivers call passengers n——s, and when asked if she had heard other expressions used, she said, "Yes, sir, heard the expression 'Apes.'"

There was little, if any, response in the courtroom other than reporters jotting down notes, their heads buried in their notebooks so no one could see their expression. There had been innumerable trials highlighting the horrors of racism, but what made this different is that it revealed, in their own words, the struggles of ordinary life for Black Americans.

The prosecution continued its effort to attack the credibility of the defense witnesses. In response to Stewart's question, Perkins admitted she had attended several mass meetings and that she knew Dr. King. Then he asked if she had spoken to anyone in preparation for this testimony. The subtext of that question was clear: Did anyone prepare you or tell you how to answer these questions? "I talked to my lawyer," she admitted. "Lawyer Gray."

"Did you go to him and tell him about the experiences, or did he come to you about them and tell you about them?" Meaning, did Fred Gray prepare this witness by telling her what to say? Della Perkins clearly was not a sophisticated or even worldly person, but rather appeared to be someone who might be manipulated. It was a challenge to the young lawyer's honesty.

"He told me he wanted me to tell the truth," she said.

And how did Gray find out about her experiences? "I went down and told him."

When Gladys Moore sat down in the witness chair, every person in the courtroom took notice. Gladys Moore had long been an outspoken activist in the community, the emphasis on *outspoken*. She said what she felt and said it loudly. She also was known for standing up to bus drivers, even answering them back at times.

Peter Hall took over the questioning. "What is your race, white or colored?"

"Colored," she said.

She had used the city buses for transportation, she told Hall, but no more. That stopped on December 5. When she was riding the buses, she often had found herself standing up when there were vacant seats in the front. "I would say hundreds of times," she guessed, "because I have ridden the buses for ten years." Hall spent considerable time going over the seating arrangements on the buses, how many seats in the back, in the front, in the middle; how they were arranged and who was permitted to sit where when. Then Hall asked, considering all her experiences, "Were you treated courteously...how were you treated generally?"

"No," she said, "not courteously... Just as rough as could be. I mean, not like we are human, but like we was some kind of animal." The drivers weren't all bad, she continued, but "They wasn't good."

"Did they call Negroes names?"

"Well, coming home on the bus...and the driver, I don't know his name now, he said, 'Don't you upset me with that racket.' I stood still. There wasn't any disorder in the back of the bus whatever. And he said, 'You n——s there'... He stopped the bus and looked back, they was just all regularly talking, and he said, 'You n——s, come on and get your fare and get off.'... Because I wanted to get home I stayed on the bus."

"Will you spell that word he used for me."

She raised her voice and spelled letter by letter starting with N.

That was too much for the solicitor. "We object to this testimony and move to exclude it until we know the time and place."

It took place sometime in 1950, she guessed. But there were other incidents. In 1952 she was on the South Jackson bus going out "and the bus driver closed the door on my foot getting off. And I had on a coat, it was a heavy coat, and landed on the highway; it threwed me clean off the bus when the door caught my foot. He said, 'The next time you catch your foot I ought to drag you all the way up South Jackson Hill.'... I didn't report the injury because I didn't think it would do any good."

She didn't report it, she continued, because a similar thing had happened earlier to her sister-in-law. "When my sister-in-law was leaving the bus...the bus driver closed the door on her. He acted very nasty about it... He said to her, 'I wasn't quick enough closing the door or you would be holding up the daisies.'

"That is what he said to her, and if he had his way only white people would be riding the buses. And two white men on the bus heard it. It would be a good way to get all colored off the buses. And that is the reason she reported it." It did no good, no good at all, which is why she didn't bother reporting her own incident.

Gladys Moore rode the buses just about every day for ten years. During that time, Hall asked, was she ever treated with courtesy? After thinking about that, she replied, "Might be a few times."

Maury Smith cross-examined her, establishing that throughout the boycott she had continued working at the Cloverland Shopping Center, commuting to and from work by taxi in the morning "and catching rides with people picking me up" in the afternoon.

"Have you ever ridden in the car pool of the Montgomery Improvement Association?"

"I sure have!"

Judge Carter interrupted to ask the witness, "Why did you stop riding the buses on December 5th?"

"Why did I stop?"

"Yes."

She understood the real question the judge was asking. "Well, no one told me to stop riding the buses."

"I didn't ask you that."

"I am going to explain it to you. I didn't have anything to do with (the boycott)."

"I didn't ask you that."

"What is it you want me to answer?"

"I asked you why you stopped on December the 5th…"

"I stopped," she said loudly, summing up the entire boycott in so few words, "because we had been treated so bad down through the years that we decided we wouldn't ride the buses no more."

Perhaps the judge believed he had pushed her into the answer he wanted to hear. "Who do you mean by 'we'?"

He was wrong. Gladys Moore literally shouted, "All the fifty thousand Negroes in Montgomery!"

The courtroom roared; the spectators burst into applause and cheers for Moore's answer. Judge Carter angrily banged his gavel, but it took him several minutes to restore order. If that happened again, he warned, he was going to put some people in jail.

The judge resumed his questioning. "When did you all decide?"

"Well," she explained to the judge, "after so many things happened. Wasn't no one man started it. We all started it overnight."

"Where did you all decide it? You said you all decided it?"

"Well, after that accident happened to Mrs. Parks, we all knowed it was unfair, and after they treated her like they did, so we just had an inward feeling, we just quit riding the buses."

The judge persisted. "Where did you all meet to decide that?"

And she resisted. "We didn't meet nowhere to decide that."

"Do you mean to tell the Court there was no meeting in which you decided? When did you decide to quit riding the buses, was it decided on the night of December 5th?"

Moore may have not been studied, but she knew exactly what she didn't want to say. "It wasn't decided that night. It came out in the paper, the bus company announced it in the paper that we stopped riding the buses."

Judge Carter grew increasingly frustrated as she seemed to be avoiding answering his questions directly. "When did you make up your mind?" he finally demanded. "That is what I am asking you. When did you make up your mind not to ride any more, or since December 5th?"

"Because Mrs. Parks was mistreated on this bus, that is why."

"You haven't answered my question." He tried even harder to pin her down. "Why did you decide particularly on December 5th, not December 6th or December 1st, or any other time?"

She repeated, "Mrs. Parks was riding the bus and we didn't think she was treated fairly, that is why. She wasn't justly treated."

"You *still* haven't answered my question. Why you decided on December the 5th? That is what I was asking."

"I think I answered that clear enough."

The judge was not going to give up. In doing so, he seemed to shed the cloak of impartiality he had been attempting to display during the trial. Judge Carter was determined to get not just an answer to his question, but the answer. "What caused you to stop riding; why did you decide not to do so on December 5th, that particular date?"

Mercifully, Orzell Billingsley spoke up. "I think the witness has given an answer... I think her answer relates to the question. I think she said why."

"She has given her reason for it," the judge responded. "The only date I asked her about particularly was December 5th."

"I think she has answered it," Billingsley said.

"I don't think so."

Gladys Moore interrupted to comment, "I think I have answered it in as clear words as I can."

One more time. "I want you to tell me why you picked this particular date, December the 5th. You told me why you quit riding. Why December the 5th?"

It was obvious, finally. "Because that is the day of this Mrs. Parks's trial, and after they mistreated her the way they did and fined her; we didn't think she was guilty of what they accused her of. That is why we quit riding the buses." Then she asked the judge, "Is that clear enough?"

"That is clear enough," he agreed. And with that, the court recessed for lunch.

As the parade of defense witnesses came on and off the stand, one thing was becoming clear: the decision by the state of Alabama to put Reverend Martin Luther King on trial had backfired spectacularly. The protesters' resolve had strengthened, and worldwide attention was now focused on a local bus boycott and the man leading it.

CHAPTER ELEVEN

Reporters from more than sixty news outlets had come to Montgomery to cover the trial, ranging from the *Press Trust of India* to the Communist newspaper *Daily Worker* in New York. "If this movement is successful," editorialized the *Hartford Courant*, "as it appears likely, the Reverend Dr. King will become not only a national hero among his race, but the continuing spearhead in the fight against segregation." When the trial was not in session, the media followed King and Ralph Abernathy and Rosa Parks and filmed, photographed and interviewed the ordinary people who had stood up against institutional oppression, telling their stories and transforming them into heroes.

A reporter driving downtown wrote of picking up an elderly woman walking to her job and asking her why, at her age, she was participating in the protest. "I am not walking for myself," the woman replied, "I am walking for the young people coming on behind me."

Another elderly woman told a different reporter, "My feets is tired, but my soul is at rest."

Magazines printed photographs of boycotters soaking their feet, of pharmacist Richard Harris cradling a phone between his shoulder and ear, arranging transportation while busily fulfilling prescriptions, of shoemaker James Bailey at work repairing a small mountain of worn shoes, and an especially poignant photograph of one-legged Horbbie Ridge making his way down the street on crutches. "So," he told a reporter, "we can be free."

"Richard Harris played an essential role in the protest," Gray remembers. "Whenever there was a bottleneck and somebody needed transportation and nobody else could solve it, Richard Harris would get it done. In fact, he was furious that he was not indicted."

It also was a well-known secret that throughout the city white men and women were finding means to transport their Black maids and cooks; their "help." According to white civil rights activist Virginia Durr, when Mayor Gayle warned residents to stop assisting the boycotters, they had responded, "Tell the Mayor to come and do my work for me, then." Both Black and white people invented excuses to explain why they were riding together. Durr remembers overhearing the Black woman who worked for her mother-in-law telling someone that her family "Don't have anything to do with the boycott at all."

"'You know,'" Durr said to her when they were alone, 'you have been the biggest storyteller in the world. You know everybody in your family is involved in the boycott.'

"'Well,' she replied to Durr, 'when you have your hand in the lion's mouth, the best thing to do is pat it on the head.'"

The success of the protest had inspired Black people in other cities and countries, as far away as South Africa, to organize their own boycotts—and it also had given rise to loosely organized counterboycotts; some Southern whites, for example, were boycotting companies like Ford, Falstaff beer, Coca-Cola, Kraft foods and Philip Morris tobacco because they supposedly had supported organizations fighting for Black equality.

Americans were being forced to deal publicly with the racism that had been ingrained in society. While politicians argued about it in Washington and state capitals, polls showed that a majority of Americans favored a peaceful, legal, although undefined, resolution, and in some areas people were becoming comfortable with a somewhat integrated world. The same issue of the *Advertiser* reporting on the trial, for example, also featured articles on its sports pages about New York Giants outfielder Willie Mays and quoted Milwaukee Braves manager Charlie Grimm predicting his young outfielder Henry Aaron "has a chance of being a great hitter," without mentioning that both players were Black Alabama natives.

When the trial resumed in the afternoon, the defense continued its effort to prove the Black community had sufficient legal reason to boycott the bus system. Its witnesses had each volunteered to testify; in fact, there were far more witnesses than necessary, but the defense team wanted to give people the opportunity to tell their stories to the world, to make certain white America learned about the indignities Black citizens dealt with every day. Leola Bell, for example, remembered coming home from work, tired, and walking "up to the corner...to catch the bus; it was a wide road and I always caught the bus there... and on this day the driver opened the door to let us on and he closed it, and he told us he hadn't been picking us up last year and wasn't going to pick us up there this year, and he went on."

Martha K. Walker testified that she had stopped using the buses the previous November. Just before Thanksgiving, she told the quiet courtroom, "I went out to get the bus on North Ripley Street coming to town; I guess about four buses passed me up with about five or six colored people in the back." With a mixture of sadness and bitterness in her words, she continued, "They had plenty of room up front to have gotten on them and sit back there on all of them. I had my husband with me, of course.

"He is blind and I was taking him to the Veterans Administration this particular day. So it took so long to get a bus, although the bus situation out that way is bad anyway, so I turned around and went back to my apartment and called the manager of the bus company. I got him on the phone and told him we had been passed up by four buses. The fifth bus stopped and we got on and rode to town."

They took seats one row in front of the long bench at the very back. At Decatur Street two white girls got on the bus. At that moment, Mrs. Walker continued, "the front part was filled except two empties. And I was looking up toward the mirror because I was expecting some unruly words. He stopped... I was still in a nervous strain there, and he looked back again, and then he pulled off and stopped...in the middle of the block and said, 'Don't you n——s see that empty seat behind you?'

"I said, 'Yes, I see it.'

"He said, 'Well, get up and get on back there.'

"Well, that just tore up my husband. We got up and got off the bus... We walked from there to the Veterans Administration, with me leading him." Five or six blocks, she added.

That was just the beginning. A year before that, her husband, a soldier who had lost his sight in Germany, was coming home from the Veterans Hospital in Tuskegee...

The solicitor objected to "all the preliminaries," which had nothing to do "with this specific incident." His point was that there is no place for sympathy in the law; he did not want the fact that this Black veteran had been blinded while serving his country to interfere with the application of those laws.

"It was about three-thirty in the afternoon and we pulled the cord. Different times I had to pull it to stop before it stopped... and when I got ready to get off he...slowed down, he didn't stop, he slowed up... What made him stop crossing Dickerson Street...he had to stop for a car and he opened the door; I got out ready for my husband to step down and just as my husband put his left foot down the driver started on out with his right foot still on the bus. And I screamed, and a white lady was in there and she said to wait a moment. Well, finally I jiggled his foot free, he couldn't get loose by himself, and with me helping him he did, and got his foot out. He (the driver) didn't stop and didn't wait to see what happened. He never got out of the bus to see what had happened and if anyone was injured…

"I ran in a store at the corner…and said—I was crying—I said, 'I just had trouble with some bus operator.'" Her husband had been cut on his right ankle. After a few minutes they crossed the street and, "When the bus came back toward town, I knew, I recognized the bus, I waited for him and when he came back I stopped him. I said, 'Look yourself what you just done to my husband.' He said, 'I don't ever remember seeing you n——s on the bus.'"

Hall interrupted, "I believe you said he used the word n——s?"

"Yes."

To emphasize the point, Hall asked her, "Spell that word for us."

"N-★-★-★-★-★-s, n——s."

"…Did you report the accident to the bus company?"

"I certainly did."

"Did you hear from them?"

"They promised me I would, but I never did… Never did."

Hall once again asked Mrs. Walker to talk about her husband's condition, but the court refused to allow her even to answer the simple questions "Is he a veteran?" and "Is he still blind?"

Stella Brooks, the twenty-six-year-old widow of Hilliard Brooks, took the stand. There was not a person in the courtroom who did not know her story, but now she would tell it to the world. "I believe your name is Stella Brooks," Orzell Billingsley began.

"Estella Brooks," she corrected. She was a lifelong resident of Montgomery and "a member of the Negro race." Living in Montgomery, she had in the past often ridden the buses, but "I haven't ridden the buses since they killed my husband in 1950."

"What month?"

"Twelfth of August."

"For what reason did you stop riding the buses?"

She did not hesitate. "Because the bus driver was the cause of my husband's death."

"We object to that," the solicitor interrupted.

Judge Carter was more sympathetic, urging Estella Brooks, "Tell what happened."

"He just got on before the bus driver told him, the bus was crowded, he asked for his dime back and he wouldn't give him his dime back." Stella Brooks's eyes watered as the impact of that memory hit her.

"What happened then?"

Her tears were running down her face as she replied, "The police killed him."

"Did the bus driver call the police?"

"The bus driver called the police and the police came up and shot him."

In a disbelieving manner, Billingsley asked, "And shot him?"

"Yes, sir." She began sobbing.

The solicitor asked one question in his cross-examination. "Were you there when your husband was shot?"

"No."

He turned to Judge Carter. "We move to exclude that part of the evidence."

"Yes," the judge agreed, "if she wasn't there."

Billingsley tried to get that back into the record, asking, "Was your husband shot?"

"Yes, sir."

Judge Carter cautioned him, her testimony would have to be confined to personal knowledge.

Billingsley continued, "But he was killed?"

"August 12, 1950."

"And according to your best knowledge he was killed while he was boarding…"

Thetford stood. "We still object to this testimony." The law was clear. "She couldn't testify to anything that happened if she wasn't there. She doesn't know what happened… The state moves to exclude that part of her testimony connected to the shooting of her husband."

"Yes," the judge agreed, "the Court wouldn't regard that. She wasn't there."

The fact that Stella Brooks's testimony was not permitted into the record did not lessen its impact. The *Times* reported simply, "Stella Brooks testified she had stopped riding the buses in 1950 when her husband had been shot to death, when he refused to obey a driver's order to stay off the bus." No one present in that courtroom could unhear her anguish. She was crying as she left the witness stand, replaced there by Henrietta Brinson. Dressed plainly in a light-colored dress and a white cardigan sweater, she settled into the chair and crossed her arms sternly in front of her and looked up at Billingsley as if to say, go ahead. The last time she rode the buses, she told him, was December the 4th. Before that, "I rode all the time. I used to ride the trolley before the buses, twice a day. I ride in the morning and ride in the afternoon. I got two places to go." Two jobs, is what she meant. And during that time she had several "unpleasant encounters," as the defense described them, beginning in 1953.

"When I would go to get on the Court Street bus you had to push to get on the bus on account of the school children, so many white children going to Lanier school. I wasn't able to get in unless I pushed to get in with the white children; and so I started in with the white children and left my transfer at the door and went on back and stood up in the aisle of the bus. And he (the driver) stood up and said, 'Who gave me this old transfer?' I cannot tell you the awful name he called me. He is the meanest man I ever saw in my life…and why he had such a nasty way with the colored, I just don't know.

"He looked at me and said, 'You gave me that transfer. I saw you give me that transfer.' I said, 'You just laid that transfer up on top of the other transfers…'"

At moments like this, it could easily be forgotten that Dr. Martin Luther King was on trial. Dr. King sat mostly still at the defense table, watching the witnesses, sometimes nodding in agreement with them or silently urging them to go ahead, tell your story. The defense had succeeded in putting the City of Montgomery, the state of Alabama and much of the South, where such stories were simply part of life, on trial.

Henrietta Brinson continued, "He said, 'Who are you talking to?'"

Suddenly she became far more animated. "I said, 'I am talking to you. Every time I catch the South Cloverdale I always have to worry with you about something; I don't see why you always keep on griping about something…'" The women sitting in the spectators' section quietly urged her on. An occasional "Amen" slipped out and danced to the high ceiling. "So he looked at me…and said, 'Who do you think you are talking to? You are just getting off this bus, all you n——s behaving like a parcel of cows.'

"I said, 'Well, that is all right. Just as long as I get to work.' And that is what I did. We have had a lot of trouble with bus drivers because they are all working together and they don't want to treat us the right way."

She described her next "unpleasant encounter," during which the driver screamed at her for opening a window, "'I am talking to you, all you n——s know we got a law in Alabama.'" She then began to let out her emotions, looking at Billingsley and saying, "This is what I would like to know, when they charge us dimes on the buses…"

Stewart stopped her. "We object to any argumental part by the witness."

Brinson didn't care about that at all. She turned to the judge and demanded, "Can I speak?"

"Just a moment," Judge Carter replied, instructing her, "You are supposed to answer any question. Don't give us any discourse." He was almost pleading when he told her, "Just answer the question."

She ignored him. She had been waiting too many years for someone to pay attention to her. For someone to understand, this is wrong. This is indecent. And now that she had that opportunity, she was not about to easily give it up. She continued, "...because we all feel we need the buses."

"Just a moment," the judge warned her, getting testy at being ignored. "We are not going to hear any sermon from you. You are here as a witness. Just answer any question."

"I believe you all feel like we all ought to work together. Don't you want to hear what I have to say?"

Judge Carter replied sternly, "No."

While several people were hiding their smiles, Billingsley tried to calm down the courtroom. "Just answer any question," he instructed her. Then he asked, "You had numerous unpleasant experiences?"

"Correct, I had," she answered his question—but then kept going. "And I am just fed up with these bus drivers, I am just fed up to my neck."

The judge got her attention. "Do you understand you are on the witness stand now and I have told you to answer the questions that are asked of you," and then he threatened, "and I will tell you what I can do if you won't do that."

Billingsley cautioned her again, "Don't volunteer any information, answer the questions I am asking you." Seeing the pent-up emotion and to avoid getting Ms. Brinson into any trouble, he got her off the stand as rapidly as possible.

Frances Rutledge had lived in Montgomery for only three years, but it was sufficient time to have "plenty of trouble" with the drivers. They had refused to let her on their bus, they had lied about their destination and they had insulted her. In 1954 one of them, a "red-headed, freckle-faced, got a big mole on the side of his nose, he told me, 'N——r, all of you are going to have to stand up as long as I am getting a load on going downtown.' I said, 'You got my dime, I don't want to stand up, give me back my dime and I will walk.'" The driver "didn't give me my dime back."

She seemed disappointed when Billingsley thanked her for her appearance, volunteering hopefully, "I can answer some more."

In September 1955, Lula Mae Hopper recalled she was getting on a bus when the driver told her, "You all act like a bunch of cows." In December, "the bus driver looked at me and said, 'I hate n——s.'" She had often had to stand while seats in the front of the bus remained empty.

Leona Perkins, "a member of the Negro race," had been living in Montgomery "ever since I have been old enough to know myself," and on three different occasions had been thrown off buses because she was standing by a seat, apparently too close to the front. "We only had a place in the back of the bus, and when the seats are full back there you got to stand up back there, even if they got empty seats up front. You weren't allowed to sit in them, no, sir."

Irene Dorsey told Peter Hall she initially had stopped using the buses a decade earlier, although "I occasionally went back when I had to ride...when I couldn't get to work no other way, and the time I stopped riding the buses was after they arrested Mrs. Parks. They could have arrested me for the same thing they had arrested her for."

She had stopped riding in 1945, she explained, because "getting off from work, I had a nickel and five pennies and let one penny fall. It was between the driver's wheel and his foot... He said, 'N———r, you don't have but four pennies.'"

Hall asked, "Are you sure he said 'Negro' or 'N———r'?"

She was sure. "He said, 'N———r.'"

"How do you spell it?"

"I don't know how you spell it," she admitted.

"You don't know how you spell it, words like 'n———r'? You don't know how to spell 'Negro'?"

She ignored him. This wasn't about correct spelling. It wasn't about education or knowledge. It was about fundamental human rights and she was not backing down anymore. "He said, 'N———r, you have four pennies.' I said, 'I had five pennies and one of them fell, you stepped on it.' He said, 'You better stoop down and get that penny, or get another and put it in there.'

"I said, 'I will not do it.'" *I will not do it.* Simple words, but a revolution was built upon it. Irene Dorsey had said those words a decade earlier, when the attention of the nation was occupied by the end of World War II. She was alone, as every person at that time who had stood up to racism was alone. But it was a stirring, the first slight breeze of the coming storm. The escaped slave, historian, philosopher Frederick Douglass once said, "A slave is someone who sits down, and waits for someone to free them." People like Irene Dorsey would no longer allow themselves to be abused, to wait for anyone else, and gradually what had been a light shower was becoming a torrent.

"He said," she continued, "'If you don't shove it in there I'm going to put you off the bus...'"

"After that occurrence you quit riding the buses?"

"I did."

The defense was crafting its case for both the verdict and the appeal. Fully aware that a trial transcript does not record anything other than the words that are spoken, and even then those words as they appear on a page carry none of the emotion with which they are spoken, when Janie Pace took the stand, Hall asked her his usual question. "Are you white or colored?"

"I am colored," she said.

In November 1955, she testified, "I was asked to give up my seat, and I was by the door here and walked off the bus."

"You were asked to give up your seat?" Just like Rosa Parks. "You were very near the rear of the bus where you were sitting... Was all the rest of the seats back there...were they all occupied?"

"They were, and people were standing as packed as they could stand."

"...By whom were you asked to get up out of your seat?"

"The driver."

"For what reason?"

"Because white people were getting on the bus."

"And what happened?"

And then she explained why Parks and Colvin and several other women had simply had enough. "I got up and got off and walked home...at least two miles... After that, I didn't give him a chance to say anything else to me, if I couldn't get a seat back there, I stood up."

Pace also testified to an experience no one else mentioned. While riding the Boylston bus, white people were sitting "where we were supposed to sit... Only on one occasion I remember (the driver) asked them to come up front..."

Judge Carter lived in the Boylston area, and he seemed so surprised at this that he wanted to confirm it. He interrupted to ask the witness, "I understood you to say on one occasion he asked white people to move so you could have a seat?"

"Yes, sir. A man was sitting in the seat in front of the rear door, and the bus driver asked him to come up front where they were supposed to sit."

No one had any additional questions.

The next witness, sixty-year-old Arreta Burney, explained she had been riding the buses only occasionally. "It was not so very long ago when I got hung in the door... I got off at the corner of Clay and Dickerson Street, and I had two children, and I put the children off, and when I got off I didn't have my foot all the way out the door and the bus driver shut the door on my foot and, of course, I yelled and he opened the door and let me out."

The children with her were seven and five years old. The bus was not crowded, the driver had a clear line of vision to the door, "so there wasn't any excuse for him not seeing me when I was getting off."

Solicitor Thetford clarified, "You testified on this Maxwell Field bus you got your foot caught in the back door?" making it appear to have been her fault. Actually, she had testified the driver shut the door on her foot.

That did not matter to the judge, who explained, "The Court don't regard that as being discourteous." He offered no further explanation of how the court did regard it.

Thetford continued, "Then you yelled out to open the door and you got off?"

"The passengers in the back of the bus yelled to the driver to open the door, and some lady who was in a hurry or something, and..."

The solicitor verbally waved it away. "Never mind about that."

Hall made certain there was no misunderstanding about what had happened: "On this particular bus the driver did have a mirror in the front of the bus, didn't he?"

He did. "He had a perfect view... He had plenty of time to hold the bus until I got off. He wouldn't wait." Then she made a simple statement that resonated throughout the entire courtroom and beyond, into the community and beyond, throughout the entire country. She wasn't asking for special treatment, she wasn't taking advantage of anyone. "All I wanted," she said, "was time for me to get off."

The parade of witnesses continued with fifty-seven-year-old

Rosa Lee Murray, who had lived in Montgomery her entire life. "You are a Negro?" Hall asked.

"Yes, I am."

She had stopped riding the buses on December 4. Prior to that, she had "a lot" of unpleasant experiences. In January 1955, for example, "I got on the Washington Park bus and when I stepped up in the bus I asked for change for a dollar, and the bus driver looked down at me and he grabbed my dollar and I waited right there on the platform for my change. He didn't tell me he didn't have change for a dollar. I said, 'You never told me you didn't have change for a dollar.' He said, 'No, I didn't.' And I continued to ask him for my change but he wouldn't give it to me. I said, 'You give me my dollar back and I will get off the bus'… He handed me my dollar and I got off."

The prosecution finally had a witness who admitted honoring the boycott. Stewart asked her "Why did you quit" on December 4?

"Well, I quit because I thought if the other Negroes in Montgomery could stop riding the buses, I could too." A textbook definition of participation in a boycott.

"Then you knew all the others were stopping?"

She knew. "They didn't ride the buses on Monday morning, and I didn't ride them either." She knew about the boycott, she explained, because "I seen it in the paper, advertised in the paper, and I said if they don't ride I won't ride either."

"Is that the reason you haven't ridden the buses since then?"

"Yes, sir," she said, but before Stewart could gloat, she added, "Because I was tired of all the unpleasant things being said on the buses."

Stewart then established Rosa Murray had attended several mass meetings and had "possibly contributed if I had any cash."

Stewart asked if she had attended any meetings in which the defendant, Dr. King, "has made the talk?" Perhaps he believed this witness would provide additional evidence Dr. King was the boycott leader. Or perhaps he was mistaking her casual use of the English language with a lack of cleverness.

Whatever he had hoped for with that question, he did not get the answer he wanted. "At so many mass meetings," she replied, "so many people has made speeches."

"Have you heard Dr. King make talks?"

"Yes, sir," she agreed, "he has made talks."

"At how many mass meetings have you heard him talk?"

She wasn't sure about that. "Couldn't have been more than two."

"Or three?"

She corrected him, "I told you two."

"Tell me what he said."

"I couldn't remember all that, what he said."

Judge Carter tried to help her. Or Stewart, advising, "In your best judgment. You cannot remember his exact words."

"Couldn't say what he say."

Stewart asked, "What was he talking about?"

"He said, 'Just let us all sing and pray.'"

"Is that all he said?"

"No, that is not all he said," she said flatly. "I told you I couldn't recall all he said."

Once again, Stewart persevered. "Was he talking about the bus boycott?"

"No, he didn't talk about the bus boycott."

"Didn't talk about the buses at all?"

"No, sir."

"Didn't talk about riding or not riding?"

"No, sir. He said it was everybody's pleasure what they wanted to do."

Stewart thought he had caught the witness. "Then he did talk about the buses?"

"No, he didn't."

"You said he did talk about riding or not riding." After Hall's objection to the question had been overruled, he asked again, "He did talk about the buses."

She shook her head. "He didn't talk about the buses."

Stewart's exasperation was obvious in his question. "He said it was everybody's pleasure whether they rode the buses, or not?"

She agreed. "Everybody's pleasure what they wanted to do. That is what he said."

"Then he did talk about the buses?"

"That is what he said."

"He did say something, didn't he?"

"Yes, sir," she agreed; he definitely had said something.

"Did you hear him talk about transportation? About getting a car pool set up?"

Of course not. "I wasn't interested. I was only interested in singing and praying."

His final question was more a statement of the obvious rather than a serious question. "You stopped riding buses because of the existence of this bus situation, bus boycott or protest?"

She replied with impeccable logic, "If fifty thousand Negroes don't want to ride the buses I don't want to ride them either." Like Gladys Moore had done earlier, she had described the miracle that was taking place every day in Montgomery. There had been several legendary protests in American history, beginning with the Boston Tea Party and including the actions of the women's suffrage movement, but never before had so many people participated in a protest for so long. Even more astonishing was the level of personal commitment; this wasn't simply a matter of attending rallies or a few marches or signing petitions; participation in the boycott required people to risk losing their jobs, it forced them to literally take the hard road in their daily lives. A year earlier the prospect of even a majority of Montgomery's very independent Black community agreeing on just about anything would have been considered implausible, but the fact that the entire community had united behind this protest had become historic.

DON CRAVENS/GETTY IMAGES

Gray used this simple diagram of a Montgomery bus to attack legally segregated seating on public transportation. The Supreme Court decision in Browder v. Gayle *essentially overturned* Plessy v. Ferguson, *which had created the doctrine of "separate but equal," and led to the successful integration of buses and trains throughout America.*

On redirect examination, Peter Hall had the witness point out on the rough diagram that Fred Gray had prepared, the seating arrangement on the city buses. No one disagreed that the seats in the front of the bus were legally designated for white passengers and the seats in the back were for Black riders; so it seemed like the entire question could be boiled down to who gets to sit on the seats in the middle.

Orzell Billingsley asked the next witness, Geneva Johnson, "You are a member of the Negro race, are you?"

To which she replied firmly, "I sure am." She remembered a Black woman carrying several packages getting on the bus and the driver "started the bus off with a jerk before she could even get to her seat...she fell in the aisle. I don't know a thing about her injury." She had stopped riding the buses in 1949, after buying a car.

At different times Odessa Williams had been told to give up her seat to a white person, had watched the bus leave after paying her dime but having not yet reboarded through the back door and been called derogatory names. Billingsley asked her, "Have you ever been present on buses when the driver referred to Negro men and women, have you heard them called Mr. or Mrs.?"

It appeared every spectator knew the answer to that question. "I never heard a bus driver never call no Negro Mr. or Mrs.; I never heard that... I heard 'girl,' 'boy,' and 'n——r.'"

Witness Odelliah Garnier said her first "unpleasant experience" on the city buses had taken place in 1945, while she was in high school. Judge Carter had ruled previously that he would only allow testimony for the last decade. So while she was not permitted to tell that story, the point was made once again that this mistreatment had been consistent and ongoing probably since City Lines got the franchise in 1938. She was allowed to tell the court that she often had been forced to stand squashed in the back of the bus while seats in front were empty. "It seemed like millions of times...well, if I had to give it my best judgment I would say, hundreds of times."

After Bessie Logan had taken the stand simply to say she hadn't been on the buses since 1946, the defense called Raymond A. Parks. "Parks," as he was well-known in the community, was Rosa Parks's husband, a popular barber and a lifelong civil rights activist. He was very light-skinned and might have "passed," the word used to describe someone with skin color light enough to be taken for white, but he had always proudly self-identified as a Black man. He was, Rosa Parks would write, one of the first Black men she knew "who was never actually afraid of white people." At times, he carried a pistol, and "Parks said he always did his best to get along, but whenever white people accosted him, he always wanted to let them know he could take care of business if he had to. They (white people) didn't bother you so much…if you just spoke right up. But as soon as you acted like you were afraid, they'd have fun with you… In other words, Parks believed in being a man and expected to be treated as a man."

While Parks had little formal schooling, he was well-read and self-educated, and both led and supported his wife's activism. He had become active in the civil rights movement as early as 1931 when he raised money to help defend the Scottsboro Boys. The nine Scottsboro Boys were Black teenage hobos who had been riding the rails in the Deep South when they got into a fight with white men. They were arrested and taken to jail in Scottsboro, Alabama. A white woman, who also had been on that train, claimed she had been raped and beaten. She identified six of those young men as her assailants. Police assumed the other three had raped and beaten a second white woman on that train, although she did not identify them. While two doctors testified the women showed no signs of any assault, much less a rape, an all-white jury found the nine defendants guilty; eight of them were sentenced to die in the electric chair.

Rarely had the term "railroaded," an 1873 word meaning "to convict quickly and perhaps unjustly," been more appropriate. Even in a nation used to seeing—and generally accepting—Black men regularly abused by the legal system, this case attracted national attention. With appeals, the case wound its way through the legal system for more than a decade, even going to the Supreme Court, and eventually all the young men were either released or escaped from prison. It was considered one of the most egregious miscarriages of justice in American history and galvanized Black Americans like Raymond Parks to join the civil rights movement—although in Alabama any work done on their behalf would encourage vigilante organizations to threaten their lives. Raymond Parks had been waiting to have his say. When he took the stand, as always, he was fashionably dressed and perfectly coiffed. Billingsley began by establishing, "You are a member of the Negro race, are you not?"

"Yes, sir." Several years earlier, he had been on a bus, and after the last white passenger had gotten off, "I pulled the cord to get off at Cleveland Avenue and he didn't open the door. Somebody else pulled the cord to get off further down the street and he didn't open the door. Two or three of us began pulling the cord trying to get him to let us off…he opened the door for us at Washington Park, and I had to catch another bus and pay another fare. I told the bus driver when I was getting off—I was really warm—'You carried me about ten or twelve blocks from my destination. I know Mr. Bagley really well and… I'm going to report you to him.' He said, 'I don't give a capital D what you tell him.'"

"He said he didn't give a D what you told the manager of the bus company?"

"Mr. Bagley had nothing to do with it…"

Parks also had heard all the name-calling other witnesses had mentioned and had been on another bus when the driver refused to let two Black women board his bus.

Solicitor Thetford cross-examined Raymond Parks. As one of the highest-profile witnesses, if he could get him to admit he was participating in the boycott, that would go a long way both inside and outside the courtroom. He began by confirming that Parks had not told Bagley but instead had reported the incident to a different bus driver. Then he asked an important question to which he already knew the answer. "Is your wife Rosa Parks?"

"Yes, sir." At that moment, Rosa Parks's defiance was making news. Fred Gray had appealed her conviction and was waiting for a Jr. hearing to be scheduled, but there was little reason to expect she would become an iconic, historic figure. Parks testified the last day he had taken a bus was the day of his wife's trial. "I went to Maxwell Field in the morning and came back to her trial…"

Apparently, the prosecution did not know the outcome of her case, asking, "Did the judge announce he was going to hold the case under advisement and would decide it when he got back to his office?"

That was not correct. "Ten dollars and costs, he announced."

"On Monday?"

"Yes, sir, whatever the day of the trial was."

Thetford refused to believe that. "He made no statement that the case was held under advisement?"

"No, sir, he made no statement." Parks hadn't ridden the buses since that day, he explained. "…They took the bus off, couldn't ride one now if I wanted to because they are not out there."

"Did you quit riding the buses," the solicitor asked, "because of the boycott or because they discontinued the bus?"

Parks replied evenly, "I stopped riding the buses because they don't have anything I want, and for that reason I remain off the buses for that same ground. They don't have anything I want."

Thetford pressed for an answer. "Do you mean they don't take you where you want to go, or you don't want the buses?"

"I don't want the buses, period."

As the solicitor complained Parks had not answered his question, Judge Carter asked, "You don't want to ride, period?"

"That is right."

Thetford claimed a minor victory. "You don't want to ride, that is the answer I want." And then he thanked the witness and sat down.

There was no way of knowing how many trials were taking place in how many courtrooms in how many cities and towns and villages throughout America that afternoon. Trials of every type, from property arguments to brutal murder trials, were in progress. Every one of those trials, whether they were criminal or civil, whatever the outcome, would have an impact on the lives of the litigants. But the only trial that would have a profound and lasting influence on the entire country, the *State of Alábama v. Martin Luther King Jr.*, was moving into its final stages.

Several more defense witnesses were scheduled to testify before the climax, when Dr. King would tell his story to an increasingly interested nation.

CHAPTER TWELVE

In 1954, unemployed teacher Inez Baskin had been hired by the *Montgomery Advertiser* to type up items sent to the paper from the Black community for its special "Negro page," making her the first—and for a considerable time, the only—Black female on the staff. Normally her page of news and features from the community replaced the stock market report in papers distributed only in the Black community. "There wasn't very much you could read about blacks at that time, unless they were really famous," she explained years later. "The rest of us only ended up on the front page if we stole a can of sardines and a box of crackers. Then we ended up on the front page."

Within several months she had convinced editors to allow her to actually cover the community and report the news. Her objective was clear, she once explained. "Whites got the bad part, but they didn't know the good things about the blacks." She wanted to change that. Less than two years later she became the "assistant editor" of that Black "section." In fact, she was the first to spread the news that a protest had been approved.

She quickly became the local Black community's voice, helping spread the story to the rest of the country.

In addition to reporting on the boycott and trial for the newspaper, she also became a correspondent for *Jet* magazine and the Associated Negro Press agency. Only months earlier, Chicago-based *Jet* had established itself as the conscience of the Black protest movement by publishing a photograph of Emmett Till's brutalized body in his coffin; it was this photograph, Rosa Parks said later, that made her cry, and it was what she was thinking about when she refused to give up her seat.

Historically, the Black media played a vital role in knitting together Black communities across the country. *Freedom's Journal*, America's first newspaper for Black readers, was published in New York (though by two white editors) in 1827 bearing the motto, "We wish to plead our own cause. Too long have others spoken for us." It eventually reached a weekly circulation of fifty thousand. By the time the Civil War started, there were more than forty newspapers published specifically for Black communities, a number that continued to grow for decades. As Black journalist Vernon Jared explained, in other newspapers "We didn't exist. We were never born, we didn't get married, we didn't die, we didn't fight in any wars... We were truly invisible unless we committed a crime." By the 1950s, when the larger newspapers began reporting events from the Black community, Black newspapers were being published in every major city in the country, and many of them carried Inez Baskin's stories about the protest and trial.

Even after reporters descended on Montgomery, she remained the essential outlet for the movement. E. D. Nixon had introduced her to Fred Gray, who gave her access to strategy planning sessions. In addition to appearing in America's most popular Black magazine, her reporting was published in more than one hundred newspapers, helping transform this local story into national and international news. It was at least partially through her reporting that Black men and women around the country became aware of the boycott and were able to vicariously participate—and, in at least a few cases, initiate their own local protests.

Black leaders in other states and cities tried to connect to Montgomery. As Dr. King's trial continued, the flamboyant Harlem congressman Adam Clayton Powell sent a long telegram to Judge Carter, pleading with him to make the righteous decision. Powell, who had spoken at Alabama State in 1954, at E. D. Nixon's invitation, wrote, "As Pilate's wife warned him concerning the justice of Jesus over 1900 ago, so today...a cross section of the Christian churches and synagogues of each major faith in the United States...also warn you concerning the justice of the twenty-five Negro ministers who await your ruling in their case. As Christians we feel that these ministers are the conscience of these United States...and it would be a shameful blot upon the American way of life should you find it convenient to hand down a condemnatory verdict upon them for exercising their constitutional rights as American citizens...

"We shall pray...that you may not be persuaded by the prejudice of those who would turn back the clock to the days of chattel slavery. We humbly pray that God will direct you toward the rendering of the right decision."

Among the other letters the judge received was a plea from New Yorker Dr. Richard Day, then well on his way to becoming one of the nation's leading pediatricians. "No matter what the history of Negro-white relations have been in the past," he wrote, "and no matter how happily the two races might be able to live under segregated conditions, it cannot be right that one race should give its bus seats to another. The world knows this. The world is watching you... Just now, our reputation in the eyes of the world is seriously worsened because of what is happening in your city, in your own church and in your court. Surely, right will win..."

The boycott and trial were revealing a bitter reality about social justice in America. The Soviet Union, in particular, attempted to use it to attack the United States by highlighting segregation and the oppression of Black citizens. Black Baptist bishop D. Ward Nichols coincidently was making a long-scheduled visit to Moscow while the trial was still in the headlines. Asked several times to describe how Negroes lived in America, he told an audience of more than 2,500 Russians "The United States government is seeking to assure first-class citizenship to all. The Supreme Court, the highest court in our land, has just made it possible for every Negro to attend school anywhere in the United States of America.

"…Negro life in America is like the life of any other people. We have our difficulties and problems…and we are working them out in a spirit of Christian brotherhood. There are some people who are not sympathetic toward us and our problems, but the official American policy is to guarantee equality regardless of race, creed or color."

Fred Gray, like all the leaders of the protest movement, knew he had to be very careful to avoid even the slightest connection to communism. "One way segregationists tried to fight the civil rights movement," he explains, "was to try to associate us with the Communist party. Right away they tried to claim Dr. King sympathized with the Communist party, which was not at all true. America was at war with communism, so the real meaning of that message was that we were not patriotic Americans. In addition to everything else, we all had to be very, very careful to be sure we had no contact or connection in any way with those people."

Yet it was the "official policy," as Reverend Nichols referred to it, and law of one of its cities and states that was the subject of this trial. Witnesses' personal stories were being amplified throughout the world, with the composite of them all creating a vivid portrait of life in a segregated city. Mrs. Inez Ricks, "a member of the Negro race," had lived in Montgomery since 1920, and like witness Georgia Gilmore, when the boycott began she had created a fundraising organization, although her club was on the west side of town. Like Gilmore's Club from Nowhere, volunteers in Ricks's Friendly Club cooked and sold fried fish, cakes and pies to both Black and white customers, with all profits going to the MIA. It was a well-known secret in the city that sympathetic white people could support the boycott by buying food from these groups, rather than risking retribution by making a direct donation.

A few years earlier, Mrs. Ricks remembered, she had handed her transfer to the driver "and started back in the bus and he said to me, 'What are you trying to do, trying to ride my bus free? I am on to you.' I said, 'You have my transfer right there.' He said, 'You never had no transfer.' I said, 'Yes I did and I handed it to you.' With that he drove off as fast as he could go right through town, jerked the bus this way and twisted it that way and did the best he could to throw me down..."

On another occasion "I put my packages in a seat and still couldn't sit down in the seat."

Orzell Billingsley asked, "Did you try to sit down in the seat?"

She had, and "The bus driver told me, 'You cannot sit there.'"

"Was it an empty seat?"

"Yes, it was an empty seat, with my packages on it.... (The bus driver) didn't object to the packages."

Mary Harris had stopped using City Lines buses in 1954, when the driver simply refused to stop for her to get off. "He paid no bit of attention," she said. "Kept going...he never did stop till about ten blocks later...and I got off at Jackson and High, and I waited there with two or three others who had to get off, and when he come back I started to get on and I had my right foot up and my left foot down and the door shut, and I was skinned up, the skin was off my right leg from the door, and I had an erysipelas condition (an infection), where my hip was cracked."

Mary Harris gave several examples of the mistreatment she had suffered, but also pointed out, "Then another thing. I would be telling other people things that happened to me and they would say they happened to them."

When asked if she had heard drivers use derogatory language, she said, "I have heard all of them call you ugly names… 'N——r,' and 'Old N——r,' 'Old damn N——r, shut up, quit your talking'… And they tell you, you cannot get in the front door, and tell you to go to the rear, and when you go up to the rear door and the rear door is closed, and sometimes they open it and sometimes they don't, and they leave you standing there and drive off… They treated us like dogs."

That ended the testimony for the third day of the trial, but the ugliness of what had been heard in the courtroom throughout the past days was not easily forgotten. As *Boston Globe* reporter Charles Whipple wrote, "Today was one to make a white man who heard it all a little ashamed of his race, or a part of that race.

"The tales went on and on—of aged Negro women ejected from filled buses when whites entered, having to walk miles to their homes, of drivers purposefully closing to catch Negro coattails… Many a white observer was asking on what meat did these, our bus driving Caesars, feed…"

The initial goal of the boycott, that Blacks would be treated decently and with respect on the buses, that the seating arrangements would be modified and the company consider hiring Black drivers, had long been dismissed. Instead, during his regular Sunday sermon, Dr. King told his congregation at the Dexter Avenue church, it had become "A great moral and religious crusade against racial discrimination."

As the British government had learned to its dismay in India less than a decade earlier, and Americans were now seeing for themselves, there was no effective weapon against passive resistance when it was employed by large numbers of people. The great British Empire had been helpless against Mahatma Gandhi and his followers. Montgomery's city government had tried all the strategies that previously had been used successfully to coerce the city's Black residents into obeying the laws of segregation, and the result was a stronger, more cohesive, more committed movement.

Any chance for a compromise agreement had disappeared weeks or even months earlier, Reverend Ralph Abernathy told a large crowd of eight thousand people in Los Angeles, who had been aroused by the trial and contributed thousands of dollars to the boycott. "They can run the buses as long as they want to, but they won't run with Negroes on them until they give us justice... We are tired of being dragged from buses and thrown in jail... The Southern way of life is crumbling. The Southern white man is sick. And we are going to receive our rights or die fighting for them.

"Before we will be slaves, we will be buried in our graves." But in addition to winning the economic fight, the brutal testimony in this trial was enabling the MIA to win the battle for public opinion. Journalists like Whipple were spreading the message that no longer could be ignored. These incidents weren't anomalies, they weren't isolated events or the actions of a few bigots, this was a way of life for countless thousands of people who had been silently suffering and forced to accept this treatment.

The trial resumed on the fourth morning with a sense of expectation; at some point during the day, Martin Luther King was going to take the stand. The defense team had not prepared him for this testimony, Fred Gray recalls. That just wasn't necessary. Dr. King's great strength was as a speaker; the plan was to let him speak. The defense team knew its job was simply to put him in the best possible position to tell his story.

Oddly, while the trial had gone very well for the defense—the solicitor thus far had great difficulty even proving that King was leading this law-breaking conspiracy and Thetford and Stewart had been unable to show that the defendant was making strategic decisions or giving directions to boycotters—they had little confidence that they would actually win. Gray had worn his lucky red, white and blue tie to court that morning, but he was under no illusions. Judge Carter was a highly respected citizen of Montgomery and would have to live there after rendering his verdict. The pressure on him to defend the system was enormous.

The morning was overcast; occasional showers were predicted, with the temperature climbing to a comfortable sixty-five. The first witness called was Miss Willie Elmore, who said she had ridden the buses "quite often" since arriving in Montgomery in 1939. She recited the now-common experiences. "I have been asked to move to the rear, there wasn't any seats…" After two blocks the driver yelled, "N——s, get back in the rear…" As usual, she was dismissed without any cross-examination.

William Jones worked at Maxwell Field. "I goes on out… and gets off at the rear of the bus, and he gives me time to get one foot out of the bus and pulled off and throwed me almost down. If I hadn't been supple I would have fell and got hurt… I was trying to not be late getting to work. I was taking care of patients' narcotics."

Mrs. Willie Chisholm was next, telling Billingsley, "The reason I stopped riding the buses (in 1954) I had been doctoring for my condition. At the time I got on the bus I was pregnant…. I rode the Washington Park bus… I got a transfer because that is as far as the bus was going; I got off and got on the Oak Park bus and…"

Each story was an encapsulated human drama. The impact of this treatment on each of these witnesses had been so intense that the details were imprinted on their memory. And as they related their stories, it was easy to visualize the event.

"…I sat at the last seat by the door, and the bus driver told me, 'You cannot sit there, you got to get in the back…' There were only three or four people on the bus, so one of these men helped me get back up. When I did sit down, I was so tired and feeling so bad."

"Did he make any remarks to you?" Billingsley asked softly.

"He said, 'Damn nasty n——s,' and cursed."

"Did he call you a n——r?"

"He called me a n——r," she responded. "Then I did sit down I was so upset. I rode as far as I could near my destination and then I got off the bus."

Dr. King once described many of these witnesses as "untutored," meaning they were not especially well-educated and spoke the common language of their community. It often wasn't grammatically correct and was peppered with slang. Those people who grew up with it often added their own verbal punctuation: "Amen." "Yessir." "You tell him." "Oh year." But the words were clear and unambiguous and often laced with strong emotion.

Mrs. Chisholm had been cursed at by drivers several different times, she said. Once, she remembered, she was standing on a crowded bus when the driver ordered, "Get on back, n——s, and let those white people sit down." At other times she had heard drivers refer to adult Black passengers as "boy" and "girl."

In his cross-examination, Robert Stewart went through the normal seating arrangements on segregated buses with the witness: who was allowed to sit where, and where people were allowed to stand. Willie Chisholm finally admitted, "I didn't understand it then."

"What is your understanding of it?"

"My understanding of it is, as far as I am concerned..."

Judge Carter stopped her. "He didn't ask what you thought," he explained. "What was the arrangement, if you know, of the system? If you don't know, tell him."

Okay. "I don't know."

It appeared Stewart was trying to show that Mrs. Chisholm was sitting in the wrong place according to the law. It was a simple matter; people of color were permitted to sit in designated seats and she had apparently taken the wrong seat. He asked her to point out on the diagram where she was sitting. "This is the seat I was sitting in," she finally decided.

"That seat isn't one of the back ten in the back of the bus, is it?"

"I don't know."

"Count them," he told her, then scolded her. "That isn't one of those ten seats, is it?"

"It doesn't look like it," she admitted. Then she changed her mind. "I just cannot recall exactly, but I think it was this seat." She pointed. "Right here."

A seemingly exasperated Stewart said, "You are changing your mind again. Which seat was it?"

With her finger, she indicated a spot on the diagram. "I think it was this seat right here."

"You are pointing to the red line." The line that separated the Black and white sections of the bus. "Which seat?" There is another line, this one an imaginary line, between asking tough questions and trying to confuse or catch a witness in a misstatement, and outright hostility or harassment. Attacking in that way is commonly referred to as "badgering"; it is derived from the late-eighteenth-century activity known as "badger baiting," in which dogs would be sent to harass badgers in their dens, forcing them into a defensive position, hopefully to lure them out. Stewart was attacking; the defense could have objected but instead chose to let Mrs. Chisholm handle him.

She said, "This seat right here."

"That is not a seat," Stewart corrected. He handed the witness a pencil and asked her to mark her seat.

She made her mark. "As near as I could estimate, this seat right here." Then, she said, "I moved back in the last seat." She pointed to the last seat in the bus. That certainly was a legal seat for a Black person.

"That is different from the testimony you gave originally. You said you were sitting in the first seat behind the door originally."

"This is where I sat," she said firmly.

Perhaps Stewart believed he finally had a witness he could control. He moved to a different subject, asking Mrs. Chisholm if she was a member of the MIA. "No, I am not," she responded, although she had attended at least three mass meetings.

"Can you tell me where they were?"

She could not. "I cannot recall where they were…because at that time the person that carried me, I am not familiar with that person."

"I didn't ask you who took you, I wondered where you went."

She gave a verbal shrug. "They were at night on the other side of town. I cannot recall the streets."

"What was discussed at those meetings you attended?"

She was finding her footing. "Usual routine discussion at meetings." What was said? "I cannot recall now, there was so much said." In general, though, she admitted, the meetings were about riding the buses.

"Can you recall anything said about riding the buses?"

Not that she was sure of. "No, I can't."

It is possible Stewart believed this was the witness who would finally confirm that Reverend King was the leader of the boycott. He pointed at the defense table and asked if she knew "the defendant in this case?"

"I know him when I see him." She had seen him before, she said. At any of the meetings she attended? Stewart wondered. "Well, I think I have seen him. I am not so familiar with him, but I do know him when I see him." She might have been speaking for the rest of the country when she added, "I just learned his name and who he was."

Did he speak at the meetings?

That was not a question she intended to answer. "I don't know anyone who spoke because it has been some time." In fact, she said she couldn't recall a single person who spoke at any of the meetings. How about Reverend Abernathy? Did she know him? "I know him. I attend his church." Did he speak? "I cannot recall because there were speakers, different other speakers."

Did she know Reverend Abernathy when she saw him?

"I know him when I see him."

Did he conduct any of the meetings?

"I think he conducted the prayer. I don't know."

She also admitted she knew Reverend Uriah Fields; she had attended religious classes he taught. Well, did he speak at the meetings?

"I probably saw him at some of the meetings, but whether he spoke or not, I'm not sure."

"Can't recall anybody who spoke?" Stewart asked with disbelief.

"I cannot recall anybody," she insisted.

As he finished his direct examination, he said, more of a comment than a question, "You can recall incidents that happened in 1953 and 1954 but not anything that happened in 1955?"

"Yes," she agreed, "I can."

When Orzell Billingsley began his redirect examination, he noted that since December 5 Mrs. Chisholm had "observed the buses" on the streets of the city. She had seen mostly empty buses, she had seen buses partially filled with white passengers, she had seen buses crowded with white people, but, he asked, "Have you seen a bus which white people occupied, and in which the first ten seats from the rear were reserved and white people were standing up?" As the system dictated.

"No, I haven't."

In Stewart's recross examination he tried to inject reality into the testimony. "You know, as a matter of fact, there just haven't been any Negroes riding the buses, don't you?"

Oh yeah. "Yes, sir. Because they were treated unfairly."

But Billingsley gave his witness the last word, asking, "You don't mean Negroes started walking because they wanted to?"

"No. Negroes wouldn't expect anyone to walk—they won't get on the buses."

While Mrs. Willie Chisholm represented a sizable segment of Black America as it existed, Dr. King's "untutored" people who had been deprived of opportunity and education under segregation, the next witness was a harbinger of what was to come: Joseph Alford was a veteran studying at Alabama State. Having served this country, he had moved to Montgomery from Anniston, Alabama, to begin classes at the university the previous September. A month later, he told the court, "I was catching a bus on Jackson and Hutchinson Street; I was helping a prominent lady on the bus, and she had a box, and as I passed the bus driver I put the money in the box, in the meter, for the lady, and as I went by him the lady went back to her seat, the first seat available in the colored...from the back. The bus driver said to me, 'Oh, Shine...'"

"Shine" was another ethnic slur for a Black man. It first appeared in the early twentieth century, likely derived from the fact that many Black men earned their living as "shoeshine boys" serving mostly white people. Fred Gray's very first job, for example, was shining shoes at Big's Barber Shop on Greyhound Street—and later he shined shoes in a white barber shop. Ten cents a shine. Whatever its derivation, it was never meant kindly.

"...I heard him the first time," Alford continued, "and I ignored him because I knew that wasn't my name. Then he said, 'Boy.' I turned around to him; I said, 'Are you speaking to me?' He said, 'I am.' I said, 'Let me tell you, my name isn't no boy nor a Shine. My name is Joseph Alford and I want you to call me that.'"

The courtroom stirred.

"And then he accused me of not putting enough money in the meter. I said, 'I beg your pardon. I most certainly put twenty cents in the meter.' I went back and sat down... After I rode several blocks...he said, 'You cannot sit there. Get up and get to the rear.' There wasn't any more seats available in the rear, only one white person was on the bus...a man who was sitting near the front. I said to him (the driver), 'If you will stop the bus I will get off...'

"He stopped the bus in the middle of the block. And I got off the bus first in order to help this lady off; by the time she went to step off the bus he pulled off and didn't give her enough time to get off the bus. She kind of stumbled but didn't fall because I caught her...

"I haven't been on the buses since."

Once again, Stewart began his cross-examination by referring to his diagram, trying to specifically locate Alford's seat. When he was convinced Alford was sitting in the seats reserved for Blacks, he asked, "What do you do for a living?"

"I am a veteran," Alford responded. "I don't do anything."

"You are a professional veteran," he asked, the lack of respect obvious in the question. "Do you do anything besides being a veteran?"

"I don't work anyplace. I go to school." He was not a member of the MIA, he testified, but when asked what he knew about that organization, he said, "I believe it is an association whose members are fighting for things that is right, and nothing more than right—and equal rights."

Stewart asked this witness essentially the same question he had asked Mrs. Chisholm, but framed it in an entirely different manner. "Is it your understanding that the Montgomery Improvement Association was organized for and is sponsoring the bus protest?"

And got the same answer. "No... I don't know anything about the Montgomery Improvement Association any more than I told you first. I think they are fighting for equal rights." He had attended several meetings, he replied to Stewart's questions, and the main topic discussed there was nonviolence. "To have non-violence whatever the program might be."

"What is the program?" Stewart demanded. "Let me get this straight. Have you a program of not riding the buses?"

"No, sir, it isn't necessarily a program." What it was, he explained, "For example, if something came up like (the bombings) at Dr. King's house, or Nixon's house, not to take violence."

Stewart was becoming frustrated at his inability to get even one person to acknowledge the boycott and the MIA's role in it. That leaked out as he asked Alford, "Do you know there is a bus protest going on? The Negro citizens of Montgomery are continually and deliberately not riding the buses?"

Alford certainly was not going to help him. "I don't understand that," he said. "Give me that again, please?"

"Do you understand there is such a movement, a bus protest going on?"

"What I read in the papers I would have to understand it, I suppose..." And then he proceeded to give Stewart the lesson that he had learned from Martin Luther King that was beginning to take hold in largely Black cities throughout the country. "I remember reading the papers from time to time. I can remember this was early, because what stimulated them most was the time Reverend King's house was bombed and the attitude he had taken toward it, and he came out front and said he didn't want any violence whatsoever. He said, 'You folks go home, the ones that live by the sword will die by the sword, we don't want any trouble whatsoever.' That is the main thing."

Many people looked over at Dr. King sitting at the defense table, his hands clasped in front of him. His facial expression offered little for those seeking a hint of his thoughts. He just continued to look at the witness and pay close attention.

Stewart ignored that, instead asking Alford if he had heard Dr. King speak at a mass meeting. He had, Alford said. "He came in and he started off with what he usually started off his talks with... He didn't want any violence in any manner, he said it was a 'Christianity movement, we haven't harmed anybody, although there were quite a number of incidents that happened that could be considered unfair, but we are going with this movement,' because he believed and we believed it was a Christianity movement."

The assistant prosecutor presented a very different picture of reality, asking, "Did he mention times that buses had been shot at, bricks and things thrown at the buses, and tell them he didn't want any violence like that to occur?"

"That is right. He said, 'We won't have any violence.'"

"Did he call those incidents to the attention of the people, buses shot at and knocked and so forth?"

Alford took that opportunity to make the most important legal point: "To the best of my telling, he didn't. We didn't even talk about the buses."

Stewart refused to accept that. "At none of these meetings you attended, you tell us, the bus situation wasn't discussed? Is that what you're telling me?"

"I am telling you what I heard him say at that particular time...just more or less of a Christianity sermon."

These witnesses had not been coached on how to answer, or avoid answering, the prosecutor's questions, and yet each one had, in his or her own way, artfully avoided implicating Dr. King. They didn't need to be told what the prosecutors were trying to do here nor trained in how to avoid crossing the line. They had lived with similar lines, legal and practical, throughout their lives and had learned how to deal with them. From the beginning of the defense case, its witnesses had skirted committing perjury. Actually proving that a witness had heard Dr. King make a certain statement was almost impossible. The prosecutors had little choice but to continue asking the questions and leaving it up to Judge Carter to decide if the witnesses were responding truthfully.

R. T. Smiley, "a member of the Negro race," had stopped riding City Lines buses in July 1955. He was riding a bus being driven by Mr. Ben Jones that day, he recalled. "The bus was crowded with white peoples, most of them schoolchildren, and they were occupying most of the seats in the bus... I sat in the next seat and he told me, 'N——r, get out of that seat, don't you see white passengers in this seat?' I said, 'This seat is vacant.' Well, he cursed and...stopped the bus and he told me to get off, which I did...

"...And I stayed off the buses and I bought me a car to keep from riding the buses."

"He called you a n——r in front of white schoolchildren?"

"He did." And, as everyone in that courtroom, in the entire community, knew, and felt, and at one time or another had experienced it, the white bus driver, Mr. Ben Jones, could do that with impunity. There was nothing R. T. Smiley could do except accept the humiliation. And get off the bus.

Mary Banks, "a member of the Negro race," got on a full bus and "when some white people get on the bus he said, 'You n——s get on back.' So after that peoples don't move back, he gets out of his seat there and walked back to the back and then he told us, everybody to get back and called us everything. What he was saying, I don't know...

"I said, 'You got a lot of Negroes on the bus and you got a lot of vacant seats up there, and I am as far back as I can possibly get, and when I get on the bus I got to stand.' Some of the bus drivers ask the white people to move up and let the Negroes occupy what vacant seats there are. Some will not move them up, just let them sit there, and we got to keep on standing until we get off the bus."

The last time she had ridden the bus, she said, was in November, when the driver stopped the bus and announced he was going no farther. He gave people transfers but, Mary Banks

DAN ABRAMS AND FRED GRAY WITH DAVID FISHER

said, "I told them, 'I am tired of a lot of trouble. I am going to quit riding buses'; when I first knowed myself I was walking."

When he made everyone get off, Billingsley asked, did that include both "white and colored?"

"Wasn't no whites on there..." Banks told him. "...and wasn't no whites to get off."

Louise Osborne was given the wrong transfer by a driver; when she asked for the correct transfer, he erupted. "He said, 'You dumb n——s, you don't know what you want.' I said, 'I am sorry, but I am not a n——r.'" After handing her the correct transfer, he started mumbling. "I couldn't understand everything he said, but I heard the word 'n——s' more than once...

"The next time I saw him—I always rode on this bus—I was in a hurry, and he said, 'Step back, you big baboon, and wait until I get ready to let you on,' and with that he slammed the door and pulled off, and he refused to let me in... I could see there were plenty of seats inside."

Asked if that driver had any resentment against her, she said she didn't know, but "I know he acted like crazy."

The final story of abuse she told by now was familiar. "I was sitting in the second straight (seat) in the rear of a Washington Park bus... He said, 'All of you get up out of your seats and let the white people sit down.' I got up and moved to the back." Summing up the feelings of the entire community, feelings that had been festering for many years, long before the boycott began, she concluded, "The longer I rode the madder I got, and I got off and started walking."

The defense had only two more witnesses to put on the stand, two of the most controversial and despised men in the city. And one of them was white.

CHAPTER THIRTEEN

While some white residents of the city supported the protest, it was far too dangerous for them to admit it. They did so silently, anonymously contributing money or creating excuses to drive Black people to a destination. But the most visible white participant in the boycott was the Reverend Robert S. Graetz, the white minister who had been assigned to the predominantly Black Trinity Lutheran Church only six months before it began. Initially some parishioners had reservations about choosing a white man to advise them on how to live their lives and interpret what the Bible should mean to them. After all, life in Montgomery was starkly different for those with white skin. But Graetz worked hard to gain the trust of his community, and his actions spoke louder than even his sermons.

Reverend Graetz became one of the few white men and women actively and very publicly involved in the quest to end segregation. "I don't believe he came to Montgomery to work in the civil rights movement," Gray says, "but once the protest started he felt it was his duty as a minister to become involved.

He not only encouraged his parishioners to join in the boycott, but also told them, 'If you need a ride, call me. I'll come and get you.' He drove regularly for months." He was so deeply committed to it that eventually he was elected secretary of the MIA—and even served as a groomsman in Fred Gray's wedding. The NAACP Youth Council held its meetings at his church, which enabled Reverend Graetz to get to know its chairperson, Rosa Parks.

Being a white man in Montgomery in 1956 was to have a stake in the power structure. Even the lowest white man had rights and privileges denied to the most accomplished Black man. So many mystified white Montgomerians just couldn't understand why a good Christian man like Graetz would throw away his position to take such radical positions defending Black people.

He knew and accepted the risk he was taking, saying once, "If anything, a white person who was helping a Black person was seen as worse than a Black person." Later he added, "We often had good reason to be afraid… There were times I was scared to death." His life was threatened many times and his wife, Jeannie, and their preschool-age children were harassed. In public people would chastise him as a "n——r lover," and several months after the trial his parish home was bombed twice. To soothe his young children's fear, he created a game in which they would quickly hide behind furniture when he heard an unusual sound outside. And when he drove he made a point of regularly changing his route—just in case.

A vast number of white Southerners considered him a traitor to his race. While still in college at Capital University in Columbus, Ohio, he had joined the NAACP in 1950, a radical step for a young white man, as many white people considered that organization somewhat akin to the hated Communist party. He was a very important witness for the defense. The color of his skin instantly made him more credible to the white community—which intensified their hatred for him. Reverend Graetz was a man of average size, although he was a bit thin, and when he took the witness stand he was wearing his trademark bow tie.

Arthur Shores would question him. "You are a member of the white race?" Shores began.

"That is right, sir," he replied.

In response to Shores's questioning, he acknowledged he had attended several MIA meetings and had heard Dr. King speaking. "At those meetings," Shores continued, "have you heard Dr. King or any of the other speakers who took part urge citizens not to ride the city buses?"

In other words, were they part of the conspiracy? "I cannot recall what was said by them all. I recall there were times that they referred to the fact that people didn't want to ride them, and they all said, 'We are going to see what you want us to do, and we are going to leave this thing up to you...' I recall on at least one occasion Dr. King said, 'We are your representatives and we will have to do what you want us to do, and it is up to you whether we want to ride the buses or not.'"

Shores then asked the key question that could determine the defendant's innocence or guilt. "And did he urge them positively not to ride the buses on any occasion?"

The courtroom was silent as he responded, "I don't recall that he ever said it that way. No."

As a member of the MIA, Shores asked, had Reverend Graetz heard people requesting that others not use the buses? "Very likely I have," he admitted, "because I have talked to so many people. I am certain I must have heard some people talk to others and urge them not to ride the buses. That would be an isolated conversation, as far as I can remember." But he had never heard any member of the MIA making a threat. "Oh, no." He was sure about that, and as he continued, his very boyish demeanor grew into a quiet maturity. "As a matter of fact, right from the beginning Dr. King and others constantly urged, 'If someone wants to ride the buses, let them ride; we are not suggesting to threaten them, coerce them, or intimidate them, or anything else.'"

There was nothing else to say, so Shores turned his witness over to the solicitor. Stewart immediately went on the attack, asking, "Did you attend the meeting of the ministers alliance on December 5th at which the Montgomery Improvement Association was organized?"

No, he had not, but he did speak to Dr. King later that week—and he didn't "recall that he said anything about the organization." However, Reverend Graetz did attend the first mass meeting at the Holt Street Baptist Church. And did he recall Dr. King speaking that night? His answer was surprising, considering all that had happened in the previous three months. "I didn't know Dr. King; someone who was there told me at one time, I believe, that is Reverend King speaking. But I didn't know."

"You know him now?"

"Yes, sir," he replied, as a smattering of laughter echoed through the courtroom. Did he speak at that meeting? "I believe he did. However, I was in the basement and I just heard it over the loudspeaker."

"Was there someone introduced as the Reverend King?"

"I don't believe so."

From these first answers, it seemed that Reverend Graetz was not going to try to avoid answering the solicitor's questions. So it was up to Stewart to ask the right questions. "What was the general subject matter discussed at the Holt Street Baptist Church?" It was obvious the prosecution believed that meeting had been called to announce—and begin organizing—the bus protest.

Instead, Graetz replied, "The thing I recall most vividly was the discussion of grievances of Negro people against the bus company, and about conditions and discourtesy on the buses."

He had heard the Resolution read, he testified, although he did not know who prepared it and when they did so. "I was under the impression that during the first part of the meeting someone had prepared it and then presented it later in the meeting." Asked who presented it, he replied, "My recollection is that it was Reverend Abernathy. And I didn't know him either at that time."

That Resolution focused on "the abuses of Negro people on the buses, and the attempts of all those to try to get something straightened out with the bus company." But then he came closer than any previous witness in linking the MIA to directing the boycott. "As I recall it, calling on the people to refrain from riding the buses."

Did Dr. King support the Resolution?

"As I recall, he had to leave the meeting before...my recollection is that Resolution was passed after he had gone."

Still trying to establish Dr. King's responsibility for the boycott, Stewart asked, "He has been during the weeks and months of the bus boycott its primary spokesman?"

"Of the so-called boycott, yes."

After joining the MIA, Reverend Graetz had attended several meetings of the Executive Committee. Dr. King did preside at those meetings, he acknowledged. And what was discussed? "Well, there were two or three compromise proposals discussed at the meetings...and I believe there were some matters discussed about the transportation system."

It must have been a relief for Stewart to have a witness actually responding to his questions. He began edging closer to the connection he needed, wondering, "What was his personal feeling as expressed in these meetings about the compromise?"

Reverend Graetz didn't recall Dr. King expressing his personal feelings about it. Although, in later conversations, "It seems to me he just expressed a feeling some kind of compromise might be worked out. And he has also expressed the feeling that the masses of people would be highly unfavorable, would be opposed to most of the compromises that you could present." That message was clear: it was the people, not the MIA board, who would make the decisions.

Stewart asked him to describe the transportation system that had been set up by the MIA. He did so, agreeing that he had been among the volunteer drivers. And while he was aware that some drivers had been paid for their gasoline, he had not been paid.

"You have been losing out," Stewart chided him. "Have you received any free gasoline?"

"No, I have not. I voluntarily said I didn't want any of the free gasoline."

In earlier testimony, witnesses had claimed the boycott was only one of the MIA's several projects to help the community. Stewart asked if that was true. "Do you know of any purpose that it served, any function that it performed other than the conduct of this bus boycott, this protest, whatever you prefer to call it?"

Calmly, Reverend Graetz replied, "My understanding is there were several grievances the association was planning to go into and this is the first one."

After dickering a bit about those other "planned projects," Stewart wanted to know if "the Montgomery Improvement Association had performed any function other than to conduct the boycott" from December through February.

"None that I know of."

"Do you know if any of its money was spent for a purpose other than the bus protest?"

"None that I know of, no."

"Do you know from your conversations with this defendant who actually organized the Montgomery Improvement Association?"

He did. "My understanding was at the time this Interdenominational Ministerial Alliance organized it...a group of Negro ministers." And yes, Dr. King was a member of that organization.

As for those violent acts, buses being shot at, rocks and bricks being thrown at them, "Do you know about that condition?"

He was aware of it. "I read that in the newspapers; it is the only way I am familiar with it... I heard it discussed at mass meetings," but not at Executive Committee meetings.

Stewart continued to ask about the committee, specifically if Graetz had from "time to time (presented) a compromise offer in an effort to adjust or settle the bus situation?"

He had, he said, "but none has been completely acceptable."

Was it true that the original demands made on the bus company and the city "the very first time" had not changed? That was correct, Graetz agreed.

The protest was about to begin its fifth month with the Black community settled in and functioning. People were getting to work, to their appointments, even saving that dime when they did. The convenience they were surrendering had proved to be a small price for the pride they were gaining. Stewart asked, "So far as you know, the Montgomery Improvement Association intends to continue this boycott, or protest, until their demands are met?"

"Until the demands are met," Graetz agreed, "or until some workable compromise is reached."

But no one had the slightest concept of what that "workable compromise" might be. Lost in the focus on the trial was the reality that the City Lines bus company could not have settled with the protesters even if it had so desired; whatever the despicable actions of certain drivers, the company would be breaking the law if it agreed to particular protesters' demands. The bus company was bound by law to segregate its buses. In fact, there were rumors the city was prepared to sue the bus company if it changed its policies. And years later Bagley claimed that Mayor Gayle had warned him that he would put the bus company out of business before he allowed its buses to be integrated. This was a constant reminder that what had begun as a dispute over where Blacks could legally sit on a bus had escalated into an assault on the future of segregation.

Neither side could afford to back down. Stewart, defending segregation, defending the city government and the bus company, tried to place the blame for the stalemate directly on the MIA. "There have been several compromises offered from time to time... Those compromises had in every case come from one group or another of white citizens, hadn't they?"

No, Graetz disagreed. "Some from white and some from colored." That surprised Stewart; when he asked for examples, the reverend replied, "Privately one or two people advanced a compromise to me in confidence so that I might advance it to the other group." As the white member of the MIA board, he was an acceptable go-between. He was hazy, though, about the nature of those suggestions, explaining, "There have been a number of discussions concerning compromise by officers of the Montgomery Improvement Association—but I don't recall any of those were definite compromises."

That testimony was somewhat different from what he had told the grand jury, Stewart pointed out. Didn't he "recall telling the grand jury you didn't believe too much of an attempt had been made along that line?"

"Yes."

The solicitor then placed the blame squarely where he believed it belonged. "Would you say the Montgomery Improvement Association at the present time has been standing in the way of submitting to this compromise?"

Shores objected, pointing out it asked for an opinion from the witness. The judge sustained the objection but it didn't matter. Stewart's question had made his point.

During his redirect examination, Arthur Shores asked the witness what had happened to the proposals for a compromise. They were not brought up for a vote, Graetz said. The only proposal that had been presented to a mass meeting had taken place in the last few weeks. Although he was not at that meeting, he said, "I understand the people there were so upset at the proposal they shouted it down before it was completely read." Once again, suggesting the movement had no real leaders.

What about all that violence directed at the buses? Shores wondered. "Have you had actual violence perpetrated against you since this (began)?"

"Yes... Three of my tires were slashed, and sugar put in my gasoline tank, and I have been threatened a number of times."

Thank you, Shores said, referring to his testimony, but it certainly could have covered considerably more than that.

Stewart had only a few more questions, just to clarify the reverend's testimony. Wasn't it true that "the police commissioner called on you immediately after the threat on your life and offered you city police protection should you need it?"

That was correct.

Then, "You said the only compromise you knew about was shouted down before it was ever read...(but) didn't you tell the grand jury you believed if this compromise had been presented and explained just exactly as it is, it would have been an acceptable compromise?"

"That was my feeling at the time," he replied honestly, then explained. "After I had been to the grand jury I was talking about the compromise with some people, and will still like to advise the people, if they would go over all the elements in there they would find it more favorable than they had originally believed."

Reverend Graetz was committed to the civil rights movement. He was willing to risk his life in the fight for racial equality. But he was white. He could empathize with Black Americans, but he could never experience what it felt like to be a Black man or woman in America. Without knowing exactly what compromise was offered, it is impossible to know what he believed could have been acceptable. But now the bus to compromise had left the depot and was never coming back.

The final witness for the defense was the defendant, Reverend Martin Luther King. When his name was called, he walked confidently, his head held high, to the witness stand. He was wearing a light gray suit jacket with a white shirt and slightly patterned tie, his hair and small mustache neatly trimmed. In a few months this young local Alabama minister had emerged as the leader of a new movement. At the end of 1955, almost no one outside Montgomery had ever heard his name. Now he was being profiled in the national magazines.

According to *Jet*, he had emerged as "the pacifist leader of the city's thousands of footsore Negroes, who have traded their crushed spirits for new dignity and tired feet." They described him as "a symbol for divinely inspired hope, a kind of modern Moses who has brought new self-respect to Southern Negroes."

The magazine pointed out that he was not always a pacifist. Growing up, they wrote, when his younger brother hit their older sister, "M.L. Jr. let him have it—right on the head with a telephone receiver."

While he had grown up in Atlanta, years earlier his father had come to Montgomery and been humiliated on public transit. During a stopover in that city while returning from a church convention in the 1920s, Martin Luther King Sr. had boarded a streetcar. After paying the fare in the front, he and his friends were told they had to go to the back door to get back on board. Martin Luther King Sr. was incensed and demanded his money back. The driver refused to refund his fare, and King's friends had to convince him to get off rather than fight.

But Daddy King developed important relationships in both the Black and white worlds. His Ebenezer Church Choir even performed at a 1939 event celebrating the big Atlanta premiere of the film *Gone with the Wind*, with a nine-year-old Martin Luther King Jr. singing on stage in front of a replica of "Tara," the fictitious plantation and home of the central character Scar-lett O'Hara.

Not surprisingly, King Jr. had his own experience with seg-regated transportation. Coming home to Atlanta after finish-ing second in an oratorical contest in Valdosta, Georgia, he and his classmates had been forced to give up their seats when white passengers boarded their bus in Macon. They initially refused to stand, doing so only after the driver called them n——s and threatened to call the police. "I could never adjust to separate waiting rooms, separate eating places, separate restrooms," he wrote, "partly because the separate was always unequal, and partly because the very idea of separation did something to my sense of dignity and self-respect." King had attended, and grad-uated from, Crozer Theological Seminary in 1951, a rare inte-grated school. Unlike many others in the South who may have only known life as segregated, King had worked and studied with, dated and lived with white people.

Now being thrust to the center of the bus boycott had given him a platform to attack segregation, and he had taken advantage of it. Fred Gray had gotten to know Dr. King well during the protest. As Gray recalls, "We had legal problems almost every day and he was in the middle of every one of them." They were close to the same age and had started their careers in Montgom-ery at the same time; Dr. King had arrived in the city the same month Gray was admitted to the bar. Gray had become both his lawyer and his friend. Throughout the protest, they spoke every day, often several times a day, as together they dealt with seem-ingly never-ending problems. "He was," Gray remembers, "a very kind, compassionate, considerate, easygoing, easy-talking minister. He could talk about anything. He had a fine sense of humor," Gray recalls, "and was not adverse to telling the type of colorful stories he could not tell from the pulpit. He was one of those people who never met a stranger. He was a good, kind person—and he enjoyed sitting down with a group of friends and just enjoying the fellowship. He never tried to monopolize a conversation, and he was a good listener. I never had any concern when he was testifying because nothing would upset him. I never saw him angry; I never saw him show hostility or hate toward anyone.

"During the trial, we would discuss legal strategy, and he would state his opinions but generally he accepted advice. Our primary goal was that whatever the outcome of the case, that Martin Luther King would come out of it a winner. He had never testified in a trial before, but I had great confidence in him. We had prepared him well for both his direct testimony and cross-examination: Dr. King understood what the law was, what the facts were, what our theory of the case was and what the prosecution would try to do. Their goal was to prove that he was the leader, the man making decisions, rather than the spokesman for all of the others. He was aware of the legal traps that Mr. Thetford would set for him and how to avoid them. He sat quietly through all the testimony, listening attentively. After each day we would all get together in my office to review the day's proceedings and plan for the following day. We never told him how to respond or what to say, we never rehearsed. But Dr. King understood that sometimes there was a difference between the law and justice, and he had spent his whole life believing in justice for our community. He was firm about that, and that made him completely confident. He wasn't the slightest bit nervous as he took the stand. He knew what they were going to try to get him to say and he knew what we wanted him to say. I suspect many of the people in that courtroom were far more nervous for him than he felt."

Arthur Shores was handed a delicate task; he had to allow Dr. King to make his statement without acknowledging he was the leader of the boycott. He also had to anticipate those areas the prosecution would attack and preempt them. Unlike many of the earlier witnesses, who could cloud the truth without penalty, his reputation as a man of the Gospel, as an honest and truthful person, was at stake. Somehow, he had to answer all the questions as honestly as possible, but without directly implicating himself. Shores began by asking him to state his full name. "Martin Luther King Jr." He was a minister at the Dexter Avenue Baptist Church. "Are you one of the organizers of the Montgomery Improvement Association?" Even on this question, he would offer a slightly nuanced response. "Yes, I was in the meeting when it was organized."

"For what purpose was this organization formulated?"

"Well," King replied in a voice that seemed soft but was carried easily throughout the entire courtroom, the mastery of projection typical of the great preachers, "the name itself covers the basic purpose of the organization, to improve the general status of Montgomery, to improve race relations and to uplift the general tenor of the community."

There were no dues or fees to join, he continued, and any citizen was welcome. There were no race restrictions of any kind. "It is just a matter of being interested in improving Montgomery."

He had attended MIA meetings, presided at some of them and spoken at them. "During the course of your speeches," Shores asked, "have you urged any of the listeners or members of the MIA to refrain from riding the buses of the Montgomery City Lines?"

That was the essence of the trial. "No, I have not," King replied evenly. "My exposition has always been 'to let your conscience be your guide.' If you want to ride, that is all right."

"Have you urged any violence, or any of those violent acts that have been testified about here in court? Have you urged any members to perform any of those acts?"

"No, I have not. My motivation has been the exact converse of that; I urged nonviolence at all points." In fact, he had never heard anyone suggesting acts of violence.

Shores was preparing Dr. King for the cross-examination, getting him on record before the prosecution could ask these questions in a much-less friendly manner. "I believe there have been several proposals mentioned," Shores said. "Have you attended any of the meetings called by the Mayor or other groups who tried to solve the bus situation?" He had. He had presented those proposals to the members. "And what was the reaction?"

"Well, they were always rejected by the people. We made it clear we couldn't make any final statement on any of the proposals and they had to be taken back to the people, and we did that through the mass meetings. And when they were rejected, I would make contact and let the officials know what happened."

Those proposals, he continued, "To the best of my recollection the main proposal...we took back was the proposal to reserve ten seats in the front for the Negro passengers and ten seats in the back for the white passengers. Also included in that was a guarantee of courtesy. Now that is about the substance of the proposal."

Shores corrected him, "Did you say ten seats in the front for Negroes or whites?"

Perhaps Dr. King was slightly more nervous than his demeanor or voice revealed, but he corrected himself, smiling shyly, "I mean white passengers, ten in front for white passengers and ten in the rear for Negro passengers."

In response to Shores's next question, he explained, "We presented three proposals. The first dealt with the question of courtesy; that is, more courteous treatment from the bus drivers themselves. The second proposal dealt with the whole question of seating; that we requested a seating arrangement based on a first come, first served basis, Negro passengers seating from the rear of the bus to the front, and white passengers from the front to the rear, with no reserved seats for anybody. And the third proposal was a request to hire Negro bus drivers on predominantly Negro lines."

And the reaction to those proposals from the bus company and the city?

"...those proposals were rejected. There was some concession on the first proposal—that is the question of courtesy—the others were rejected outright at every meeting we attended."

They then discussed the car pool, which Dr. King described as "just a matter of individuals volunteering to give their cars for the purpose of transporting persons to and from their jobs and their business...these cars will be there (at the pickup and dispatch stations) at certain hours..." None of the drivers were paid, none of the passengers were charged fees. But... "There is a payment...for the wear and tear on the cars. We have all day drivers, about twenty all day drivers that start at six o'clock in the morning and work throughout the day, and there is a bonus given for the purpose of wear and tear on the car—and no one is paid a salary for driving."

In fact, he reiterated, no one, including himself, was paid a salary.

Vandalism? Violence? "I am sure I know of no one in the organization who has anything to do with it or is responsible for it."

But, Shores asked, "Have any acts of vandalism or acts of intimidation or worrisome nature been perpetrated against you?"

"Yes, very definitely...my home has been bombed on one occasion and I have received numerous threats. I couldn't really give the number. I received numerous threats."

Because no one was injured in this bombing, there were people who believed it was meant as a warning. But throughout the South, participating in civil rights movements was becoming increasingly dangerous. Three weeks before the trial began, for example, Dr. Thomas Brewer, a vocal Black leader who had filed a voting rights lawsuit, was gunned down in Columbus, Georgia. Even this soon after the boycott had begun, there were few Black men with a greater national profile than

Martin Luther King. His sudden rise to prominence had made him a high-profile target.

Shores continued, in response to the prosecution claiming the MIA somehow was responsible for the violence against buses, "And at the time your house was bombed, did you or any member of your organization, to your knowledge, urge any member of your organization, or anybody else, to commit violence?"

"No, just the opposite."

Shores asked Dr. King about Mayor Gayle's claim that Dr. King had agreed to his compromise proposal, then later rejected it. Was that true? Did he receive a proposal and later reject it?

"No, I did not," he said, essentially calling the mayor a liar. "I have never received a proposal that I accepted. I have always contended that I could only take it up with the people, and that is what I said to Mayor Gayle, when he offered the proposal over the phone, I would take it up with the people, and that is as far as I would go. And he was to call me back on Friday to discuss it, but he never called back."

"And have you always taken the proposals to the people to have them decide whether or not the proposals would be accepted?" In other words, Dr. King was more of a representative, carrying the decision of the members of the MIA, rather than a leader influencing that decision.

"Yes, sir, I have." And the results of taking proposals to the people? "Well, to this point all of the proposals I took to the people and put before them, they felt were not satisfactory, so they have rejected the proposals to this point."

As for the claim that the Montgomery Improvement Association simply was a fancy name for the leaders of the bus boycott, Shores suggested that Dr. King's "activities in connection with the MIA constitute a part of your effort to improve the Negro status in Montgomery?"

"That is right. Quite right."

As for the protest, "Was Reverend Glasco paid any amount in connection with transportation?"

"Yes," the defendant replied, although he could not recall how much he had been paid.

The reason for that, Shores established, is that "The finances are not handled by you, are they?"

"No." The MIA had a finance committee. It also had employees. "How many office workers that you pay a salary?"

"I think it is seven."

With that, Shores had completed his direct questioning, having covered the essential material. The solicitor, William Thetford, would conduct the cross-examination himself. Dr. King sat patiently in the witness chair.

For the spectators, the main event was about to begin. While Thetford would question King, the two men actually were the stand-ins for what really was on trial, white Montgomery vs. its Black population, with the future of segregation in the balance.

CHAPTER FOURTEEN

In lore and entertainment, the cross-examination of the defendant or key witness often is the climax of a trial. It is the confrontation the trial has been building toward, the last opportunity for a clever litigator to attack and poke holes in testimony detrimental to their client, and on occasion to powerfully discredit a witness. Verdicts often are determined by compelling cross-examinations.

In this case, however, the impact could be even more far-reaching and potentially significant. Dr. King's rising star was more and more becoming a threat to the segregated South. It was possible that the embryonic civil rights movement, which until then had been primarily a series of local challenges, could coalesce behind a charismatic leader and become a more unified national crusade. The outcome of this trial was not nearly as important as the tremendous public exposure it already had provided for Martin Luther King. Now this question-and-answer session, which would be covered around the world, could make this local leader a critical national voice of a bursting national movement.

If Solicitor Thetford succeeded in his cross-examination, however, he could prevent that from happening. His job was to expose him. While locally Dr. King's conviction would serve as a reminder to the Black population who was in charge in Montgomery, exposing him to the world as duplicitous, a minister willing to lie under oath, would have far greater impact. Thetford immediately got down to business, and from the first question, his tone dripped with disdain. "This bus boycott, or bus protest, whatever you choose to call it, was called for the 5th of December through a series of little pamphlets—you are familiar with what I am talking about?"

"Yes, I am familiar."

"It is true they appeared on the streets a day or two before the protest meeting concerning alleged grievances?"

Describing the grievances that had been heard in the courtroom for the past few days as "alleged" was an obvious attack on the credibility of the previous witnesses. Rather than responding to that bait, Dr. King dismissed it. "I really couldn't say. I don't know if the pamphlets were put out for more than one day. I just don't recall what the pamphlet said concerning the time... I remember seeing one of them."

Thetford established that Dr. King met with numerous "other men" at the Mt. Zion A.M.E. Church and formed the Montgomery Improvement Association at "around 3:00 p.m. on December the 5th." Officers were elected at that meeting, the solicitor continued, "Refreshing your recollection..." reading from the minutes, "'Moved and second that the sixteen persons here...and a suggestion that nine names be brought up in making twenty-five which constitutes the Executive Committee.' Do you remember the Executive Committee of twenty-five with nine others to be named?"

"Yes, that is right. I remember that."

After a brief discussion about the various committees created at that meeting—"I really don't remember about these committees," Dr. King said—Thetford began asking the questions that mattered; his objective was to show that the boycott had been planned at the afternoon meeting of the ministers, and that Dr. King played a significant role in that initial planning. "Did you have anything to do with what I will refer to as the first boycott, the boycott called for December 5th?"

"No." Flatly, no. "Do you mean if I had anything to do with calling it… I didn't."

Did he know who called the meeting? "No, I don't. It was a spontaneous beginning, one of those things that had just been smoldering."

Did he know that "according to all the testimony we have had here up to now (the MIA) has spent of this money it has collected, some $30,000 in supporting the boycott or protest?"

"That would be impossible to say. I don't know enough about it."

"…You sign all the checks, don't you?"

"Yes, I do. I would say most of it has been used for that."

Moving to another subject, poking, looking for an opportunity to dig deeper, he said, "I note in your minutes of that first meeting, 'It is recommended that Resolutions would be drawn up,' and a Resolutions Committee was appointed… You were on that committee, I take it?"

"I don't believe I worked on the Resolutions Committee. That committee was appointed."

Thetford wondered, "Your minutes show, 'The President, Reverend M. L. King, Attorney Gray and Attorney Langford are on the committee.' Is that true?" Believing he may have caught Dr. King in an inconsistency, he added, unnecessarily, "They are your minutes, aren't they?"

Dr. King conceded, "It might be true I was on the committee and I had worked with the committee."

"That drew up the Resolution?"

"This committee, this Resolutions Committee."

Like any good attorney, Thetford had found a small opening and proceeded to try to drive an 18-wheeler through it. "Who was on the Resolutions Committee at that time?"

"I don't remember."

"When was the Resolution drawn up?"

"Sometime during the meeting at the Holt Street Baptist Church."

"You are telling the Court that the Resolution wasn't drawn up at the afternoon meeting, but it was drawn up that night? Is that what you are telling us?"

"That is right," Dr. King responded. In fact, after that meeting, Fred Gray had returned to his office and transformed the general objectives that had been agreed upon into a formal written Resolution.

"And it also was agreed at the afternoon meeting that the protest would be continued; is that correct?"

"I don't know."

"Let me read it to you to refresh your recollection, or you can read it."

He handed Dr. King a copy of the minutes. The courtroom was anxiously somber as he read them, then finally said, "Well, that is true according to the minutes here. I don't remember the discussion at this point."

Thetford got the defendant to admit he had previously seen the minutes, then said loudly, "You stated that you have never asked anybody not to ride the buses. Let me read what the Resolution says. It says: 'That the citizens of Montgomery are requesting that every citizen in Montgomery, regardless of race, color or creed, to refrain from riding buses owned and operated in the City of Montgomery by the Montgomery City Lines, Incorporated, until some arrangement has been worked out between said citizens and the Montgomery City Lines, Incorporated.' You said this was made up on that night. That is what the Resolution says."

Without drawing attention to it, Thetford had casually attributed the work of the entire committee to Dr. King personally. Dr. King said, "I didn't read the Resolution."

"You heard it read," Thetford countered.

"This was done by the committee." Not by me, he meant. "Oh yes," he had heard it read. To the best of his recollection, it was read aloud by Reverend Ralph Abernathy.

"In other words, what the Montgomery Improvement Association did, as I understand it, is to back an existing one-day boycott and by this protest, or whatever you want to call it, has extended over a period of several months and is still in existence; is that substantially true?"

"Yes and no." Dr. King explained, "The last part is true, it is still in existence. Now as to the first part I would say the Montgomery Improvement Association came into being in an attempt to improve the general status of the city plus the…"

Thetford interrupted, "That is not in response to my question at all."

"I was fixing to give the other part of it."

The solicitor appealed to the judge. "That wasn't responsive to my question."

"Ask it again," Judge Carter suggested.

So he did. "I ask you this. I said the Montgomery Improvement Association…backed an existing one-day boycott and has through its transportation committee and others urged people not to ride the buses, and that situation is still existing today?"

This was the heart of it: Was there a conspiracy—organized by the MIA—to boycott the buses? Technically, within the Black community, this was always considered a protest, not a boycott. So Dr. King could answer truthfully, "No, I wouldn't say so."

"Isn't that the way it came about?"

"No."

Rather than contesting that, Thetford tried a different approach. After establishing that Dr. King had lived in Montgomery only a year and a half, he asked, "Since you have been here how many times have you ridden buses?"

"Only one."

"How many white members have you at this time in the Montgomery Improvement Association, to your knowledge?"

"I really don't know," King replied somewhat dismissively. "We don't keep records by race. I couldn't say how many white members we have."

How many white people did he *think* belonged to the MIA?

"Well, I don't know," he repeated. "I know Reverend Graetz is a member, and we probably have some other. I know we have some other."

"Who are they?"

If there were any others, answering this question might well put them in danger, so Dr. King replied, "I don't recall at this point."

"How many members do you have?"

"I don't know. We don't keep a record of that."

Thetford returned to the main thrust of his cross-examination. "Coming back to the minutes of your first meeting: 'It was passed that the recommendations from the committee be given to the citizens at the night meeting.' That is right, isn't it?"

"That is right."

"The recommendation they are referring to there was the recommendation that the protest or boycott be continued; is that correct?" When King said he didn't "catch the question," Thetford repeated, "You testified that 'It was passed that the recommendations from the committee be given to the citizens at the night meeting.' You say that is right?"

Dr. King deftly avoided answering that question. "What Resolution does that refer to?"

Thetford read it again. "'It was passed that the recommenda-tions—'" he held up the Resolutions "—as you see this here."

"What recommendations does that refer to?"

Thetford sabotaged his own attack. "I don't know. I wasn't at the meeting."

Indicating the minutes, Dr. King pointed out, "This don't say about what. I really don't remember what transpired at that there."

"Don't know what it means?" Thetford mocked.

"No, I really don't."

"As a matter of fact, you remember being at this organiza-tional meeting on the afternoon of the 5th?" Although there had been previous testimony that he had arrived late and had already been selected president by the time he got there. "Did you draw up this agenda for the meeting that night on the afternoon..."

"I don't remember for sure when that was drawn up."

"Look at this right here," Thetford insisted, again indicating the minutes, "and you read that."

Dr. King agreed. "I imagine so, that it was drawn up there." Thetford then asked if he had attended the MIA meeting on the ninth of December. Dr. King didn't remember. "What was the nature of that meeting?"

Referring again to the minutes, Thetford read, "'The contact committee of the...association.'"

Dr. King had no idea what he was talking about. "The con-tact committee?"

"The contact committee."

The defendant examined the minutes, then shook his head. "I don't see anything about a contact committee. I don't know anything about it."

"I am reading from your minutes," Thetford insisted.

Arthur Shores objected, asking, "From whose minutes?"

Dr. King told the judge, "I didn't write these."

"Take a look at your minutes," Thetford told him, "and see what they say."

Billingsley also objected. "You are using 'your' and 'we' sometimes. 'Your.' You are using your organization."

Thetford instructed the witness, "Look at it and see what it relates to and give an answer to my question."

"I am not familiar with that name. I guess that's the name the secretary used. However, that committee was appointed by the executive board."

The solicitor asked, "Did the Executive Committee at that time formulate the demands that would be made upon the bus company?" And who formulated them?

"I think that was done at the Holt Street Church, as I recall… I don't really remember, as I said, the people made the demands."

"What people?"

"More than four thousand people at the Holt Street Baptist Church."

Thetford doubted that. "Those four thousand people formulated these three specific demands? Is that what you're telling us?"

"Well, it is according to how you interpret the word formulate," Dr. King agreed. "If you mean they wrote them…no, not four thousand people."

"Who did write them?"

"I don't know. I don't remember who wrote them." In fact, Fred Gray had drawn up the Resolution containing those three demands. As he remembers, "At the meeting on the afternoon of December 5th, we talked about the three things we wanted: to be treated with decency, Black drivers in Black neighborhoods and, of course, the seating arrangement. Those were all the things Jo Ann Robinson and I and several other people had been talking about since Rosa Parks's arrest. We didn't spend a lot of time discussing demands, though. We spoke mostly about how to get the message out about staying off the buses. At that point, none of the other lawyers were involved, so I drew up a draft of what we would discuss at the meeting that night. Those demands were presented to the people that night and that is what we all agreed upon. I doubt Dr. King knew who had prepared that draft."

The two greatest active prizefighters were the white undefeated heavyweight champion Rocky Marciano and the already legendary Black former middleweight champion Sugar Ray Robinson. In some ways their styles mirrored Thetford and Dr. King. Marciano was a slugger; he had won forty-three of his forty-nine victories by knockout. In the ring he would bide his time, taking punches and throwing jabs as he searched for an opening—and once he found it, he attacked relentlessly, until he delivered a knockout blow. In contrast, Sugar Ray Robinson was a boxer, who would trade punches, look for combinations while frustrating his opponent with his dexterity. He was a dancer, bobbing and weaving, fast on his feet, making his opponents miss, avoiding the big hit while he piled up points. Or waited for his opponent to make a mistake, to leave himself exposed.

Thetford had been jabbing, but he hadn't landed a big blow. He continued pursuing his elusive witness. "When is the first you heard of the three demands?"

"Well, as I stated, I believe it was the Holt Street meeting. I don't remember. I don't like to go to that extent."

"Anyone ever tell you the three requests were going to be made to the bus company?"

"Who told me?" He shook his head. "I cannot recall. I think I heard them at the mass meeting. There were so many speakers at that meeting I don't know who mentioned them."

"Who was it got up and said, 'These are the demands we are going to make on the city and the bus company'?"

"It was one speaker," Dr. King replied.

"That is what I am trying to get at," Thetford said. Who was that one speaker?

Dr. King bobbed. "I don't know."

That was hard to believe. "You just don't know?"

And weaved. "I don't know."

"How much money have you in your bank account over in Atlanta now?"

"I really don't know."

"We object," Shores said loudly, "to the wording of the question, 'In your bank account.'"

Judge Carter dismissed it. "He has already said he don't know."

Thetford tried again. "Let me change that. You have a bank account in the name of the Montgomery Improvement Association in the Citizens Trust in Atlanta?" Correct. "I believe $5,000 was deposited in that bank in Atlanta, the same $5,000 you drew out of the Alabama National Bank?"

The implication was obvious. If Thetford could even raise the possibility Dr. King had personally profited from the boycott, his credibility, and most likely his future as a leader, would be destroyed. Dr. King responded in a casual tone. "That is right…it was sent over." Depositing those funds in an out-of-state bank, a Black bank, prevented local law enforcement from having any access or knowledge of it. While Dr. King was one of three signatories to the account, it was in the MIA's name.

"On February 21st do you know the amount you had put into the bank?"

Shores tried to stop him. "We object to that. It has nothing to do with this case."

"Overrule your objection," Judge Carter said, then explained, perhaps for the edification of an appeals court, "The reason I am going to let it in, this is money spent by the Montgomery Improvement Association and collected for the purpose of helping out with the so-called boycott. For that reason I will let it in."

"The amount wouldn't make any difference," Shores argued.

"Show how much they collected at the time," Judge Carter

advised Thetford. Then to Shores, "He said voluntary contributions were given for the purpose of aiding the boycott."

Shores continued, "We concede money was collected and put in the account."

Thetford spoke up. "We would like to know the amount."

"This is fishing," Shores complained.

Overruled.

Thetford turned to Dr. King. "Do you know?"

"No, I don't know."

"I believe that you have stated that the Montgomery Improvement Association is being run on a budget of about $3,000 a week."

"Approximately that."

Thetford kept jabbing. "The Montgomery Improvement Association is spending approximately $400 a day?"

"I wouldn't say that exactly, but it might be in that area."

"And whatever is being spent by the Montgomery Improvement Association, so far as you know, is being spent for the continuance of the protest or boycott?" In other words, this was the only project the MIA was supporting.

Dr. King demonstrated his rhetorical footwork. "Well, I don't know exactly what you mean by the continuance of it. When you say continuance, I don't exactly know."

The solicitor ended his cross-examination without delivering the knockout punch. Dr. King had walked a fine line. He hadn't distanced himself from the MIA while providing precise, highly legalistic nonresponses to direct questions about his role. And with that, the defense ended its presentation. Dr. King stepped down.

The spectators began applauding—but Judge Carter instantly gaveled them quiet.

That was not the end of the trial. The state began presenting its rebuttal evidence, its response to the defense case. Thetford began by putting another bus driver, Joseph B. Sadler, on the stand. He had been driving for the company for twenty years, he said, the last ten of them on predominantly Black routes. Thetford showed him the diagram showing a bus interior and asked him to explain the seating policy. While every public transportation company throughout the South adhered to segregation, the way that was enforced differed from city to city. There were no uniform rules or regulations, just local policies that kept the races separated; on buses Black passengers were relegated to the back, on the trains Blacks sat in the first car closest to the noise and dirt from the engine. "Do you reserve seats on Montgomery City Lines buses for Negroes?" They do. Pointing at the diagram, the solicitor asked, "What seats are reserved for Negroes?"

It wasn't exactly a black-and-white answer: "There is a question there. The rear section of ten seats is reserved for them; at all times it is reserved for them."

"Now, is there a section reserved for white people?"

"...this front section up here.... Twelve in that section."

"What happens in the center?"

"In the center we try to follow the City Ordinance which reads colored to sit from the rear forward, whites will sit forward toward the rear, and wherever the meeting line is, is where they will stop at. Now, you understand that leaves the responsibility on the bus driver. I will try to make this plain, if I can: We allow them to sit in that section... Now, in the case they are standing we allow them to sit first come, first served until the bus is filled up to here..." He tapped a spot in the middle of the diagram. "That varies. It would be here, or would be there, or would be up here..."

There was no firm policy, he admitted, and then continued to explain that policy.

"...It is every driver's responsibility to allow them to sit until they have filled up this section wherever it might be. We allow colored persons in these seats and white persons in these seats."

But, he added, "We don't allow colored persons to sit forward. That would be breaking the law… That has been the custom for the full twenty years I have been here."

"During the past ten years as a bus driver, have you, or not, ever requested colored people move to the back of the bus?"

"Yes, sir," Sadler said. Rather than clearing up any confusion about the policy, his explanation confirmed it was entirely at the driver's discretion: "When the seating would begin at any particular end of the line—the Day Street line was predominantly colored; the same bus goes through to Highland Avenue, which is predominantly white—the colored passengers have filled it plumb to this line here…when you get to the Bell Building on Lee Street quite a number of colored will leave, and sometimes the front seats are still occupied. We don't ask them to move back unless there is room up here for whites. When the whites begin to get on sometimes we find one or two still up there with ten or fifteen seats back yonder, and all the seats up here are filled with white people, so the whites won't have to be standing then we ask them to kindly take their seats back."

Kindly? There was light snickering from the spectators.

"Have you ever asked or requested white people to move from their seats?" As incredible as it seems, it appeared the solicitor was trying to make the argument that the law was applied equally to both races.

He had moved white people, the bus driver claimed; or more specifically, a white person. "I couldn't name the specific date, but it has been five or six years ago, I had one to refuse to move and I asked him either to get off or I would have to call the police if he sat back, because he was sitting back when there were enough seats in front of him for colored to fill up behind him."

And he had never referred to colored passengers as "black apes," or "black cows," or anything of that nature. He had never sworn at them or cursed them. But he had been reported to the bus company "for showing favoritism to colored passengers…by white people."

Lawyer Billingsley began his cross-examination by asking Sadler if he was a member of the White Citizens Council of Montgomery. He was not, he said. Then Billingsley referred to the diagram. "I believe you testified on direct examination that one end has reserved seats here for whites and reserved seats in the rear for Negroes…and if there was any moving done the white people would move to the rear instead of the Negroes moving to the front… I believe you said that complies with the law."

His response was chillingly accurate. "With *our* law."

Billingsley didn't flinch. "Will you explain to the court what you mean by that, by that statement."

The driver explained it as if this were some kind of natural law, handed down through generations, rather than an effort to segregate races made by white men. "Well, if all these ten white seats up front are filled and no more white seats are needed, then if there is room forward back of the white seats the colored are permitted to seat right on up."

Billingsley asked for a clarification. "Are you saying the law says ten seats?"

No. "I am not saying what the law says. That is our instruction."

It was an astonishing claim: the bus company was making its own regulations that may or may not have been consistent with the city and state laws. Billingsley asked him, what were those instructions?

"To reserve a section in the rear for colored and reserve a section in the front for whites." When other people got on the bus, they could take seats in the middle, first come, first served. Where had those instructions come from? "Our superintendent."

Driver Sadler was still working for the company, although on a different route since the boycott began. "Are there Negroes riding your bus?" he was asked.

"No regular Negroes." Since he had been covering that route, he had averaged about thirty-three people. Did any of them have to stand? "No, because we didn't have any colored on."

That interested Billingsley. "Ten seats were not reserved?"

They were not, "Because no colored person occupied them."

So, "If one colored person got on he would have ten seats reserved?"

"Ten seats cleared."

"Suppose a Negro took a seat in the rear of the center...would you ask a white man to get up out of this seat if he was sitting here?... A hypothetical case." He pointed at a seat in the middle of the bus.

Sadler confused his instructions and the law, replying, "If a colored person gets on that colored person goes to the rear because that is the law, I say to you."

"Assuming all these seats (in the rear) are filled, he has to stand then?"

Incredibly, the driver replied, "If these seats are filled with white people and a colored person gets on the white people have to stand."

That was hard to believe. "All of them (the white people) have to stand."

"Yes."

Switching subjects, Billingsley wondered, "Have you ever called a Negro a 'n——r'?"

"No."

"Do you know Mrs. Henrietta Brinson?" He did not, he said. Nor had he ever had any "unpleasantness" or "difficulty" with Black passengers. At Billingsley's request, Judge Carter gave him permission to bring Mrs. Brinson into the courtroom. While cameras were not permitted to record the scene, young artist Harvey Dinnerstein captured her. Henrietta Brinson was a plain-looking middle-aged woman, wearing a cardigan sweater over a simple dress, a woman of average size but with sparkling eyes. She stood quietly, arms crossed, looking dispassionately at the witness. She didn't say a word.

"Do you recognize this woman?" Billingsley asked.

"Yes."

"Did you at any time refer to her as a 'n——r'?"

"No." He became defensive, adding, "I want to say that she has only been asked to take a seat back, something like that, and I never had any difficulty with her, and I never referred to her as a 'n——r.'"

Okay then, "How do you refer to Negroes?"

"Colored people."

"What do you say?" Billingsley asked. "'Colored, get back'?"

"I said, 'Colored, kindly take the seats back,' or in the rear..." Kindly?

"Suppose a Negro boarded the bus you knew by name, how do you refer to him?"

"Call him by his name, 'Willie,' 'John,' 'Pete.'... I have never called any of them 'n——s,'" he insisted. He was always polite, he always spoke to them kindly. The spectators listened silently, without doubt comparing that testimony to their own experiences. Sadler continued, "When I get to know a colored man, I call him by his given name."

Billingsley did not say it, but it was clear in his next question that he wondered, with such polite treatment, "Why do you think the Negroes stopped riding the buses?"

Sadler didn't know. "I haven't any idea," he said. But according to his best judgment, "The colored people will always kick about the buses." Asked to explain that, he defended himself. "I conducted myself to gain the respect of the better type of people, and if any difficulties ever come up on the bus I have had colored people speak up and say, 'Mr. Sadler is a man who treats us right, he is all right, and you do what is right and don't argue about it.' I have had them speak that way more than one time."

In those few words, Sadler accurately described the mindset of the white population of the city toward the Black community. Negroes were "treated right." They were not entitled to equality but rather they were treated right, as defined by the white establishment. Similar words might have been spoken in Montgomery a century earlier, before the Civil War.

Billingsley's composure never wavered. "You stated you have been reported to the bus company by white people?"

Sadler explained, "...I was called into the office. I was running Day Street and Cloverdale... It was about seven forty-five and it was heavily loaded with colored people... Going down Hull Street I had stopped for an old colored woman...so she wouldn't have to wait for the regular bus because it was thirty minutes between buses. I wouldn't pass her up, she rode with me regular and I knew her. And the colored people were already standing up to the last seat reserved for them, and just had to stand in the aisle alongside of the whites that were seated... This one white lady got up and told me I was standing colored people in front of her, and I was called in the office about it."

Billingsley homed in with his last few questions. "Have you ever had an occasion to have a number of Negroes on the bus, some of them were standing and there were no white people at all on the bus?"

"We don't allow them to sit down in the areas where we are liable to pick up white... When I was running Day Street, until I reached Mobile Street, if colored people wanted to sit down, I never suggested they sit down, I didn't tell them not to sit down or ask them to move."

"And suppose a white person got on in a Negro area?"

"I tell them I had to have a seat for him."

"Just what would you say?"

"I would tell them to get up."

"Wouldn't let him stand up?"

"No."

Another bus driver, O. T. Rainwater, was the next witness. He had been driving "Ever since they first put the buses on in 1936, March the 8th." He too had never had "trouble" on his bus, and because he had always driven a predominantly Black route, to his recollection he had never asked a Black passenger to move back. "Not if there was no seat or standing room there, or would be packed full, I never asked them." Although, "a few times" he had asked white people to move up when they were sitting in the Black section.

And no, he had never called anyone a derogatory term.

C. H. Williams had been driving for City Lines for two decades, mostly on a white route. He testified he had never asked Negro passengers to move to the back of the bus—unless there was a seat available for them, while he had asked white people to move up "Quite a lot of times." And "never in my life" had he referred to a Black passenger by an insulting name.

In his cross-examination, Billingsley took on a somewhat disbelieving, derisive tone about the benign portrait the solicitor was trying to paint with these witnesses. The drivers were nice, they were benevolent and courteous. In fact, he asked, "You were very kind, you say, to Negro passengers?"

"Yes, sir."

"You didn't speak to them in a rough tone of voice, did you?"

"So far as I know, that is right."

"Didn't find it necessary to have any Negroes arrested?"

"No, sir."

"You knew how to get along with Negroes, did you?"

"That is right."

Driver W. H. Mills told Thetford that he had been assigned a "most of it is colored" route for the last decade. And "On account of the heavy riding on the Washington Park route we let them (Black passengers) occupy all of the seats except the ten seats up (front) for white people."

"When you are on Court Street," he was asked, "that was predominantly white, wasn't it?"

He replied casually, "Early in the morning you had lots of n——s, or colored people, going out there. In fact, I was running it back, must have been seven or eight years ago didn't have as many working out there as they do now."

Oblivious to the word Mills had just used in his previous answer, Thetford asked, "Did you ever use any of this language?"

Never "black cows" or "black apes"? No, he wasn't raised that way.

"Have you ever cursed or used profanity?"

"No, sir."

"Or had any trouble with them?"

"Never have."

C. E. Mosley, who also had been driving for twenty years, never referred to any passengers in derogatory terms and "never had no trouble" on his bus. Peter Hall took charge of the brief cross-examination. "Have you on occasions had a number of colored people and all the seats occupied with colored persons standing in the aisle and the first ten seats vacant?"

"I have had that," Mosley acknowledged, as if it was perfectly normal.

"You have had a bus that was completely filled up with colored people?"

"In their section, yes."

Hall repeated this to make his point. "In their section they were sitting...and those who couldn't get a seat were standing... and there were no white persons in the first ten seats?"

"That is right, in the first section." He explained, "In other words, we have to have a white section there for the white passengers that get on the bus." And sometimes there were white passengers, he continued.

And sometimes there were not, Hall said. It didn't matter. "If no white persons were on your bus you would have those seats vacant, wouldn't you?"

"That is right." Even if people were standing in the rear? "That is right."

O. O. Martin, who had been driving twenty years, had been president of the bus drivers' union "during the war," he pointed out. Normally he drove a route that in the morning was "one way predominantly colored and the other way predominantly white." In the afternoon it would be reversed because, he told the solicitor, "In the morning maids would be going to Cloverdale to work and in the afternoons coming back home." Martin testified that he had asked Black passengers to move back or change a seat, but only if there were "enough seats and whites standing." He also did the same for white passengers, asking them "to move in order to give seats to colored passengers."

Martin went further than that, he said. "When I was on Cleveland Avenue coming to town every morning and an understanding with the passengers as they got on they were privileged to take all the seats provided they would get up without making me ask them and give them up to a white person."

"In other words," Thetford emphasized, "you just ignored your company rulings; is that what you are telling us?"

"Yes, sir, that is what it was." He would grant them the privilege of sitting in the front of the bus as long as they understood their place, he repeated, "and they were very cooperative."

And no, he had never called any person, white or Black, an insulting name, and the only trouble he remembered having was with an older drunk white lady who "was knocking colored people." But she got off the bus without being asked to leave.

In his cross-examination, Peter Hall asked Martin approximately how many drivers were in the union. Approximately ninety, Martin guessed, and yes, all of them were white. And no, he had never asked a Negro sitting in the middle section to

give up his seat to a white person "if there was no vacant seat…
not my practice." He went even further than that, allowing Negroes to sit in the front ten seats. "In case of an old person, or
one that was carrying a lot of things, and the back of the bus
was filled up and nobody else would…give her a seat. Then I
would let her sit there until she reached her destination."

As it turned out, Martin's route was the same route on which
Rosa Parks had been arrested, although, as he said, "I wasn't involved in that. I cannot give that information so I couldn't answer that question." He knew of the situation "Only through
rumors and what I have seen in the paper."

"Who relieved you on the afternoon of December the 1st,
1955? Do you recall that?"

Strangely, as the identity of the driver was well-known, Martin replied, "I couldn't answer that…because we change every
three months."

City Lines manager and superintendent James Bagley was
recalled. Bagley had been involved in this since the first meeting at city hall, when Dr. King explained that the boycott had
been precipitated by the arrest of Rosa Parks, but that it actually was the culmination of years of "injustices and indignities."
Mr. Bagley had not responded to that. Now he was testifying
once again for the prosecution, claiming the company fired employees when they were discourteous or abused passengers. The
company had an average of ninety employees, he told Thetford.
During the previous ten years, thirty-eight of them had been
"discharged," some of them fired, some of them permitted to
resign. Twenty-one of them had been discharged after "abus-
ing" passengers, although he offered no details about specific
incidents.

Peter Hall wondered if any of the "ninety-three or ninety-
four" drivers regularly employed by City Lines, "Were any of
those drivers Negroes?"

"They were not."

"They were all white?"

"They were."

Hall was asking about the third of the original requests. "Does your company have a policy of not employing Negro drivers?"

"It don't," Bagley claimed.

Then, he wondered, "Why do you only hire white drivers?"

"Because the company leaves it to the transportation superintendent of properties to hire anyone he feels like would qualify for doing the work we have for him to do." It's not my decision, Bagley wanted it known.

"So," Hall summed up, "your company has no objection to the employment of Negro drivers at all; is that true?"

Earlier in the trial, it had been the Black passengers who navigated around the truth without directly committing perjury. Now it was the white drivers who had to carefully maneuver about questions without giving direct answers. Bagley had talked himself into a corner. "They have never told me not to," Bagley said.

Hall knotted together this testimony with the original requests. "So then the fact as you have testified here, when you met with the delegation of Negroes, do you recall your first meeting with the Negro delegation up on Decatur Street..."

Thetford jumped in to protect his witness, objecting "to this line of questioning. This is not relating to anything he testified to in rebuttal."

Carter overruled him, and Hall continued, "Was it at this meeting that you first were presented with the request that Montgomery Negroes have more courtesy, and the arrangement of seating be different from the one you had at that time and for the employment of Negro drivers on buses that served predominantly Negro areas?"

Bagley desperately tried to avoid answering that question. "Was that the first I had been approached about that?... In order to separate the requests, I had a number of requests that you now make before that meeting—but not all of the requests that you now make were made then." He did admit, though, "At the city hall we did hear the three requests that I stated here before."

"You were the spokesman for the bus company?" He was. And "you were in a position to grant the requests for employment of Negro bus drivers, weren't you? Did you object to that request?"

"Ask that again."

He did.

"At the time it was made?" Bagley asked. Yes. He objected to the question. "I didn't state that I had no objections to hiring anybody."

"Well, let's see," Hall mused. "You just testified a few minutes ago your company has no policy of employment of bus drivers predicated on race; as I understand it, that was the substance of what your testimony was. Your company would employ anybody as drivers depending on their ability to drive. If that is true, when you met with the Negro delegation...you as superintendent of the bus company had no objection to the request of employment of Negro drivers, did you?"

"I haven't said."

Okay, did you or did you not? Hall was pressing him now.

"I said I had a right to employ anyone that I would think would qualify to do the job." He wouldn't hire Negro drivers, he continued, if they couldn't qualify. And if they could? Bagley flailed about, trying to not answer the question. "At such times as, understand, they are employed in other positions over the city. Then I would have no personal objection, if they are employed in other places." Basically, he appeared to be saying, when Montgomery was no longer segregated he would consider it. "It has never been the custom here to employ colored drivers, and we have never had a colored person make application to me for a bus driving job."

Then Hall said, moving to the logical conclusion, "Then the

fact is your policy for the past twenty years has been not to employ Negro drivers?"

"Not to employ anyone who don't qualify to drive a bus."

The conversation was turning nasty. "And in your opinion no Negroes could qualify, is that it?"

Bagley repeated, "I haven't had any applications from any colored people."

Thetford tried to stop this debate, objecting to Peter Hall "arguing with the witness."

Hall pleaded innocence, explaining, "We would like to know from you, did you object to the request made at the meeting of guaranteeing…more courtesy from the bus drivers?"

"I didn't object to them asking for courtesy." At that meeting did he object to a request for a first come, first served seating policy? "I had to…we couldn't do it and live within the law that we are required to operate under."

Hall asked Bagley to "tell us specifically which laws" he was citing. It was a simple question that Bagley could not answer. He didn't know, exactly. "I couldn't name where you could find them. Anything I do is the way our attorneys would interpret the law, and I would operate under the city ordinance, not interpret it. I couldn't interpret the law, but I would operate under it the way it was interpreted for us."

Bagley had been put in the middle of a situation he had no power to change. He was, he said in essence, only following orders. It was not his job to understand or interpret those laws, just follow them as directed by other people.

Peter Hall pressed him even harder. "Then I understand the answer you made…was the opinion of the legal adviser that the city law and the state law—I am just trying to understand what you said…prohibited you from meeting the requests of the Negro citizens as to the seating arrangements; is that right?"

"I cannot say whether or not it was either or both. It was his advice I couldn't meet the demands under the law."

DAN ABRAMS AND FRED GRAY WITH DAVID FISHER

Which attorney? Your attorney? The attorneys for the city? The bus company's attorneys?

"My attorney advised me it was his and the city attorneys' opinion. The city attorneys didn't let me know their opinion."

Hall established in his next few questions that the company owning and operating the bus lines in Montgomery also owned and operated the buses in the city of Mobile, Alabama.

Thetford saw where this was going and objected, trying to stop it. Judge Carter let Hall continue.

Bagley admitted he was familiar with the operation of Mobile's bus lines. "Isn't it a fact," Hall asked, "that (in Mobile) Negroes seat from the rear toward the front and whites from the front to the rear and no seats reserved on the bus?... Isn't that what the Negroes of Montgomery asked of the Montgomery bus line?"

"They asked for it," Bagley had to admit.

"Isn't Mobile a city situated in the state of Alabama?"

"I cannot testify what they would do in Mobile, or what they can do, but I know what we can do in Montgomery."

"You do know that the state law would bind every city in Alabama equally as much, don't you?"

"I wouldn't know that," Bagley insisted. "I am not a lawyer and I cannot argue any point of law."

Peter Hall reviewed that initial meeting at city hall. "At that time," he asked, "did you know the Mobile bus line was operating on a first come, first served basis...?"

"I didn't know it at the time of that meeting." And now, "That it wouldn't have been possible (in Montgomery) under the law."

Hall then began to question the witness about the current situation, asking, "Have Negroes been riding your buses since December 5th, 1955?"

"A very few," he replied—not mentioning that the woman who worked for his family actually had been one of the few Black people who had continued to use the buses during the boycott—after boarding the bus through the rear door she would sit on the floorboard so no one could see her, a practice that was secretly continuing as he testified, and was not revealed for decades.

The point Hall was trying to make was that the boycott was entirely voluntary. "Have your lines been picketed, have you seen anybody carrying signs picketing your lines or your buses... Have you seen anyone physically restrained from riding..."

He admitted, "As far as I know, the people can ride the buses if they want to."

"Has anybody threatened anyone if they don't accept the demands, made any threats to the bus company...made any threats to you as representing the bus company?"

"They haven't," he said, which apparently was not true. Years later, it would be revealed that he had received several threats, both by phone and mail. After Dr. King's house was bombed, for example, he was warned there would be retaliation and his family lived with that fear.

Hall finally began questioning Bagley about the situation leading up to the boycott, suggesting the company had received "numerous complaints" about the conditions on the buses before December 5. Bagley disagreed. "I wouldn't say it was numerous. The complaints that you could expect to receive when you haul as many as twenty-one million people in a year...we have had complaints all through the operation...the normal complaints have always been running... I would say the last two years it has been nearly all seating."

They responded to those complaints, he said, "In all the meetings we would tell the men to be fair with all the people when asking them to move. And I had numerous meetings with the personnel and stressed on them the company's policy as to courtesy to all passengers..." Even with that, though, he admitted, he had received "a number of complaints" that drivers were not courteous to Black passengers.

Finally, Hall once again tried to get a witness to testify about the bus company regulations on seating. There seemed to be no uniform application of the rules; bus drivers appeared to move people around based on their own code. Sometimes Black passengers were permitted to stand in white sections or even, in unusual conditions, sit down. Other drivers restricted them to the rear and some seats in the middle of the bus. It seemed haphazard, confusing, sometimes flexible. "Did you not get a report and check on what happened very recently when a person was removed from the bus, placed under arrest and prosecuted?" When Bagley didn't recall that incident, Hall reminded him, "You made such a report in this court a day or two ago pertaining to one Rosa Parks?"

"I don't recall it stating where she was sitting."

"Claudette Colvin? The report said she was seated in the middle...and she refused to get up when she was requested to get up, and the driver had her removed and arrested."

"That is true."

"That would be contrary to company policy?"

"It depends," Bagley equivocated, "on whether there were vacant seats available. We have asked white and colored to move if there is vacant seats for the whites forward or the colored back behind...it wasn't the company's policy if there were no vacant seats."

As Hall ended this cross-examination, the witness testified that the bus company's policies in regard to seating and hiring had not been changed in the last decade—even after numerous complaints. With that, at 1:30 in the afternoon, the State of Alabama rested.

As it turned out, the end was only the beginning.

CHAPTER FIFTEEN

As the closing arguments began, the journalists took an informal poll among themselves. By a three-to-one margin, they voted that the defense had presented the stronger case—but, understanding reality, they also voted five-to-one that Dr. King would be convicted.

It was Martin Luther King, Solicitor Thetford exclaimed in his summation, Dr. King and sixteen or eighteen other "Negro leaders" who had promoted the boycott through "hysterias built up at mass meetings...to gain personal power and influence." The law was clear and unambiguous, he continued. An organized boycott was illegal and Dr. King had broken the laws of the state of Alabama by "engaging in a conspiracy to hinder and prevent the operation of the bus company without just or legal cause." And no matter what Dr. King said, he was directly responsible for the attacks on the city buses. As evidence of that, he reminded Judge Carter, the Montgomery Improvement Association, of which Dr. King was president, had spent more than $30,000 for the sole purpose of keeping the bus boycott alive.

And, he warned, if these leaders were permitted to get away with this attack on the law and tradition, well, there was no way of telling where it would stop. His argument was that the boycott was illegal and Dr. King had to be convicted.

Arthur Shores and Fred Gray gave the summation for the defense. While Shores was the far more senior of the two, Gray had been there at the beginning, even before Rosa Parks had been arrested. He was there when the MIA was formed, when the protest began, and from the beginning on December 1, he had provided legal advice and protection to the protesters. He had drafted the Resolutions that were the key point of contention and, finally, organized and participated in Dr. King's defense.

Shores and Gray insisted that witness testimony had proved the Black population of the city had "just cause" to protest the buses, which made the boycott legal under the statute. Rather than Dr. King being the leader of the boycott, Shores contended, he had been drafted by the Black leadership to be their spokesman. And contrary to the solicitor's claims, "Dr. King didn't volunteer to be a rabble-rousing crusader, as the state attorneys have presented him."

Rather than making an impassioned plea about the morality of segregation, a system that guaranteed less than equal treatment based on skin color, Fred Gray reviewed the legal arguments in his respectful courtroom style. He argued the law, not justice; he argued that Dr. King and the Black community had not violated the law in seeking justice. Black bus passengers had complained about being mistreated for more than a decade, he told the judge, drawing on specific testimony, and the bus company had ignored them. While the bus company claimed it had to follow state law, in fact Alabama law mandated no such seating policy, as had been proved by the fact that in Mobile the same bus company previously had adopted the seating policy requested by the MIA. In addition to that, "just cause" provided "legal excuse" mentioned in the statute.

Generally in a bench trial, after hearing all the evidence and arguments, the judge will return to his chambers to review the record and make his decision. Whether it is necessary or not, it at least provides the appearance of deliberative justice. But Judge Carter delivered his decision from the bench almost immediately. "The Court is of the opinion the defendant is guilty of the illegal boycott, and I find him guilty and fix his fine at $500."

He added an additional $500 in court costs. The judge added that while he had little doubt about Dr. King's guilt, he was levying a fine substantially lower than the maximum of $1,000 and six months in jail because the defendant had "discouraged violence."

"Once again, we were neither surprised nor discouraged by this verdict," Gray recalls. "Actually, we were happy the trial had gone as well as it did. Our witnesses had done very well in telling their stories to the whole country. Dr. King had done well protecting himself. On some level, we felt we had won, because our people recognized that this decision was not consistent with the law. Whatever this trial had started out to be, it had become a significant moment in our legal attack on unconstitutional laws. And we were more certain than ever that eventually we were going to win. In addition, the trial had allowed the media to bring considerable attention to the protest and had put Dr. King on front pages throughout the world."

The defense immediately announced its intention to appeal. Judge Carter suspended payment of the fine pending the appeal. Because the defendant chose not to pay the fine immediately and to appeal instead, it technically was converted into a jail sentence of 386 days—but that too was suspended. Solicitor Thetford told the court that he had agreed with the defense lawyers that, pending the outcome of that appeal, all of the other boycott cases would be "continued," or put off until there was a final decision. An appeal, Shores estimated later, that could take as long as three years before it was heard by the Alabama Court of Appeals.

Perhaps surprisingly, Judge Carter supported that agreement. "I think that is fair," he said. "They have a perfect right to take this appeal to the Supreme Court to find out if my ruling is right or wrong, and on account of the many witnesses, the amount of time and all, I believe that is perhaps the better procedure." Left unsaid in these seeming accommodations and niceties from the judge and prosecutor was the fact that bringing the eighty-eight additional people to trial would be an enormous burden on the city, and immediately jailing King would have been an enormous risk. Montgomery's Black community was prepared for the verdict, but not for seeing their leader hauled off to jail for organizing a protest.

As soon as Carter left the bench, journalists gathered around Dr. King, who told them, "I was optimistic enough to hope for the best but realistic enough to prepare for the worst. This will not mar or diminish in any way my interest in the protest. We will continue to protest in the same spirit of nonviolence and passive resistance, using the weapon of love."

A boisterous crowd of more than three hundred people was waiting for Martin Luther King and Coretta King as they left the courthouse. Those people seemed far more celebratory than upset. As television cameras and photojournalists recorded the scene, they surrounded the smiling Martin and Coretta King, chanting, "Long Live the King," "Behold the King," and sang "We Ain't Gonna Ride the Buses No More." When they quieted, Ralph Abernathy shouted, "Don't forget the mass prayer meeting tonight. You gonna be there?"

The crowd roared its approval.

Someone in the crowd yelled, "You gonna ride the buses?"

The crowd, as one, responded, "No!"

That night, about three thousand people attended the mass meeting at the Holt Street Baptist Church. Additional meetings

AP PHOTO/GENE HERRICK

Outside the courthouse after the verdict was announced, Dr. King and Coretta King jubilantly joined supporters—including Fred Gray to their left—to celebrate the fact that their local protest had been transformed into a national movement.

took place at other churches to satisfy the overflow crowds, and the main speakers, Dr. King, Reverend Abernathy and several others, visited each of them and repeated their statements. As usual, loudspeakers were set up outside the Holt Street church to make sure everyone could hear the proceedings. Martin Luther King had been convicted and, in the process, had been anointed a leader, soon to be *the* leader, of the new civil rights movement. He was introduced by Baptist layman W. C. Lee, who said, "Here is the man who today was nailed to the cross for you and me."

After being greeted by "a thunderous ovation," according to the *Advertiser*, Dr. King told them, "Freedom doesn't come on a silver platter. Some of the things we have to go through are a necessary part of our campaign. There can never be growth without growing pains... This conviction and all the convictions they can heap on me will not diminish my determination one iota… The protest will continue no matter how many times they convict me… God is using Montgomery as his proving ground, and maybe here in the cradle of the Confederacy the idea of freedom in the southland will be born…

"And let us not lose faith in democracy. For with all its weaknesses, there is a ground and a basis for hope in our democratic creed."

And, perhaps symbolic of the city's desire to put this trial behind them as quickly as possible, none of the local papers reported any comments from Solicitor Thetford or his assistants. In fact, even *Advertiser* columnist Joe Azbell, who had reported and commented extensively throughout the trial, did not write a word about the verdict.

Rarely had the losing side in a trial gained so much. Usually, a victory in a courtroom carried with it some significant benefits to the winning side. Not in this case. Dr. King had been convicted, but he had walked out of the courthouse a free man without having paid a fine. The actual impact of the trial appeared on the front page of the *New York Times* the following morning: a story headlined "Negro Minister Convicted of Directing Bus Boycott." The fact that this story made front-page news in America's most respected newspaper far outweighed any benefits of a conviction.

And rather than ending the boycott, as the *Times* reported a day later, "Conviction Spurs Negro Boycott: Action Against Minister Only Adds to Grievances in Dispute on Buses." According to this story, the buses remained empty while the car pool continued transporting as many as forty thousand people each day. "The only change," wrote reporter Wayne Phillips, "was the increased determination of the Negroes."

In fact, the conviction proved to be incredibly damaging for proponents of segregation. In New York two days later, for example, minister and congressman Adam Clayton Powell Jr. urged the almost ten thousand people jammed into Harlem's Abyssinian

Baptist Church to join in "massive public resistance to everything that's wrong... Montgomery, Alabama, is an example of what Christian men, marching together, can accomplish... Montgomery has made a deep impression."

Contributions to support the boycott increased. The *Asbury Park Press*, announcing a fundraising campaign to pay Dr. King's fine and court costs, called the verdict "a disgrace...which must be shared, in part, by the whole country." People made their voices heard in any way possible. For example, a New Jersey business owner made public the telegram he sent to Judge Carter. "Have cancelled plans for building in Alabama," he wrote, "150,000 sq ft manufacturing space upon the conviction of Rev Martin Luther King Jr."

The *Alabama Tribune* summed up the trial in its editorial: "The Negroes of Montgomery have started something that will not be stopped by the conviction of the Reverend Martin Luther King... It is difficult to see how that process can do anything but hurt the segregationists' cause. For even eventual upholding of this conviction—which is by no means certain—would not kill the idea of nonviolent use of economic power."

On the Sunday after the verdict, Dr. King flew to New York, where he was "given a hero's welcome" by an interracial audience of 2,500 people at Brooklyn's Concord Baptist Church. It was reported that the crowd "laughed and wept, cheered and prayed" and took up a collection "in wastebaskets, cake boxes, cartons, cooking utensils and other containers," raising thousands of dollars. That same Sunday morning at New York's St. John the Divine Cathedral, Dr. King was praised as "a Christian minister who, like his Lord, is now a convicted criminal."

Speaking to ten thousand people who had turned out to see this new leader in person, King likened the movement to the Jewish exodus from Egypt, saying that a new "Red Sea was opened and the forces of justice marched through to the other side."

Fred Gray never had high hopes for an acquittal and had long believed that the legal end of segregation would come from the federal courts. So while Dr. King, Rosa Parks, E. D. Nixon and Ralph Abernathy, among others, traveled around the country raising awareness and funds, he continued preparing for the May 11 *Browder v. Gayle* hearing in district court, as well as for his June 17 wedding.

Gray was proved right as the legal cracks in segregation began to fissure. The fight to end segregation on public transportation scored a major victory in late April, just over a month after the King verdict, when the Supreme Court essentially overturned *Plessy v. Ferguson*, the 1896 South Carolina case that legalized separate but equal facilities. In June 1954, a Black Columbia, South Carolina, resident named Sarah Mae Flemming was ordered by a bus driver to give up the vacant seat she had taken in the white section of the bus. She was so humiliated she signaled to get off the bus. When she tried to exit through the front door, the driver blocked her, demanding she use the rear door. She persisted, and he punched her in the stomach. With the assistance of a local white attorney, Flemming sued, claiming her Fourteenth Amendment rights had been violated and asking for a monumental $25,000 in damages.

A federal district court dismissed the case, but the federal court of appeals reversed that decision, citing *Brown v. Board of Education* in ruling that the doctrine of separate but equal "can no longer be regarded as a correct statement of the law." Among Flemming's lawyers were Thurgood Marshall and Robert Carter.

The verdict was appealed to the Supreme Court, which unanimously refused to hear the case; the outcome was so certain, the court ruled, that it "needlessly consumed our time."

While the ruling seemed clear, separate but equal facilities were unconstitutional, there was some ambiguity about exactly what the court had ruled by not actually ruling. Regardless, the application of the decision would be confusing. The City Lines bus company, from its corporate headquarters in Chicago, ordered its drivers to immediately "discontinue the practice of segregation of passengers on account of race." But before that edict could take effect, Alabama state officials insisted that ruling applied only to South Carolina and "We expect the bus company...to abide by all existing laws and ordinances." Police commissioner Clyde Sellers warned that bus drivers permitting passengers "mixing with the opposite race" would be arrested, as would those passengers.

Reverend King told reporters that the boycott would continue until there was a firm resolution and the buses were completely integrated. Solicitor Thetford issued a statement that this decision would not affect Dr. King's conviction, as that case was not about segregation but rather the violation of the statute prohibiting organized boycotts.

Legal segregation was under attack everywhere in the country when Fred Gray and Charles Langford, the only two Black attorneys in Montgomery, stated their case in front of the District Court for the Middle District of Alabama on May 11. This was an evidentiary hearing, a sort of mini trial in which witnesses are heard under oath and evidence is presented, but the strict procedures of a courtroom are more relaxed. At the end of the actual hearing, no verdict is given, rather the judge or judges take the materials presented under advisement and eventually issue a ruling. It was in a federal courtroom, Dr. King believed, that "The Southern Negro...has an honest chance of justice before the law."

Fred Gray does not remember being nervous that day, believing he was well prepared and the law now supported his position. But he still wore his red, white and blue good-luck tie.

Ironically, two days before this hearing, Montgomery circuit court judge Walter B. Jones ordered City Lines to basically ignore the Supreme Court. City Lines officials and drivers had to continue segregating passengers on its buses or risk going to jail for contempt of court. The bus company could not rely on the Supreme Court decision, he ordered, because technically there was no Supreme Court decision. The court had not ruled on the constitutionality of segregation, he wrote; it simply had sent the case back to the lower court. Contrary to what had been initially reported, the judge ruled, in the Flemming decision the Supreme Court had not outlawed bus segregation. It merely refused to review the case because the issue of damages had not been settled. Without making any moral judgments about segregation, the judge wrote in his decision that it was necessary for public safety, claiming, "A situation of tension and unrest has been created in the City of Montgomery which is likely to explode into violence at any time if not restrained."

The court had unwittingly set the stage for Gray and Langford's direct assault on segregated public transit not only in Montgomery or Alabama, but throughout the United States. They were assisted in this effort by the same group of attorneys who had worked with them during Dr. King's trial, although this time the NAACP's Robert Carter was allowed to participate. Thurgood Marshall was added to the plaintiffs' team as an adviser. The suit charged that the state and city statutes requiring segregation on public transportation were unconstitutional, as they "deny to (Negroes) those rights, privileges and immunities as citizens of the United States and equal protection of the laws." Gray and Langford charged the defendants were harassing participants in the car pool "to obtain information for the purpose of bringing pressure upon employers...to subject them to economic reprisals." They had brought this suit, the plaintiffs wrote, "on behalf of all other Negro citizens."

The suit named the Montgomery City Commission, the police chief, two bus drivers and the Alabama Public Service Commission as defendants. It was presumed, based on the type of case and the way it was filed, that the losing side would appeal the verdict directly to the Supreme Court. With the Flemming case returned to the lower courts, this might well result in the first clear-cut decision about the continued constitutionality of separate but equal facilities in public transportation.

The courtroom was again filled mostly with Black spectators, among them Martin Luther King. This time he was an interested spectator. A three-judge panel heard the case. In prehearing filings, the Alabama Public Service Commission contended it should not be a defendant in this suit, as it had no regulatory power over the bus company. The bus company claimed it had no options, as it simply was obeying the law. And the Montgomery City Commission argued that the federal court lacked jurisdiction because the plaintiffs had been subject to municipal, local ordinances, not the required state law.

Gray and Langford and Orzell Billingsley were prepared to counter each of those arguments while proving that the plaintiffs had been denied their rights granted by the Fourteenth Amendment to the Constitution. By this point, Charles Langford, who had only reluctantly been dragged into the civil rights movement, was among the men leading the charge.

The four plaintiffs testified in the relatively brief morning session. Listening to seventy-seven-year-old Susie McDonald and sixteen-year-old Claudette Colvin, it was possible to imagine the past and visualize the future. "Miss Sue," as McDonald was fondly known, had been born in 1879, at the end of Reconstruction, when the promises of the Civil War had faded into history, and nearly two decades before the government fully legalized separate but equal societies. Although she was sufficiently light-skinned to pass as white, she found joy in telling people she was a "member of the darker race." Her entire life had been defined and marginalized by racism; she had lived through forgotten massacres of Black men and women, and sometimes children, in cities like Tulsa, Oklahoma, Elaine, Arkansas, and Rosewood, Florida; through two world wars, through lynchings and humiliation, but finally she had arrived in this court-room to help end it all.

Colvin represented the possibilities of a just future; when America would be a nation, Dr. King later prophesied, in which people would be judged not by the color of their skin but by the content of their character. A great movement was stirring, and this young woman was at the beginning of it. It was the young, optimistic people who would lead this uprising. Colvin had finally gotten her day in court, testifying that she had been "drug" off a bus by a policeman and "handcuffed to a patrol car" for refusing to give up her seat. As she testified, a spectator suddenly began sobbing and screaming, but eventually calmed down.

She told Fred Gray that at the time it happened she didn't even know what laws she was breaking. When she was told by the bus driver to surrender her seat and stand in the back, she refused. "I said I was just as good as any white person and I wasn't going to get up…and then two more policemen came in… I was crying then, I was very hurt because I didn't know white people could act like that." When she still refused to move, one of the police officers "kicked me…and so I was very pitiful…it really hurt me to see that I had to give a (white) person a seat…"

City attorney Walter Knabe asked Colvin during cross-examination if the success of the boycott had caused her to change her ideas about segregation. "No, sir," she replied. "We haven't changed our ideas. It has been in me ever since I was born."

Wasn't it Reverend King who aroused that new awareness in her? Knabe asked. "No, sir," she said. "It was in the beginning when they arrested me, when they (the Black community) seen how dirty they treated the Negro girls here, that they had begun to feel like that all the time, though some of us just didn't have the guts to stand up."

Each of the four plaintiffs testified they had been mistreated on Montgomery's buses; they had been required to give up their seat to a white person. Nineteen-year-old Mary Smith and Claudette Colvin both said they had been arrested for violating the city's segregation statutes. Smith told Knabe that she didn't even know what crime she had been convicted—and fined $5—of committing.

The partisan *Birmingham (Alabama) News* reported to its white readership, "Each testified, more or less in shrill or indignant tones… One witness, the Colvin girl, spoke in a slurring tone and sought to give extensive replies to questions." One of the judges warned her to "stop trying to make speeches."

During the cross-examination, attorneys for the state and city tried, unsuccessfully, to get the witnesses to admit that Dr. King was the instigator and leader of the boycott. Knabe suggested to Aurelia Browder that Dr. King "was the mouthpiece for the Negroes, was he not?" In response, Mrs. Browder said, "We employed King to be our mouthpiece, but we are our own leaders too." Mary Smith told him sharply, "We represent ourselves. We appointed him as our leader." And Susie McDonald later testified, "I don't know who selected who to lead us. We all spoke for ourselves." Finally, it was the teenage Colvin, in her supposedly "slurring tone," who so eloquently responded to this question. "We did select (Dr. King), quite naturally we are not going to have any ignorant person to lead us; we have to have someone who is strong enough to speak up, someone with intelligence enough, we have got to have someone who can stand up and who knows the law…it is quite natural we are not going to get up there ourselves, and some of them can't even read or write, but they knew they were being treated wrong."

Speaking of knowing the law, Knabe asked snidely, "Was attorney Gray here one of those whom you felt knew the laws?"

Colvin's answer showed her restraint. "Yes, quite naturally, he is a lawyer." Fred Gray recalls smiling inside, but managed to keep a professionally straight face.

From the beginning of the hearing, the defense sought to

prove that the boycott was never intended to be an attack on segregation, but rather a quest to modify the existing bus policy. Knabe said to the first witness, Aurelia Browder, "You did not stop (riding the buses) on account of segregation, but you stopped riding before the segregation issue was ever raised, that is correct, isn't it?"

Browder was ready for that question, saying flatly and accurately, "It is the segregation laws of Alabama that caused all of it."

When Knabe asked Susie McDonald basically the same question, suggesting she had stopped riding the buses when the boycott began, she told him, "I don't follow the others. But I reach my own judgment. I stopped because I thought it was right, and we were mistreated."

"It took enormous courage for these women to participate in this lawsuit," Gray acknowledges. "By being so public, they literally put their lives on the line. I don't know that they ever received the credit for their bravery that they had earned. As the case went through the legal system, each of them got some threats, but because Aurelia Browder was the name people knew, she became the main target. One night she received an anonymous phone call, and the caller apparently told her in somewhat vile terms what he was going to do to her. They told her they were going to bomb her house. As her son, Butler Browder, later remembered, she responded in a dignified manner. 'My room is in the front of the house, right next to the icehouse,' she said. 'You got any issues, you got them with me, not with my children. My children's room is in the back of the house.' At least twice they found bombs by her house. One time it was actual dynamite; another time it was broomsticks wrapped up like dynamite. But she just refused to be intimidated."

After the plaintiffs had finished testifying, Mayor William Gayle, "Chairman of the Board of Commissioners...in charge of the general supervision of the city," took the stand. Following the Flemming decision, he said, he had given the police department orders to continue enforcing the segregation laws. "I believe in segregation," he said with no hesitation, "and I believe in enforcing the city ordinances concerning that."

When questioned by Knabe about the potential for "disorder" if those laws should not be enforced, he parroted a warning that was spreading throughout the country as the civil rights movement took hold. The mayor defended his position. His job, he said, was to protect the public safety, and "There is a danger of bloodshed or something like that unless we strictly enforce segregation laws."

Charles Langford asked the mayor how he knew that to be true. "Have you taken a survey?"

Mayor Gayle ignored that taunt, instead claiming "reliable Negroes" had told him they wanted to use the bus system but were afraid of Negro "goon squads." Since the boycott began, he continued, there had been shootings, windows knocked out, "beating up the colored women." His own mother-in-law's cook had been "cut up and beat..."

In the back-and-forth questioning permitted in this type of legal proceeding, Knabe asked if it were true that it was "Negroes who were causing bloodshed because they objected to Negroes riding the buses?" And, he continued, making a wild assertation, "Is it or is it not true that the Negroes, most of them, wanted to ride the buses, and that a few Negro leaders had kept them from riding the buses?"

Even the mayor would not go that far, responding, "Some of them wanted to get back on the buses."

Well, Langford asked moments later, as if reading a line from a movie script intended to be delivered (sarcastic), "Do you think it will ease and help the racial situation in Montgomery by your membership and open advocacy of the policy of the White Citizens Council as opposed to any rights of the Negroes at all?"

Mayor Gayle replied defiantly, "I would not join anything that is illegal or will promote violence or anything like that...

If they started anything out of line I wouldn't be a member, but I have confidence in that organization." Oddly, the court reporter originally left the word *not* out of the transcript, and it was added later.

Langford then challenged the mayor's assertion that the boycott had spread violence, pointing out for the record that in Dr. King's trial "only two Negroes testified they had been molested... only two Negroes out of twenty thousand Negroes."

"Do you say we had no bombings either?" Gayle snapped, seemingly ignoring the fact that those attacks had been on the homes of Black leaders. But then he admitted, "The only one I know of is the one that happened to my mother-in-law's cook."

Following Mayor Gayle's testimony, Fred Gray then had the rare opportunity to question his adversary in two previous legal events: William F. Thetford took the stand, identifying himself as "The circuit solicitor of the Fifteenth Judicial Circuit of Alabama."

Gray began by confirming that Thetford had prosecuted Claudette Colvin. "All I wanted to do," he says, "is get him to admit that he had prosecuted her for refusing to give up her seat. That she had been arrested for violating laws that supposedly made segregation legal. I wanted to show that he had a very high interest in this case; he easily could have had one of his assistants prosecute, but he chose to do it himself. This was a sixteen-year-old girl. Nobody got hurt. Yet he thought it was important enough, with all the cases he had, to see that she was punished for what she did."

It had been an easy case, routine, under normal circumstances quickly forgotten. A Black teenager had been arrested for refusing to obey the existing segregation laws. But in Montgomery, Alabama, in 1956, it was hardly normal.

The plaintiffs then called C.C. "Jack" Owen, the commissioner of the state's Public Service Commission. Langford began by reading a telegram Owen had sent to the bus company's

Chicago headquarters demanding that City Lines buses follow Alabama's segregation laws. "'I hereby defy ruling handed down by the Supreme Court ordering the desegregation of public carriers... All public carriers...are hereby directed to strictly adhere to all presently existing segregation laws in our state, or suffer the consequences.'"

The embarrassed Owen claimed that he had sent that damning threatening telegram as a private citizen—but under questioning admitted he had both identified himself as president of the commission and signed it in his official role. Whatever claims Owen made, in reality he was powerless to do anything about it. The state PSC had no control over Montgomery's city buses; they did not regulate rates or supervise the carrying of passengers. In fact, the only possible power they might have would be to regulate waiting rooms—and City Lines had no waiting rooms.

The law was murky; acting as president of the Alabama PSC, Owen certainly had assumed control, but technically he did not have the authority to do that. When pushed by Langford, he admitted, "I am a firm believer in segregation, and not knowing whether or not this came under my jurisdiction, I was not going to take any chances."

Commissioner Clyde Sellers was called next. Like Mayor Gayle, he too was proud of his membership in the White Citizens Council; he had joined, he admitted, to perpetuate segregation, pointing out, "They are peaceful and legal men." During his testimony, he reiterated circuit court judge W. B. Jones's warning when ruling that the Flemming decision did not apply to Alabama; in that decision, Judge Jones had written that if segregation on public transit was ended, "violence would be the order of the day... It won't be safe on the streets." Asked why he believed that, Sellers responded that the telephone calls and letters sent to his office, "not only from Montgomery but from throughout the United States," had created that impression.

Langford asked simply, "You don't think that integration would work in Montgomery?"

Sellers didn't blink. "I do not."

In fact, Sellers said, he was not aware of any areas in which integration had been successful. Langford asked if the commissioner was familiar with army camps (including Maxwell Field), or with the local veterans hospitals, or with the post office building: all of them integrated and functioning well without the slightest violence. In fact, was he aware that the building in which this trial was being held, the courtroom in which he was testifying, was completely integrated?

Sellers defended his belief, wondering, "Don't you know what's going on in Montgomery? There is a very intense feeling." As evidence of that, he pointed out, "one of your own witnesses who was up here a while ago. The hate just went across her face as she answered questions."

After listening to the series of witnesses subtly threaten that ending segregation would rip apart the city, Judge Richard Rives had heard enough. He asked their attorneys, "Is it fair to command one man to surrender his constitutional rights, if they are his constitutional rights, in order to prevent another man from committing a crime?"

The attorneys protested that was not their intent; they simply were concerned about the effect of taking such significant actions.

In his final question to Sellers, Knabe actually contended that the segregation laws benefited Black riders, asking if, "The objection on the part of the city (to first come, first served seating) was that it might result in being an all-Negro bus or all-white bus? And the position of the city was that there must be some space reserved for each race. Is that true?"

At the direct request of one of the judges, who wanted to more fully understand how the segregated seating system worked (from how Black passengers entered the bus to how the ordinances were enforced), the bus line's assistant superintendent, Reynolds Mills, took the stand. His boss, James Bagley, could not be there, he explained, because he'd suffered a mild heart attack.

Reynolds Mills patiently explained the seating policy, which turned out to be far more flexible than generally believed. Implementation of the regulations generally were left up to the driver, who could make his own decisions. Before the boycott, the company had served fourteen different lines, with somewhat different practices on them, depending on the racial breakdown of their passengers. The seats throughout the bus were exactly the same, the springs in the seats were exactly the same, the only difference was where on the bus they were located. Mills said that, to his knowledge, no Black passenger sitting in the rear section had ever been forced to give up their seat to a white person. And there had been situations in which white people were standing while all the Black riders were seated. "It works both ways," Mills offered. When both sections were filled, people stood in the section reserved for their race. As for Black passengers boarding in the rear, well, that was done only when white people were standing in the aisle in the front, making it difficult to squeeze through them to get to the back.

Not surprisingly, Mills was evasive. Asked by Gray, "Isn't it a fact, Mr. Mills, that under no circumstances can a Negro occupy the first ten seats in any bus in the City of Montgomery," he claimed that was not true. "On some of the lines…we have had buses marked Special where they have all the seats."

Gray pointed out that there were no whites on buses designed Special, then rephrased his question. "On regular buses, that are not marked Special, under no circumstances can a Negro sit in the first ten seats?" In other words, were people separated by race, or segregated on City Lines buses.

"That is right," Mills responded, then added helpfully, "That applies to the rear too."

"But," Gray persisted, "you do know, of your own knowledge, where so many drivers have requested Negroes to get up from their seats and stand so the white people can sit, don't you?"

"In some cases, I do."

The Claudette Colvin case, for example, Gray suggested. Mills was unsure, but he seemed to remember that when she was asked to move there was a vacant seat for her. Gray then put into the record the driver's statement that there were no empty seats.

When Mills pointed out that the company had asked more white people to move seats and had ejected more white passengers from its buses for refusing to do so, Gray dismissed that, then countered by asking, "Isn't it a fact that in most instances Negroes voluntarily get up without calling the police?" It was a fact, about 80 percent of the time, Mills agreed.

Finally, under questioning from Knabe, Mills testified to the success of the boycott, estimating that buses presently were carrying three hundred to four hundred Black passengers a day compared to the thirty thousand to forty thousand fares paid prior to December 5. But he never wavered in his defense of the seating policy, explaining that in Black areas "more than three-quarters" of the seats were allotted to Black passengers, and "invariably more white people than Negroes are required to change their seats to meet special demands."

After a brief lunch break, Fred Gray joined with the NAACP's Robert Carter to present the plaintiffs' final arguments. In terse, dry legalese, they attacked the laws and traditions that had created the segregated South. They did not talk about morality or human decency; they didn't discuss right or wrong; once again, they fought on the battlefields of the law.

A fundamental question that had to be answered was whether the Supreme Court in its decision in the Flemming case had outlawed segregation. In their comments, two of the three judges, Richard T. Rives and Seybourn Lynne, said they did not believe that was the intention of the court. While the defendants agreed with that, Carter and Gray said that "in view of the Supreme Court's…other segregation decisions" the doctrine of separate but equal had been overturned in every other area and "possibly in transportation."

The two other significant legal points addressed in these arguments were whether the federal panel had jurisdiction to make any kind of ruling and whether the boycott initially had been intended to attack segregation or had it been limited to a protest against specific regulations.

It was Robert Carter who made the dramatic, direct attack on segregation. This was no longer about seats in the back of the bus, he seemed to be saying, but it was about the fight for complete equality. He cited a long list of Supreme Court decisions to claim "the doctrine of separate but equal has been so weakened as to be without any remaining legal substance…. The *Plessy v. Ferguson* doctrine has been so impaired as no longer to be the rule."

State assistant attorney general Gordon Madison responded with a fiery, impassioned defense of segregation, beginning by criticizing the Supreme Court for its decision in the *Brown* case. Previously he had proclaimed, "The people of Alabama are never going to send white children to nigra schools, and the sooner these Justice Department people understood that, the sooner we can give a quality education to everyone." But he also had been clear about his obligations: personally and privately he opposed integration, "but as a lawyer I can't say that." In his arguments that the Supreme Court had ignored the Constitution in reaching that decision, he read carefully selected excerpts from Swedish economist Gunnar Myrdal's 1944 influential study of racism, *An American Dilemma: The Negro Problem and Modern Democracy.* Then he cited long passages from Virginia senator Harry Byrd's Southern Manifesto, a document promising to defy integration in education, which had been signed by more than one hundred Southern senators and representatives. And finally he focused attention on Judge Jones's injunction preventing desegregation of the city buses.

By the conclusion of the hearing, reported the Black *Alabama Tribune*, "All of the side issues were cut away and the bare issue of segregation was left under fire."

To no one's surprise, the three-judge panel announced, "This is an important case and will be studied and deliberated." Then everyone went home to await their momentous decision.

Meanwhile, Southern segregationists were preparing to fight for their way of life. A day after this hearing concluded, a commission set up by the Mississippi legislature announced publicly it intended to hire secret agents—"including Negroes"—to check on the activities of anti-segregationists. According to reports, "the commission agreed upon secrecy because among other things 'it's possible we may want to hire a Negro' to spy upon Negro activities in Mississippi."

But it was too late. The strategy was spreading. In Tallahassee, Florida, for example, a bus boycott had been launched when two young Black Florida A&M coeds were arrested for insisting on sitting near the front of a bus. Heeding the message of Montgomery, Tallahassee city officials refused to prosecute, but the boycott had caught hold across the city. An action filed by the NAACP in Memphis, Tennessee, asked a federal court to declare state laws protecting segregation on buses unconstitutional. Similar actions were being prepared in major cities through the South.

A new American civil war had begun, but this time it was being fought in courtrooms across the nation.

CHAPTER SIXTEEN

Fred Gray and Bernice Hill were married at six o'clock on the evening of June 17, 1956. It was a joyous affair. The Protest Wedding, it was called, because in addition to honoring the union of two popular young African Americans, it celebrated the unexpected success of the movement—and Fred Gray's contribution to it. More than two thousand invitations had been printed and mailed; not enough, as it turned out, and Fred and Bernice had to retrieve them from family members and close friends and forward them to additional people who asked to be invited.

The Holt Street Baptist Church was overflowing three hours before the ceremony began. The unity of the boycott was applied to this wedding. So many people in so many ways contributed their efforts to the occasion. Fred Gray was dressed formally in a white dinner jacket and dark pants, while Bernice Hill wore a traditional wedding gown with a short train. Tom Gray served as his brother's best man. Older brother Hugh Gray, a florist, provided flowers for the ceremony and reception. Bernice's brother, Elbert Hill, was a groomsman. And Tom's daughter Karen was the young flower girl—who was halfway down the aisle before remembering she was supposed to toss the petals. Following the ceremony and dinner, the newlyweds got into Gray's 1954 two-door Ford, shifted the manual transmission into gear and set off on their honeymoon to Cleveland, where he had attended law school and another reception had been planned. They were accompanied by Gray's stepbrother Curtis Arms and his wife, Minnie.

Two days after the wedding, just after the newlyweds arrived in Cleveland, and exactly six months to the day the protest had begun, they learned that the district court had issued its decision in the *Browder* case. The court wrote, "We hold that the statutes and ordinances requiring segregation of the white and colored races on the motor buses of a common carrier of passengers in the City of Montgomery and its police jurisdiction violate the due process and equal protection of the law clauses of the Fourteenth Amendment to the Constitution of the United States."

It was a monumental victory, the equivalent of the *Brown* decision but applied to public transportation. This was the first federal civil rights case Fred Gray had won, although as he recalls, initially no one was certain exactly what rights they had won. Their excitement with the ruling was tempered by the knowledge that this would not instantly change anything. This decision would be appealed to the Supreme Court.

Coincidently, *Browder v. Gayle* also was the first major civil rights case in the career of Judge Frank Johnson Jr., who would become a major ally in the legal quest for equality. The majority decision, 2 to 1, laid out the legal case for ending segregation. The court ruled that it had jurisdiction and that the complaints were "clearly sufficient to constitute this as a class action on behalf of the four individual plaintiffs and of all other Negro citizens similarly situated." The actual ruling on segregation was a little trickier. The court agreed that "in the conduct of their private businesses, it is clear that people themselves have the liberty to select...the person with whom they will do business," but then wound its way through the circuitous legal history of the doctrine of separate but equal concept, from its beginning "prior to the adoption of the Fourteenth Amendment in the decision of a Massachusetts State Court relating to public schools" in 1849 through its repudiation in the 1954 *Brown* decision. As a result, the majority wrote, "We cannot in good conscience perform our duty as judges by blindly following *Plessy v. Ferguson*...when our study leaves us in complete agreement...that the separate but equal doctrine can no longer be safely followed as a correct statement of the law...

"In fact, we think that *Plessy v. Ferguson* has been impliedly, though not explicitly, overruled...and there is no rational basis upon which the separate but equal doctrine can be validly applied to public carrier transportation within the City of Montgomery..."

Because the court did not issue any formal order to integrate the buses, but rather asked each side for guidance how best to accomplish that, Gray told an *Advertiser* reporter on the phone from his honeymoon that "the protest will continue" until an injunction was handed down. Dr. King, declaring this "a victory for justice and democracy," agreed with Gray that the boycott was going to continue until "it becomes possible to go back on the city buses on an integrated basis."

From Cleveland, the foursome drove to San Francisco to attend the NAACP's annual convention, Gray as the representative of the Montgomery branch. At this gathering, his client and now-friend Martin Luther King, who had been just a minister of a somewhat conservative Black church in a segregated Southern city less than a year earlier, would join legendary crusader A. Philip Randolph as the featured speakers.

In his speech to the convention, Dr. King referred to his trial, telling in excess of one thousand delegates, "(M)ore than a hundred persons were indicted, including all of the members of the

DAN ABRAMS AND FRED GRAY WITH DAVID FISHER

executive board of the Improvement Association...on the basis
of an old anti-labor law of doubtful constitutionality... It was
on the basis of this law that I was convicted, and whether you
know it or not, a convicted criminal is speaking to you tonight."

Gray recalls one particularly proud moment when Dr. King
jubilantly referred to the *Browder* decision and the lawyer who
won it, telling the delegates, "(W)e discovered that the City
Commission didn't even want to work within the framework
of the present segregation law. So it was necessary for our brilliant young attorney, who is here tonight, attorney Fred Gray,
to go into the federal court with the case, and it went into the
courts, and as you know the federal court ruled the other day
that segregation in public transportation in Alabama is unconstitutional." Gray received a large ovation.

Gray was abruptly forced to return to Montgomery from San
Francisco earlier than originally planned, when his draft board,
after changing his status in retaliation for his leading the legal
charge against segregation, ordered him to appear for a preinduction physical. Weeks later, the night before he was to report for duty, General Hershey, the head of Selective Service,
ordered Gray's 4-D ministerial exemption restored. But sched-
uling him for a physical while he was on his honeymoon was
an all too routine type of petty harassment.

The protest continued through the summer and into the fall,
as white city and state officials searched desperately for some
legal way to end it. The city did not press for a ruling on Dr.
King's appeal of his conviction. Martin Luther King had quickly
become a worldwide symbol of resistance to segregation, and it
would not benefit the city to add more fuel to an already rag-
ing fire. Instead, they put pressure on local agents to cancel the
auto insurance policies on the MIA's growing fleet of station
wagons, making it illegal for them to continue transporting
passengers. That was averted at the last minute when Lloyd's of
London decided to issue the necessary policies.

In late October, city leaders finally accepted the advice of their attorneys and asked the court to enjoin the operation of the "car pool or transportation systems growing out of the bus boycott." The lawsuit contended that Dr. King, the MIA and fourteen Black churches had created "a private enterprise" that violated city and state laws by failing to obtain a license to operate a franchise and had failed to pay license fees. They went further, claiming it was a "public nuisance," that some of its drivers were not "morally qualified" to carry passengers and were not properly licensed.

It was the wily legal way to attack the boycott, presenting a strong legal argument with a significant chance the city would prevail. As Gray acknowledged, if the city had adopted this strategy months earlier, it might well have stopped the boycott before it gained the momentum that transformed it into a movement. He tried to block the suit by asking the federal court for a restraining order preventing the city from interfering with the car pool, describing it as a voluntary share-the-ride service that provided transportation without charging any fares. It was turned down. A hearing was scheduled in front of Judge Carter for November 13.

King and Gray were resigned to the outcome. The car pool, which Gray described as "the lifeline of our operation," was going to be shut down. Without transportation, the boycott would have to end; as much as people might want to, it simply was not possible for forty thousand people to walk the miles back and forth to work every day. After almost a year of dedication and hardships, the protesters had failed to change the system.

The night before the hearing, Dr. King spoke to the regularly scheduled mass meeting, telling them, "This may well be the darkest hour before the dawn...we must believe that a way will be made out of no way."

When the hearing began, the only witness Gray and Langford called was Mayor Gayle, who testified the illegal operation prevented "a comprehensive traffic survey" from being done "with this artificial transportation going on." The Negro boycott, he complained, had "destroyed a safe, economical bus system."

The city showed 16 mm film clips of the boycott in action, then put several witnesses on the stand who testified they were indirectly receiving payment for driving. The first Black witness called by the city was Dr. King, who told Knabe that he had little knowledge of the MIA's financial structure. They called a bank officer who testified the MIA had deposited almost $200,000 in his bank.

During a recess late in the morning, Gray was sitting at the attorneys' table when he heard a stirring in the rear of the courtroom. Mayor Gayle and Commissioner Sellers were summoned to a private room. Something was going on. Gray was handed a note from a local broadcast journalist named Frank McGee reading, "I need to see you immediately outside the courtroom." As he got up to meet him, AP reporter Rex Thomas gave Dr. King a news release.

Frank McGee, the local NBC reporter who would use the trial as his springboard to become a nationally respected journalist, was waiting for him. A camera was set up. McGee told Gray that he had received a wire announcing that the Supreme Court had upheld the decision in *Browder v. Gayle* and asked for a comment. As always, Gray kept his emotions under control, although he was both stunned and thrilled.

Inside the courtroom Thomas had handed Dr. King a copy of the AP report. "The United States Supreme Court today affirmed a decision of a special three-judge US District Court in declaring Alabama's state and local laws requiring segregation on buses unconstitutional. The Supreme Court acted without listening to any argument; it simply said, 'The motion to affirm is granted and the judgment is affirmed.'"

It was a stunning turn; only moments earlier King and Gray, Langford, the spectators filling the courtroom had been edging toward despair. All of the work of the past year was about to be negated. Then, in an instant, the world had changed forever. It was, Dr. King told reporters, "A glorious daybreak to end the long night of segregation."

"God almighty has spoken from Washington, DC!" shouted one of the spectators as news of the decision spread.

It had happened so quickly and the decision was so explicit that no one on either side really knew how to react. What appeared to be true, the *Advertiser* wrote the next day, was that the decision "in effect also outlawed similar segregation laws throughout the South since the ruling sets a precedent for all similar cases in the future... There is no appeal from a Supreme Court decision."

Judge Carter clearly was shaken by the Supreme Court ruling. He called a recess to read and consider it, obviously aware his power to shape events had been pulled out from under him. From being the potentially heroic defender of segregation, he had become a historical footnote. But he refused to concede; when court resumed, he granted the city a temporary injunction, ordering the protesters to "halt their car pool operations" at midnight. Two mass meetings were scheduled for that evening to explain both decisions; "to educate the people," Dr. King told reporters. Court clerk George Jones said restraining orders would be issued to the MIA, to fourteen Negro churches and twenty-seven people named in the city's action. According to the *Advertiser*, "Speaking for a battery of four Negro lawyers, Montgomery attorney Fred Gray said the decision would be appealed. Negroes who had jammed the courtroom filed silently out as Carter announced his decision."

Even after Judge Carter had granted the temporary injunction, Gray maintained his usual taciturn demeanor. While expressing pleasure with the Supreme Court's decision, he pointed out that, as Judge Carter had made clear with his ruling, there remained considerable legal work to be done. His only public comment about the historic victory at that time was that "I am very happy with this decision."

That night, mass meetings were convened at two separate churches, with the speakers appearing at both. Eight thousand people joined the celebration. Georgia Gilmore was in the middle of the celebration, recalling, "We sang 'Swing Low, Sweet Chariot' and 'This Little Light of Mine, I'm Gonna Let It Shine,' and a whole lot of others. Weary feet and weary souls were lightened. It was such a night. We didn't have to walk no more. Even before Martin Luther King Jr. got up and told us it was over, we knew it was over and we knew we had won." Celebratory crowds at both meetings cheered wildly—and many wept. The *Advertiser* reported, "They held small children in their arms as if not wanting babies to be absent from the momentous occasion."

To deal with the conflicting state and federal court decisions, the MIA's board recommended ending the boycott and the now-enjoined transportation system, but while awaiting the official order, Dr. King said, "We will continue to walk or share rides with friends." As for integrating the buses, he continued, "We must take this not as a victory over the white man but with dignity... Don't go back in the buses and push people around... We're just going to sit where there's a seat...

"We must have the courage not to hit back."

At one meeting, Dr. King later recalled, Reverend Graetz's reading of the scripture was interrupted by a huge ovation. When Ralph Abernathy was asked by a reporter if this was a little peculiar, he replied, "Yes, it is. Just as it is peculiar for people to walk in the snow and rain when there are empty buses available; just as it is peculiar for people to pray for those who persecute them; just as it is for the Southern Negro to stand up and look a white man in the face as an equal."

In reviewing the history of the boycott, the *Advertiser* highlighted Dr. King's trial, concluding, "None of the other Negroes indicated have stood trial."

Many Southern white leaders were outraged by the Supreme Court decision; PSC commissioner "Jack" Owen warned once again that segregation had to be continued "To keep down violence and bloodshed." The head of the White Citizens Council turned that into a threat, saying, "Any attempt to enforce this decision will inevitably lead to riot and bloodshed."

The owner of the city of Dothan, Alabama, bus system said angrily, "No damn Yankee has a finger in this company... There will be no race mixing on my buses."

Another bus company owner seemed unable to comprehend the magnitude of the decision, telling reporters that if Black passengers occupied all the seats when whites boarded, "I am sure the Negroes would vacate the seats in the front and move to the rear."

In response to the ruling, the local chapter of the Ku Klux Klan announced on radio that a caravan would be parading through the Black community after dark. While previously that would have aroused fear, this time people turned on their lights and stood outside to watch them pass. The newspaper reported, "About forty carloads of robed and hooded Ku Klux Klan members toured Negro neighborhoods...blowing horns and shining floodlights into homes...

"Police captain H. E. Jackson reported no steps were being taken since no complaints were received." Suddenly, these "night riders" weren't able to terrorize urban Black residents.

The federal order, it turned out, would take almost a month to take effect. In the interim, the community continued proudly walking and ride-sharing to work. Although they won this battle, many people were reluctant to give up the extraordinary feeling of intense unity that had grown throughout the year-long boycott.

In hopes of avoiding violence, the MIA began preparing people for the day when the Montgomery City Lines buses were integrated. Workshops were held to teach people the techniques of passive resistance. Role players portrayed both passengers and drivers—and even these mock sessions at times ended in confrontations. Eventually the MIA issued mimeographed instructions; among them, they cautioned, "The *whole* bus is now for the use of *all* people. Take a vacant seat."

"Not all white people are opposed to integrated buses. Accept goodwill on the part of many."

"Be quiet but friendly; proud, but not arrogant, joyous, but not boisterous." And then listed specifics, including, "Do not deliberately sit by a white person, unless there is no other seat."

"If cursed, do not curse back. If pushed, do not push back. If struck, do not strike back, but evidence love and goodwill at all times," and, "The bus driver is in charge of the bus and has been instructed to obey the law. Assume that he will cooperate in helping you occupy any vacant seat."

The local white community made no effort to prepare for the potential consequences. Days before the order arrived, the City Commission issued a statement vowing to uphold segregation, promising they "will not yield one inch, but will do all in its power to oppose the integration of the Negro race with the white race...and will forever stand like a rock against social equality, intermarriage and the mixing of the races under God's creation and plan."

The court order became law on the morning of December 20, 1956, just over a year after Rosa Parks had been arrested. "It was the nicest Christmas gift I had ever received," Gray remembers. Speaking at an afternoon rally, to rousing cheers, Dr. King announced that the order had gone into effect. "These twelve months have not been easy," he said. "Our feet have often been tired..." Perhaps remembering his trial, he continued, "There have been moments when roaring waters of disappointment poured upon us in staggering torrents. We can remember days when court decisions came upon us like tidal waves, leaving us treading in the deep and confused waters of despair...now our faith seems to be vindicated." He paused, then continued, "This morning the long-awaited mandate from the United States Supreme Court concerning bus segregation came to Montgomery. This mandate expresses in terms that are crystal clear that segregation in public transportation is both legally and socially invalid…

"In light of this…the year-old protest against city buses is officially called off, and the Negro citizens of Montgomery are urged to return to buses tomorrow morning on a nonsegregated basis."

The next morning, Dr. King, accompanied by Ralph Abernathy, E. D. Nixon and white minister Glenn Smiley, the leader of the Fellowship for Reconciliation, boarded a bus. The seat clips reading "Whites front, Blacks rear" that had indicated the two sections had been removed. The driver greeted the two men with a smile, saying, "I believe you are Reverend King, aren't you?… We are glad to have you this morning."

Fred Gray did not join them, believing, "I had done what I needed to do. I had obtained the court order desegregating the buses. It was important for them to make this point publicly, but I didn't have a need to do that. And I knew that from that day forward, I could sit anywhere I wanted to sit on any bus."

The *New York Times* reported, once again on its front page, "For the first time in this 'Cradle of the Confederacy' all the Negroes entered buses through the front door. They sat in the first empty seats they saw, in the front of the buses and in the rear. They did not get up to give a white passenger a seat. And whites sat with Negroes."

Over the next weeks and months, isolated incidents of white resistance elevated into serious violence. People were beaten. One woman was shot in her leg. Shots were fired at buses. Homes and churches were bombed. A poorly constructed bomb made of twelve sticks of dynamite was found on Dr. King's porch. For their safety Reverend Graetz and his family left Montgomery.

For a brief time, all bus service was canceled. Then daytime service resumed. The KKK became increasingly active, although its power was greatly diminished; one night, for example, a young Black child was seen warming his hands near a burning cross.

The local legal system remained entrenched in the past, still trying to defend segregation. Seven white Klansmen were arrested and eventually two of them were put on trial for the bombings. Thetford diligently prosecuted them. Dr. King was called by the defense and accused of fomenting a climate of violence. Even though several of the accused bombers had signed confessions, an all-white jury acquitted them. The city's two circuit court judges publicly praised the jury for its verdict.

On February 13, 1957, Justice Robert X. Harwood of the Alabama Court of Appeals upheld Rosa Parks's conviction on a technicality, even though the ordinance she had violated had been declared unconstitutional in the *Browder* decision. With penalties she was fined $41.35.

The city wasn't quite done searching for a path to legal segregation. After *Brown* many white communities had successfully opened "private" schools to maintain segregation; in Montgomery a group of white men filed an application for a franchise to operate a new bus system, to be called "The Rebel Club," as a private club. The City Commissioners turned to the three judges who had issued the *Browder* ruling to determine if this was legally acceptable. That court refused to hear the case, stating it could not address a hypothetical situation—but two judges wrote opinions in which they stated the city could grant a franchise, but had to ensure that club operated on a "racially neutral basis."

The final legal matter was settled on April 30, 1957, when the Alabama Court of Appeals threw out Fred Gray's appeal of Dr. King's conviction in the *State of Alabama v. Martin Luther King Jr.* more than a year earlier. In his decision, Judge Aubrey Cates explained that under state law, for an appeal to be considered, a full transcript of the trial had to be filed within sixty days.

That had not been done. The defendant had not requested an extension. Therefore, the verdict was upheld. By law, Dr. King was provided the opportunity to pay the fine once again or the jail sentence would be imposed. He paid it. Despite that, King would later write of the legal system: "I have a deep and abiding admiration for the legal profession and the tremendous role it has played in the service of the cause with which I have been identified. The road to freedom is now a highway because lawyers throughout the land, yesterday and today, have helped clear the obstructions, have helped eliminate roadblocks, by their selfless, courageous espousal of difficult and unpopular causes."

The protest and the ensuing trial proved to be the beginning of so many historically important careers and moments that have shaped the American landscape. The legendary story of Dr. Martin Luther King is told in classrooms throughout the world and inscribed on statues and plaques in America's cities. Only eight years after his trial he became the youngest person in history to receive the Nobel Peace Prize, celebrating his nonviolent campaign for equal rights for all Americans. In 1968, as he had been warned, he was assassinated by a white racist. In 1983, President Ronald Reagan signed a bill recognizing the third Monday of January as Martin Luther King Jr. Day, to be celebrated as a federal holiday. This was the first holiday to honor someone who was not a president—and the first to honor an African American. The name Martin Luther King will be heard forever in American history.

When Dr. King left Montgomery in 1960 and moved back to his hometown of Atlanta, he asked Gray to join him there as counsel to the Southern Christian Leadership Conference, a civil rights organization King had cofounded in 1957. "I declined," Gray explains, "although I certainly appreciated the offer. But there was still too much that needed to be done in Alabama. I was honored and proud that I was Dr. King's first civil rights lawyer... Martin was to have many other lawyers on other occasions, but I was his first."

In 1960, once again, Gray was involved in a historic Supreme Court decision, although this time he was able to physically argue the merits of his suit in front of the entire court. As more African Americans had begun exercising their right to vote, the Alabama legislature took steps to dilute their potential power. In 1957, the legislature had gerrymandered most of the African Americans out of the city of Tuskegee. By changing the boundaries of the city limits, politicians essentially excluded Black voters, guaranteeing white candidates would be elected. The boundaries of the city that originally had been a square had been redrawn into a bizarre twenty-eight-sided figure that eliminated all but a handful of Black voters. Tuskegee Institute dean of social sciences Charles Gomillion was Gray's lead plaintiff against the city's mayor, Phillip Lightfoot. Gomillion claimed the electoral maps illegally discriminated against Black voters.

This was among the first cases to challenge gerrymandering on the basis of racial discrimination. "I almost had to beg Robert Carter to look at my complaint," Gray says. "There weren't too many people who believed we had any chance of winning. It wasn't a matter of right or wrong—it was politics. The courts had never really ruled against racial gerrymandering. Even Judge Johnson, who generally was sympathetic to attacks on racial discrimination, had dismissed it summarily, without even letting me argue my case. They all believed the law was clear—the state legislature had the power to draw election district boundaries. Maybe they do, I thought, but not when they are drawn to discriminate against an entire race. I was thrilled when we got a dissenting opinion in the United States Court of Appeals for the Fifth Circuit, because that allowed us to use that in the Supreme Court."

Fred Gray likes to describe himself as "a shotgun lawyer.

I gather a complete arsenal of weapons, take aim and shoot everything I've got. I prefer to argue as many theories as possible, and pray the court will see fit to adopt one of them. In this case, I wanted to claim the city map was a violation of both the Fourteenth and Fifteenth Amendments. My colleagues initially wanted a much more narrow focus, but I was able to persuade them to load up our argument with as many weapons as possible."

Fred Gray remembers being transfixed as he walked into the Supreme Court building for the first time, recognizing the extraordinary distance he had traveled from the Alabama ghetto in which he had been raised by a single mother with a sixth-grade education to presenting his case in front of the highest court in the nation. Gray was joined in arguing the case by Robert Carter, while Arthur Shores served as an adviser. Gray had contacted the famed Rand McNally map company to draw a map of the newly created city boundaries. He had attached that map to his original complaint, which allowed it to become evidence. That map made all the difference; as Gray began his practiced argument, a curious Justice Felix Frankfurter interrupted him. Referring to the map, he asked, "Where is Tuskegee Institute?"

Gray recalls that moment with great pleasure, explaining, "I was delighted to hear him ask that question because I knew then he was concerned about the new boundaries. It meant something to him. In response, I wanted to be sure he understood it was in the city limits, but it had been taken out of them. So I replied, 'Tuskegee Institute is not on the city map.'"

Frankfurter was incredulous. "You mean to tell me that Tuskegee Institute is not located in the city of Tuskegee?"

"No, sir, Your Honor," Gray responded, driving a truck through this opening. "It was in, but they have excluded it."

Frankfurter obviously found that difficult to accept, so he asked again for clarity. "Tuskegee Institute is excluded from the city of Tuskegee?"

"Yes, sir, Your Honor."

Frankfurter wrote the majority opinion for the court: the Alabama legislature had violated the Fifteenth Amendment, which prohibits states from denying anyone the right to vote on the basis of race, color or previous condition of servitude. This case subsequently became a landmark voting rights decision.

Fred Gray was fulfilling his college vow to fight segregation. In 1961, busloads of so-called "Freedom Riders" rode Greyhound buses down from the North to completely integrate bus terminals—including lunch counters. In several cities they were confronted and beaten by white mobs. At least one bus was firebombed by the KKK. Both Black and white Freedom Riders attempting to be served at lunch counters were arrested. Gray filed a class-action lawsuit against Greyhound, with John Lewis and several others as plaintiffs. White Department of Justice attorney John Doar joined him in filing *Lewis v. Greyhound*, which resulted in a permanent injunction against segregation in Montgomery's bus terminal facilities and set a precedent for other similar actions. It also would be the first of several cases in which Gray and the widely respected Doar would collaborate.

Four years later, Black voters were becoming a potent political force; many in Alabama were desperate to blunt this effort. To bring attention to the difficulty Black residents of Selma were encountering in trying to register to vote, a fifty-mile right-to-vote march from Selma to Montgomery was planned for Sunday, March 7, 1965. When marchers led by John Lewis, longtime voter registration activist Amelia Boynton and Hosea Williams crossed the Edmund Pettus Bridge on what was to become known as "Bloody Sunday," they were blocked by a phalanx of state troopers on horseback and sheriff's deputies. Governor George Wallace had ordered them to use whatever means necessary to stop the march. After a brief standoff, the law enforcement officers attacked, beating demonstrators with nightsticks, tear-gassing them, poking them with cattle prods and trampling them. "The next two hours (in Selma) were bed-lam," the *Advertiser* reported. Thirty-five marchers had to be treated at local hospitals, some with fractures and cuts but most suffering from tear gas reactions.

The following day, Fred Gray filed *Hosea Williams et al. v. George Wallace et al.*, demanding the State of Alabama and George Wallace protect the protesters as they marched to secure their constitutional right to vote. President Lyndon Johnson's Department of Justice joined in the suit. Judge Frank Johnson ruled that the march was a constitutionally protected right of assembly and enjoined Governor Wallace and the State of Alabama from interfering with the march. An appeals court upheld that decision and the march proceeded. The night before twenty-five thousand people marched into Montgomery, the leaders of the movement, including Dr. King, Reverend Abernathy, John Lewis, Hosea Williams and Andrew Young, met in Fred Gray's living room to finalize their plans. The massive publicity generated by the attack on peaceful marchers created the political climate necessary to pass the historic 1965 Voting Rights Bill, which allowed countless thousands of Black citizens to exercise the most fundamental American right.

Gray successfully built a large practice representing both Black and sometimes white clients, while continuing his involvement in civil rights cases. He spent much of his early career fighting to integrate Alabama schools and public facilities. But one of his most horrific cases began in 1972 when he learned about the Tuskegee Syphilis Study.

Beginning in 1932, more than six hundred Black men were unknowingly enrolled in a government-run US Public Health Service experiment to monitor the effects of untreated syphilis. About four hundred of those men had been diagnosed with the disease, although they were never provided that information. They weren't even informed they were in a study. They weren't asked for consent. Instead, they were told they had "bad

The Alabama Lawyer

Human and Civil Rights Multicultural

ASB PRESIDENT FRED GRAY AND FAMILY AT THE TUSKEGEE HUMAN AND CIVIL RIGHTS MULTICULTURAL CENTER

ALABAMA LAWYER MAGAZINE

When Fred Gray was admitted to the Alabama bar, he was one of two Black lawyers in Montgomery, one of only nine in the entire state. But because of his massive legal contributions both locally and nationally, in 2002 he was elected the Alabama State Bar's first African American president, and posed on the steps of the Tuskegee Center with his entire family.

blood." Initially they agreed to be examined annually in return for a variety of benefits, including free medicine other than penicillin—the treatment for syphilis. Even after it was proved that this disease was treatable, the men were not informed of their condition; instead, the study continued for decades. The other two-hundred-plus men, who were not diseased, served as the control group.

The study lasted until 1972; by then, more than 125 men had died either directly from syphilis or from complications related to it. One of the subjects, Charlie Pollard, upon learning what he had been put through, asked Gray to take his case. Developing

AUTHOR COLLECTION—FRED D. GRAY

Before her death, Bernice Gray made it clear Fred Gray should remarry—and in that request she accurately described the woman he met in a Cleveland church a year after her death, Carol Ann Porter. Fred and Carol were married at the University Church of Christ during an Ohio blizzard in December 2000. "It was," she once commented, "a union blessed by God."

a case of this type, which meant collecting a small mountain of records, then filing a lawsuit against the government, required substantial funds. Gray put together a small team of Black and white attorneys and eventually settled *Pollard v. United States* for approximately $10 million. But in addition, new standards—with watch guards—were established for medical studies and clinical trials involving human participants.

In 1997, Gray accompanied several survivors of this study to the White House, where President Clinton offered the nation's apology. During that ceremony, Clinton promised his support for the new Tuskegee Human and Civil Rights Multicultural

Center. In 2001, Gray was elected president of the Alabama State Bar Association—the first African American to hold that position.

On October 16, 2011, Fred Gray was invited to attend the ceremony in Washington, DC, as President Barack Obama dedicated the four-acre Martin Luther King Jr. Memorial. "Naturally, it was a very special day for me," he remembers. "I remember looking around on the large crowd as America's first African American president was speaking and appreciating the fact that Eric Holder, our first African American attorney general, was standing close by. A lot of memories ran through my mind that day, but mostly I closed my eyes and thought all the way back to those days working with young Martin Luther King in my office and Jo Ann Robinson's living room and appreciating how far we all had traveled since he had come to Montgomery not even thinking about civil rights. All we ever wanted to do was be treated as human beings when we put our dime in the coin box. Instead, we helped create the movement that changed this country forever."

That was not quite the end of this case. More than a half century later, in October 2021, eighty-two-year-old Claudette Colvin filed a request with an Alabama court to expunge her conviction for refusing to give up her seat on a Montgomery bus. Fred Gray responded to reporters' questions by explaining that he was happy Claudette Colvin had filed this petition, then pointed out that there might be others in the movement who were unjustly convicted wanting to follow suit. "On the other hand," he added, "there are some who were convicted who consider that conviction to be a badge of honor."

Two months later, a Montgomery Juvenile Court judge expunged, or eradicated from the records, her conviction. Colvin said she wasn't going to celebrate because the process had taken sixty-six years, but added that it meant "I'm no longer, at age eighty-two, a juvenile delinquent." Asked why she filed this

AP IMAGES/JACK THORNELL

Early in their relationship Dr. King told Fred Gray, "If we are arrested, we will be calling on you to defend us." In addition to this trial, in 1960 Gray successfully defended Dr. King against charges of tax evasion, although he refused King's request that he move to Atlanta, instead choosing to continue the fight for equal rights in Alabama.

request after so long, she explained, "It means I get a chance to tell my grandchildren, my great-grandchildren, what life was like living in segregated America, in segregated Montgomery. The laws, the hardships, the intimidation that took place during those years and the reason why that day I took a stand and defied the segregated law."

Also in October 2021, after many delays, the City of Montgomery officially changed the name of Jeff Davis Avenue to Fred D. Gray Avenue in honor of the man whom Dr. Martin Luther King once described as "the brilliant young Negro who later became the chief counsel for the protest movement."

★ ★ ★ ★ ★

BIBLIOGRAPHY

Alabama Journal. December 1955–December 1956, Newspapers.com.

Branch, Taylor. *Parting the Waters, America in the King Years, 1954–63*. New York: Simon & Schuster, 1988.

Civil Rights Movement Archive. "Montgomery Bus Boycott." Civil Rights Movement History 1955. www.crmvet.org.

Crosby, Emilye (host). *The Real Rosa Parks and the Montgomery Bus Boycott* (podcast). Season 3, Episode 9. www.learningforjustice. org/podcasts/teaching-hard-history/civil-rights-movement/the-real-rosa-parks-and-the-montgomery-bus-boycott.

Daniels, Pearl Gray. *Portrait of Fred D. Gray*. New York: Vantage Press, 1975.

Donnie, Williams and Wayne Greenhaw. *The Thunder of Angels:*

The Montgomery Bus Boycott and the People Who Broke the Back of Jim Crow. Chicago: Lawrence Hill Books, 2007.

Eyes on the Prize Study Guide (documentary research tool). www.socialstudieswithwarsaw.com/uploads/2/3/2/9/23296048/eyes_on_the_prize__awakenings_documents.pdf.

Garrow, David J. "The Origins of the Montgomery Bus Boycott." *Journal of the Southern Regional Council, 1978–2003* Vol. 7, No. 5 (1985) pp. 21–27.

Glennon, Robert Jerome. "The Role of Law in the Civil Rights Movement: The Montgomery Bus Boycott, 1955–1957." *Law and History Review* Vol. 9, No. 1 (Spring 1991) pp. 59–112. Published online by American Society for Legal History.

Gray, Fred D. *Bus Ride to Justice: Revised Edition.* Montgomery, Alabama: NewSouth Books, 2013.

Gray, Fred D. *The Tuskegee Syphilis Study.* Montgomery, Alabama: NewSouth Books, 1998 and 2013.

Greenhaw, Wayne. *Fighting the Devil in Dixie: How Civil Rights Activists Took on the Ku Klux Klan in Alabama.* Chicago: Lawrence Hill Books, 2011.

Houston, Karen Gray. *Daughter of the Boycott: Carrying On a Montgomery Family's Civil Rights Legacy.* Chicago: Lawrence Hill Books, 2020.

Kennedy, Randall. "Martin Luther King's Constitution: A Legal History of the Montgomery Bus Boycott." *Yale Law Journal* Vol. 98, No. 6 (April 1989) pp. 999–1067.

King, Carole A. and Karren Pell. *Montgomery*. Then & Now. Charleston, South Carolina: Arcadia Publishing, 2011.

King, Martin Luther, Jr. *The Montgomery Story* (speech). June 17, 1956, Stanford, California. The Martin Luther King Jr. Research and Education Institute. https://Kinginstitute.stanford.edu/king-papers/documents/montgomery-story-address-delivered-forty-seventh-naacp-convention.

King, Martin Luther, Jr. *Stride Toward Freedom: The Montgomery Story*. Boston: Republished Beacon Press, 2010.

Mack, Kenneth W. *Representing the Race: The Creation of the Civil Rights Lawyer*. Cambridge, Massachusetts: Harvard University Press, 2012.

McGuire, Danielle L. *At the Dark End of the Street: Black Women, Rape and Resistance—a New History of the Civil Rights Movement from Rosa Parks to the Rise of Black Power*. New York: Vintage Books, 2011.

Milewski, Melissa. "Rethinking the Role of the Courts in the Lives of Black Southerners." *American Historian* (November 2017).

Montgomery Advertiser. December 1955–December 1956, Newspapers.com.

New York Times. December 1955–December 1956, Timesmachine. NYTimes.com.

Parks, Rosa with Jim Haskins. *Rosa Parks, My Story*. New York: Puffin Books, 1999.

Pell, Karren and Carole A. King. *Classic Restaurants of Montgomery.* Charleston, South Carolina: Arcadia Publishing, 2020.

Phillips, Eddie. *The Other Side of Montgomery: Growing Up White in the Birthplace of the Civil Rights Movement.* Montgomery, Alabama: NewSouth Books, 2009.

Pittsburgh Courier. December 1955–December 1956, Newspapers.com.

Reddick, L. D. *Crusader Without Violence.* Montgomery, Alabama: Republished NewSouth Books, 2018.

Robinson, Jo Ann and David J. Garrow (editor). *Montgomery Bus Boycott and the Women Who Started It: The Memoir of Jo Ann Gibson Robinson.* Knoxville, Tennessee: University of Tennessee Press, 1987.

Rothstein, Richard. *The Color of Law: A Forgotten History of How Our Government Segregated America.* New York: Liveright Publishing Corp., 2017.

Shands, Timothy. "The Anatomy of a Social Movement: The Least Publicized Aspects of the Montgomery Alabama Bus Boycott." CUNY Academic Works: Dissertations and Theses, City College of New York, 2016.

Smith, J. Clay, Jr. *Emancipation: The Making of the Black Lawyer, 1844–1944.* Philadelphia: University of Pennsylvania Press, 1993.

Wiggins, Sarah Woolfolk (editor). *From Civil War to Civil Rights, Alabama 1860–1960: An Anthology from "The Alabama Review."* Tuscaloosa, Alabama: University of Alabama Press, 1987.

ACKNOWLEDGMENTS

Fred Gray:

When I was approached by *New York Times* bestselling authors David Fisher and Dan Abrams to join them in writing this book, I was surprised yet honored. It has been a wonderful collaboration. Thanks to Maurice Foster, interim executive director of the National Bar Association, for pointing them in my direction. Thanks also to the National Bar Association for the work it does, particularly for the minority lawyers in this country.

My wife, Carol Ann Porter Gray, has been a lifesaver to me since our marriage in 2000. Both of us had lost our spouses after long marriages, and we met at a church event in Cleveland. She sold her businesses and her home and moved to Tuskegee, Alabama, where she only knew two persons other than me. Without her help, none of this would be possible.

My children, Deborah Gray, Vanessa Gray Taylor, Fred D. Gray Jr. and Stanley F. Gray, have assisted me in everything I have done, including working on this book. Deborah is the managing director of the Tuskegee History Center; Fred Jr.

and Stanley are both attorneys in our law firm; and Vanessa is a paralegal there. Their mother, my first wife, Bernice Hill Gray, is responsible for aiding in all of the successes I have enjoyed during my legal career. Unfortunately, we lost her unexpectedly in 1997. However, her contributions continue through my work and the work of our children. Thanks also to her brother, Elbert Hill, and his wife, Pauline, who have always been there for me, whatever needed to be done. My niece, Karen Gray Houston Nesbitt, the author of *Daughter of the Boycott*, has been of substantial assistance, and so has her brother, Thomas W. Gray Jr. Thanks also to my stepdaughter, June Porter, who has been very helpful.

Professionally, I established our current law firm, Gray, Langford, Sapp, McGowan, Gray, Gray & Nathanson, PC. We have a general practice with offices located in Tuskegee and Montgomery, Alabama. The firm and its staff have contributed greatly to my career and have assisted me in connection with this book. The firm continues to render service to clients. I particularly want to thank Trudy B. Powell and Thalia R. Hardnett, who have been of tremendous assistance with this project.

I also especially want to thank our editor, Peter Joseph, who so completely embraced my participation in this project, and our literary agent, Frank Weimann, who deftly handled the business side of it. Also my sincere appreciation to the hundreds of clients who gave me the opportunity of representing them in their legal matters. Without them, I would have had no professional legal career.

I am greatly indebted to my mother, Nancy Gray Arms, for the sacrifices she made for all of her children. She taught us that we could be anything we wanted to be if we did three things: (1) keep Christ first in your life, (2) get a good education and (3) stay out of trouble. I've tried to do that and taught my children and grandchildren to do likewise. Mom died in 1992. I delivered her eulogy; however, she still lives through her children, this publication and the work of others whose lives she touched while she lived.

Finally, I thank Jesus Christ, who is the author of my salvation and whose teachings I have tried to follow as set forth in the New Testament. His teachings have governed and will continue to govern my life.

David Fisher:

As we began this book we reached out for advice to Maurice Foster, executive director of the National Bar Association. Rather than accepting our invitation, he graciously put us in contact with Fred Gray and stepped aside, a selfless action that grew into this collaboration. We are extremely grateful to Maurice Foster for that. We also greatly appreciate the contributions of our editor and publisher, Peter Joseph, who once again has perfected the delicate art of shaping a book without leaving footprints. In that effort he has been assisted by Grace Towery, whose cheerful presence, diligence and expertise continually smooths an often-bumpy process. And once again, we are appreciative of the work done by our literary agent, Frank Weimann of Folio Literary Management, who took great care of the business aspect of publishing.

Early in our research we discovered the Alabama Department of Archives and History, an incredible resource and a breathtaking depository of American history—both at its beautiful facility across the street from the capitol in Montgomery as well as in its already vast and growing online presence. They welcomed us and provided access to a troubled period of American history. In particular we would like to thank reference librarian Courtney Pinkard; it would be impossible to better represent any agency than Courtney does. She was always available, always willing to assist, and guided us down extremely productive and sometimes-provocative paths. Please visit for yourself at digital.archives.alabama.gov/.

I also was fortunate once again to have the services of Christine Sharbrough, who is everything I could ask for in a researcher. If you're looking for someone to mine history, contact her at red.sharbrough@gmail.com.

I am truly fortunate to have as my partner Dan Abrams. From inception to publication, Dan somehow finds the hours, enthusiasm and energy to make this truly a joint effort. Late at night, it is comforting to know he is also working and instantly available, and I remain extraordinarily grateful that we have collaborated in this series. And working with Fred Gray is a privilege; in my career I have been fortunate to work with many extraordinary people, but Fred Gray stands alone in his impact on this country and history. It is an honor to work with him (and it's also fun!).

Personally, I want to thank my friends David Stein for his time and valuable advice, and Richard Soll, who has acted as a no-nonsense sounding board on so many occasions. It's important to me that he knows how much I depend on him. And finally my appreciation, my gratitude and my love to my wife, Laura, who fills our days and nights with the level of adventure, happiness and love anyone has to be very lucky to find. I am a lucky man indeed. (And our dog, Willow Bay, will be upset if I don't mention her contribution to our happiness!)

Dan Abrams:
There are only so many times that I can thank David Fisher for his partnership and collaboration on all of our books without it starting to sound a bit hackneyed. But on this fifth effort together, I hope the accolades and appreciation still ring as true as ever. David is the ultimate partner, reporter and writer, and I would never have ventured into this series that I cherish so much—or continued it—without his guidance, grit and talent. And this effort may showcase David's best work to date, which is saying a heckuva lot.

But this book was truly special because legal icon Fred Gray agreed to partner with us. Fred has the humility to suggest it was an honor to be asked to work with David and me, but of course, the reality is that the honor was ours to have the opportunity to work with a legendary attorney, and person, like Fred Gray.

I have thanked our editor and publisher, Peter Joseph, as well as his deputy, Grace Towery, our publicist, Emer Flounders, and agent, Frank Weimann, so many times that let me just echo David's comments. They are all critical to making these books and making them work. But just because it becomes a bit redundant, that doesn't mean my appreciation for them is any less significant on this book than it was on our first.

I also want to thank the folks who have done such a sensational job representing me in my on-air career. Jay Sures isn't just my agent—he has become one of my closest friends and confidants. Carole Cooper has represented me for twenty-five years and has become like a second mother to me. Her sound advice and counsel have guided me through the good and the difficult, and I will always treasure her for it. Adam Leibner and Andrew Lear have done terrific work finding me some of my most exciting projects while helping me balance my various commitments. They are also just wonderful people and I cherish the social time we spend together. And because I have so many different roles and jobs, I spend an inordinate amount of time with the great Jennifer Rohrer as she deftly holds my hand through all of the contracts.

I would also like to thank my tireless assistant, Shannon Megale, who has helped me on everything from complicated research to major life decisions. I am truly lucky to have her in my life.

Finally, let me thank many of the same people I have acknowledged in our previous tomes: my dad, Floyd Abrams, for his ever-present inspiration; my children, Everett and Emilia, who are everything to me; and their wonderful mother, Florinka, whose dedication to those children while thriving in a high-powered job has always been both humbling and awe-inspiring. My mother, Efrat; my sister, Ronnie; her husband, Greg; and their amazing children, Dylan, Teddy and Finn; Ev and Em's Nonno and Nonna Roberto and Ilike; and our Geeta.

Finally, thank you to all the principled people of Montgomery and beyond who had the courage to speak up about the inequity of this government-sponsored oppression. I am sure you never got the appreciation you deserved.

INDEX

Page numbers in *italics* refer to images.